SOCIALLY RESPONSIBLE INVESTING
How to Invest with Your Conscience

Alan J. Miller

New York Institute of Finance

New York   London   Toronto   Sydney   Tokyo   Singapore

Library of Congress Cataloging-in-Publication Data

Miller, Allan J. (Alan Jay), 1936–
    Socially responsible investing : how to invest with your
conscience / Alan J. Miller.
        p.   cm.
    ISBN 0-13-156183-9
    1. Investments—Moral and ethical aspects.   2. Social
responsibility of business.   I. Title.
HG4528.M55   1991   91-7757
658.15′2—dc20   CIP

© 1991 by NYIF Corp.
Simon & Schuster
A Paramount Communications Company

Printed in the United States of America
10   9   8   7   6   5   4   3   2   1

To my father and mother, Louis and Claire, who were always there with love and understanding when I needed them most and who first instilled in me the values of productive and responsible behavior . . .

to my wife and best friend, Sue, who brought more love, passion, and meaning to my life than any one man has a right to expect . . .

and to our children, Laurie and Adam, the very best investments we ever made.

Contents

Preface

Several years ago, when I was first introduced to the concept of socially responsible investing, I thought it was one of the dumbest ideas ever to come down the pike. Obviously, it was being propounded by people with no understanding of even elementary economics—let alone any grounding in ethical principles.

Both professionally as a money manager and philosophically as a libertarian, I believed fervently that property rights derived naturally from man's basic rights to life and liberty, and I did not see how I could reconcile that belief with the ostensibly more communal values of the most vocal advocates of socially responsible investing. To expect a corporation or investment manager to balance the goal of maximizing risk-adjusted returns for shareholders or investor-clients against other *societal* values struck me not only as economically unsound but also as fundamentally immoral.

I still believe much of this. A corporation does *not* belong to society; it belongs to its shareholders. Investment managers may *not* put the interests of third parties ahead of the interests of those whose assets they are managing—even when those third parties are disadvantaged, underprivileged, handicapped or disenfranchised, or comprise major sectors of society. To do otherwise would simply be wrong.

And yet, as a human being, how can I not be affected by the horrors of South African apartheid, the threat from environmental degradation to our own and future generations, the magnitude of deaths from cancer and heart disease attributable to smoking, the injustice of employment discrimination against women and ethnic minorities, and the panoply of other societal evils that have captured the attention of advocates of socially responsible investing? If corporate America and investors have the economic power to redress or at least mitigate these problems, how can we not expect them to do so?

I was between an ethical rock and a moral hard place.

Then it struck me that there really is no conflict between my social concerns over environmental degradation, racial discrimination, or political disenfranchisement on the one hand and my philosophical convictions that (1) corporations exist for the sake of their *stockholders*, not for the sake of their employees or communities or society at large, and (2) investment managers have fiduciary responsibilities to their *clients*, not to various other segments or all of society, on the other. And the resolution really was simple.

All I had to do was recognize that the legitimate interests of shareholders and investors are not necessarily limited simply to maximizing their short-term financial returns. Rather, they may—and often do—encompass nonquantifiable and nonfinancial concerns for the *quality* of life itself—including the air they breathe, the water they drink, and the opportunity to live free. Thus, even if it is morally indefensible for a company's management to act otherwise than to maximize risk-adjusted returns for its shareholders in the absence of a mandate from them to do so, once granted such a mandate, that is precisely what a company's management *must* do.

And the same is true of investment managers and their clients: absent directions from clients to invest in a socially responsible manner, investment managers may be under no obligation to do so. However, once given such instructions, they may not do otherwise.

Having resolved my *ethical* conundrum, however, I still had an *economic* problem: even if, under the circumstances as I described them, it is not only ethically acceptable but incumbent upon corporate and investment managers to consider factors beyond the short-term financial interests of their shareholders or clients, is it also economically sound for them to do so? Or do socially responsible corporate or investment approaches significantly jeopardize economic returns?

Here I discovered that, a priori assumptions to the contrary notwithstanding, social responsibility at the corporate or investment level does *not* necessarily appear to have a significant negative effect on financial returns. Indeed, in some instances, it might even enhance them.

Finally, I put it all together and realized what had been my basic problem: neither the political left nor the political right had a monopoly on morality. All persons of goodwill, of both the left and the right, cared about the social, political, and ethical issues of our time: apartheid, equal employment opportunity, environmentalism, women's rights, and so on. What they differed about was means, not ends: *What* should be done; *who* should do it; and *how* should they go about doing it?

Traditionally, of course, the left turned to the *government* for solutions, while the right relied on *individual* initiative. And the left, consistent with its tradition, did just that on most of the major social, political, and ethical issues of our day. That is, it lobbied and politicked for *government sanctions* against trade with South Africa, *government-mandated affirmative action* and comparable worth programs, and even *government regulations* on cigarette smoking. That is just what should have been expected of it; it was consistent with the left's history—and in many cases, it was effective.

But then the left did something out of character: it took a leaf from the conservative-libertarian book and advocated individual initiative to accomplish its ends too. That is what corporate social responsibility and socially responsible investing really were about—voluntary, individual initiatives by stockholders working within the capitalist system to achieve desired social, political, and ethical goals *without* reliance on government intervention or regulation.

And that is where the right blew it. Instead of applauding the fact that liberals finally had adopted a fundamental tenet of their philosophy as their own, the conservatives opposed it on the dubious grounds that if the left favored it, there must be something wrong with it. The left effectively had co-opted one of the right's traditional approaches to solving problems and included it in its own arsenal of methods. Instead of delighting in this, the right was fearful of it.

It was crazy. It was almost as if, faced with the reality that the Soviet Union, Poland, Czechoslovakia, Romania, and East Germany were beginning to adopt democratic, free market solutions to their political and economic problems, conservatives were to oppose them on the grounds that if historically communist states could favor them, they'd have to rethink their validity!

Of course, the political right in the United States didn't do that. Rather, it encouraged the movement of Eastern Europe in the direction of democratic capitalism. But for some reason, when it came to applauding the left's acceptance of the basic value of voluntary individual efforts in achieving goals through corporate social responsibility and socially responsible investing in this country, the right had a blind spot.

And that even included the prestigious *Wall Street Journal*.

The Wall Street Journal is arguably the finest newspaper in the country. Its investigative reporting is outstanding, its economic and political analyses invariably are astute and insightful; and its editorial policy is legendary for its rigorously logical and consistently libertarian bent.

It is never a surprise, therefore, when a *Wall Street Journal* editorial opposes some new government law, regulation, or subsidy, which happens with great frequency. Had a federal law been passed mandating, say, that tuna could only be caught in a manner that did not threaten dolphins or, say, that oil tankers had to be built with double hulls, it would have come as no surprise if *The Wall Street Journal* opposed such legislation. In fact, the *Journal* has opposed efforts to pass just such laws.[1]

However, when **H.J. Heinz Company** (NYSE—HNZ) announced that it was *voluntarily* changing its corporate policy so that it no longer would market tuna caught in nets that threaten dolphins (stemming from pressure from stockholders and customers), and when **Conoco Inc.,** a wholly owned subsidiary of **E.I. duPont de Nemours & Company** (NYSE—DD) announced that it would *voluntarily* construct its future tankers with double hulls because that's what its stockholders and customers seemed to want, *The Wall Street Journal* never applauded those *voluntary* actions. And yet, isn't that just what the *Journal* should have done?

Consider the main themes of conservative political thought and how they *really* square with the socially responsible investing movement:

1. An antipathy toward government activity and regulation preempting the free market and a reliance instead on economic voluntarism. This is a main tenet of conservatism. It is also what the socially responsible investing movement is all about—the encouragement of *voluntary* action by investors and corporations to improve society in the *absence* of government action.

2. A focus on justice, fairness, and individual responsibility as opposed to communal obligations. For example, if the **Exxon Valdez** is guilty of spilling oil and thereby polluting the ocean, it should be the responsibility of **Exxon Corporation** (NYSE—XON) to clean it up, not the responsibility of society or the State of Alaska or the U.S. Government. Isn't that exactly what advocates of corporate social responsibility are demanding?

3. A recognition of property rights, which includes the demand that caretakers of owners' property (including corporate and investment managers) be responsive to the demands of owners (shareholders and investors). This is integral to the concept of socially responsible investing.

4. A belief in the efficacy of democratic capitalism to solve more problems than it creates. This has been proven time and again, most recently in any objective comparison between the depth of environmental problems in the United States (serious but surmountable and improving) and those of Eastern Europe (life threatening and far more intractable). Still, some prominent environmentalists have persisted in blaming capitalism for our environmental problems, and all too often conservatives have allowed them to get away with it.

5. An emphasis on traditional values of home, family, community, and country. Or, in tangible terms, a clean environment for ourselves, our children, and our grandchildren; a world safe from the threat of war or nuclear
accident; and a respect for the inalienable rights of individuals, whether they be homosexuals or heterosexuals,
blacks or whites, male or female. Could anything be more
fundamental?

6. Finally, a paramount concern for freedom and liberty
whether it be in the United States, South Africa, Northern Ireland, the Middle East, or anywhere else in the
world. Isn't this among the major concerns of socially
responsible investors too?

And so this book was written to put this all in perspective and to
make the case that socially responsible investing is an idea that all
of us, whatever our other political inclinations might be, can
wholeheartedly endorse. To those of you of a liberal bent, I doff
my hat—you have been in the forefront of a movement whose
time has come and you were both smart enough and flexible
enough to seize the initiative and use a whole repertoire of
approaches (including those more traditionally associated with
the political right), in pursuit of your goals.

And to those of you of a conservative bent, I salute you, too,
for it really is your ideas that have prevailed—although many of
you do not yet realize it. Open your eyes. The future is now.

PART
One

IDEAS

The Pros and Cons of Socially Responsible Investing

A BRIEF HISTORY

As recently as 1984, only $40 billion was being managed in the United States in a socially responsible manner. Today that number stands at over $450 billion—a more than twelvefold increase in scarcely six years.[1]

What began as a fringe movement appealing to a limited band of anti-Vietnam War activists has moved into the mainstream. Its advocates now include some of the nation's largest public pension plans, banks, churches, and mutual funds, as well as a growing body of sophisticated individual investors. This explosive growth seems not only likely to continue, but to accelerate in the 1990s.

What made it happen? No one thing, but a fortuitous confluence of events. For starters, the demographics were right. College graduates of the 1960s were one of the most idealistic generations in history. It was the members of that generation who integrated the South through sit-ins and marches, who chained themselves to fences to protest nuclear testing, and who burnt their draft cards rather than serve in Vietnam.

They also created the market for the nation's first socially responsible mutual fund—the **Pax World Fund** which scrupulously avoids investments in companies that are engaged in manufacturing defense- or weapons-related products. Organized in 1970, the **Pax World Fund** remains committed to investing only in those companies with fair employment practices, sound environmental policies, international development, and which produce life-supportive goods and services and are engaged in non-war related activities.

While the **Pax World Fund** (and, two years later, the **Dreyfus Third Century Fund**) provided that generation with vehicles through which they might invest in a socially responsible manner, few of the graduates of the 1960s had the capital to avail themselves of those opportunities at the time. While they were willing to put their bodies and their lives on the line from the very beginning, it was not until the 1980s that they also had the money to put where their mouths were in a major way. By then, they were in their forties and, with the passage of time, they had accumulated sufficient wealth so that they could support their beliefs financially as well as physically.

Many, moreover, appeared troubled by the fact that their wealth came through their participation in the very system they had challenged in their youth. Did this mean they had sold out? That was an intolerable conclusion to reach. A better resolution was to use the very assets which came from the system to improve that same system, thereby proving that their principles remained intact.

Over the years many of them have also moved into positions of power, or at least influence, at their places of employment (major corporations, banks, insurance companies, municipalities, and universities). In some cases, that allowed them to become involved in their employers' financial decisions—including the deployment of assets in pension plans, reserves, and endowment plans. It was another opportunity to put their 1960s principles into practice in the 1980s—this time to the tune of billions of dollars.

Concurrently, many churches began to see inconsistencies between their preaching and their portfolios. Was it not hypocritical of them to rail against apartheid on Sunday and cash the dividend checks they received on their South African investments on Monday? How could they oppose smoking while owning stock in cigarette manufacturing companies such as **Philip Morris Companies Inc.** (NYSE—MO) or **American Brands, Inc.** (NYSE—AMB)? Was their avowed opposition to war as a means to resolve international disputes credible if their own portfolios included shares of the nation's major defense contractors such as **General Dynamics Corporation** (NYSE—GD) or **McDonnell Douglas Corporation** (NYSE—MD)? And so, churches became leading players in the socially responsible investing movement.

Two other developments deserve special mention. One is the anti-apartheid movement. While the *Sullivan Principles* (see Chapter 10) were introduced as long ago as 1977, it really wasn't until 1984 that the issue moved into the center stage. In the wake of South Africa's introduction of a new constitution in 1983, black South Africans mobilized as never before to challenge the apartheid system. The government's hand was forced, a state of emergency was declared in 1985 and, day after day, Americans heard or saw reports of the brutal repression of the black uprising.

In the United States, activists stepped up their efforts on two fronts: political and economic. In the political sphere, this culminated in the passage of the *Comprehensive Anti-Apartheid Act* in 1986. On the economic front, it was reflected in an escalation of the effort to pressure corporations to stop doing business in South Africa. One way to do that was to encourage investors to divest themselves of the securities of those companies which persisted in doing business in South Africa.

The divestment campaign worked. Between April 1985 and August 1988, the number of colleges and universities that divested at least partially tripled from 53 to 155. By the end of 1989, 25 states, 19 counties, and 83 cities also had taken some form of economic action, including public pension funds' divestment of stocks of companies that were doing business in South Africa.[2]

If a socially responsible investing campaign could have that great an impact in one sphere, couldn't it have an impact in others too? Perhaps divestment of the stocks of tobacco companies, armaments manufacturers, or nuclear utilities would also make sense. And so, embryonic efforts along those lines were stepped up and the ranks of socially responsible investors swelled.

That brings us to the final development which has raised the socially responsible investing movement to new heights and that promises to catapult it to an even more prominent position in the 1990s: the worldwide environmental crusade. In the last few years, environmentalism has captured the imagination and attention not only of Americans but of the entire world. It has generated incredible media coverage; prompted the development of new products, services, and industries; and contributed to the passage of reams of legislation affecting virtually every individual and business in the country. It encompasses such a potpourri of issues—ranging from tuna fishing to acid rain to asbestos to the greenhouse effect—that its impact on the socially responsible investing movement was inevitable. New mutual funds (such as **Alliance Capital's Global Environment Fund, Oppenheimer's Global Environmental Fund, Schield's Progressive Environmental Fund, Fidelity's Select Environmental Fund**, and **John Hancock's Freedom Environmental Fund**) have been launched within the last year alone (since 1989). And this may be just the beginning.

ETHICAL CONSIDERATIONS

Virtually everyone would agree that corporations have a responsibility to maximize profits for shareholders. After all, isn't that what they're in business for? But, do they have other responsibilities as well? On that question, opinions are divided.

On one side are those who hold with Milton Friedman, Nobel Laureate in Economics, that "There is one and only one social responsibility of business—to use its resources and engage in activities designed to increase its profits so long as it stays within the rules of the game, which is to say, engages in open and free competition, without deception or fraud." Indeed, according to Friedman: "Few trends could so thoroughly undermine the very foundations of our free society as the acceptance by corporate officials of a social responsibility other than to make as much money for their stockholders as possible."[3]

According to Friedman, the concept of corporate social responsibility other than to maximize profits is inherently immoral since a corporation's assets rightly belong to its shareholders (*i.e.*, its owners) not to its hired managers. Thus, management may not use those assets ethically in anyone's interest other than that of shareholders.

It would be as if you trusted your best friend to manage your assets and he in turn gave a portion of them to the homeless. He certainly could do that with his own property if he wanted to, it might even be admirable of him to do so, but by what right can he do it with yours? Perhaps you'd prefer to donate some of your assets to AIDS research or public education. Wouldn't your friend's action be tantamount to theft?

Friedman has expressed this point by asking rhetorically: "Can self-selected private individuals [i.e., company managements] decide what the social interest is? Can they decide how great a burden they are justified in placing on . . . their shareholders to serve that social interest?"[4]

Some advocates of corporate responsibility, however, contend that this is not immoral but, indeed, is highly ethical. These people look upon the corporation as something more than the property of its shareholders. Harold Williams, Chairman of the Securities and Exchange Commission in 1978, expressed it like this:

> As a society, we depend on private enterprise to serve as the instrument through which to accomplish a wide variety of goals— full employment, equal economic opportunity, environmental protection, energy independence, and others. When viewed in light of these social implications, corporations must be seen as, to a degree, more than purely private institutions and corporate profits as not entirely an end in themselves, but also as one of the resources which corporations require in order to discharge their responsibilities.[5]

Similarly, James E. Burke, chairman of **Johnson & Johnson** (NYSE—JNJ), one of the nation's leading manufacturers of health care products, has stated that "Although public service is implied in the charter of all American companies, public

responsibility—in reality—is a company's very reason for existing."[6]

The respective positions of Friedman on the one hand and
Williams and Burke on the other would appear to be dia-
metrically opposed. Yet they can be reconciled in the following
fashion:

First, to the degree that there exists any moral imperative that
one behave in any particular way, it may be argued that the
imperative must, of necessity, extend to his agents as well (which
would include the managements of any corporations in which he
invested). If, for example, it is wrong for one to murder, lie, or
steal, then it is wrong for the management representatives of the
corporations of which he is part owner to murder, lie, or steal as
well. In addition, if one has a moral obligation to provide charity,
or not to pollute the environment, or to come to the aid of the
disadvantaged or disenfranchised, then it would be logical that
the managements of the corporations in which one invests retain
those obligations.

Of course, not everyone would agree on what an individual's
moral imperatives are in the first place. Thus, while some would
contend that we are all our brothers' keepers (meaning that we all
are obligated to give charity or support the arts or generally do
more than the free market would require), others would argue
that the only moral imperative we really share is the *negative*
injunction to do no gratuitous harm. As they see it, it is incumbent upon us not to murder, lie, or steal, or in a broader sense,
not to initiate the use of force or fraud in any way, but we are
subject to no *positive* moral imperative to do good.

If you are in the former camp (the brothers' keepers group),
your problem is solved. You don't have to imbue the corporation
with any responsibilities beyond those which derive from its
shareholders; those shareholders themselves have such an array
of obligations that, by extension, corporate managements who
act on their behalf must behave in a socially responsible manner
in virtually every area (*e.g.*, apartheid, environmentalism, smoking, animal rights, or affirmative action).

If you're in the latter camp, this reasoning will only get you
part way home: it might justify why a company should not pollute

the environment (because it would *force* individuals to suffer the consequences of such pollution involuntarily), or why a company should not manufacture or market tobacco products (because of the hazards of second-hand smoke to those who do not wish to smoke themselves), or why a company should withdraw from South Africa (because it should not participate in the apartheid system which survives only through the use of unjustifiable force). However, it wouldn't help us to understand why a company should be obligated to make charitable contributions, or support the arts, or pay above-average wages to employees, or provide daycare centers, affirmative action, or comparable worth programs. If, as an individual, one is under no obligation to do any of those things, whence would a corporation's moral obligation derive?

Well, one answer would be if those responsibilities were *voluntarily* assumed by the stockholders. For even if there is no moral imperative that an individual care for his neighbor, one may assume such a responsibility. And if one voluntarily assumes an obligation, then he may delegate it to his agent—in this case, the management of the corporation of which he is part owner.

We think that even Friedman might agree to this, since the corporation actually belongs to its stockholders. Therefore, management is obligated to carry out the stockholders' will. So if, for instance, it is the will of the corporation's shareholders to act in a socially responsible manner (e.g., by contributing some of its profits to charity, paying higher wages, withdrawing from South Africa, or by reducing the level at which it pollutes the environment *even at a cost to the corporation*) then it would become the obligation of management of the corporation to carry out those shareholder mandates.

Now return for a moment to the analogy in which your best friend was giving away some of your assets to the homeless as tantamount to theft. Suppose that instead of your friend's having done that on his own, you had instructed him to do it. Or suppose that you had simply directed him to distribute some of your assets to worthy causes as he saw fit. In those cases, his action would not have been theft at all. In fact, in those instances he would have had a social responsibility to do just that, the responsibility having devolved directly from your instruction.

This, then, would be the answer to Friedman's questions about whether corporate managements may decide what the social interest is and whether they may decide how great a burden is placed on shareholders to satisfy that interest. The answer is two-thirds *yes* and one-third *no*. For example, the answer is *yes* if they simply are acting to fulfill their shareholders' own moral imperatives to do no harm. The answer is also *yes* if they are acting to fulfill their shareholders' mandates. It is only *no* if there is no inherent obligation to do so and no direction from shareholders to do so.

When stockholders do direct the managements of their companies to act with a sense of social responsibility, that direction may either be by *implicit* endorsement of actions initiated by management, as reflected by their reaction to such initiatives, or *explicitly* through the shareholder resolution process.

Ben & Jerry's Homemade, Inc. (OTC—BJICA). An example of *implicit* endorsement would be the consistent level of shareholders' support accorded **Ben & Jerry's Homemade** management for their broad array of avowedly socially responsible corporate policies. The company is a manufacturer and marketer of super premium ice cream through supermarkets, grocery stores, restaurants, 78 franchised ice cream parlors, and 5 company-owned outlets. Its annual revenues nearly tripled in three years from $20 million in 1986 to $58.5 million in 1989 and its earnings almost doubled from 40 cents a share to 79 cents. But it is not the company's superior ice cream product, good as it is, that has earned it nationwide recognition and publicity. Rather, it is the company's consistent leadership role in matters of corporate social responsibility.

Indeed, it probably would not be excessive to say that **Ben & Jerry's Homemade** is *the* quintessential example of responsible corporate citizenry in action today. **Franklin Research and Development Corporation**, a leader in the socially responsible investing movement and publisher of *Franklin's insight*, is an investment advisory service that evaluates companies from both a financial and social standpoint; in that regard, **Franklin** gives **Ben & Jerry's Homemade** its very highest social assessment rating on all counts: South Africa, employee relations, environment, citizenship, energy, product, and weapons. In **Franklin's** opinion, "The company's dedication to the creation and demonstration of a new corporate concept of linked prosperity continues to be the key ingredient that sets the firm apart from all others."[7]

As examples, **Ben & Jerry's Homemade** contributes 7.5% of pretax profits to charity (compared to a corporate average of 1%) and pays no employee more than five times what it pays its lowest paid worker. Had they been so inclined, shareholders might have challenged the charitable contributions policy as a waste of corporate assets and the employee compensation policy as insensitive to competitive market realities, but shareholders have done no such thing. It is evident that they *like* the way **Ben & Jerry's Homemade** does business and that is one of the main reasons they became shareholders in the first place. Their *implicit* endorsement of the company's extraordinarily socially conscious behavior is overwhelmingly evident.

Exxon Corporation (NYSE—XON). At the opposite end of the spectrum is **Exxon Corporation**, the world's largest integrated oil company, which has annual revenues more than 1,000 times those of **Ben & Jerry's Homemade**. But size and product lines are not the only differences between the two companies. Unlike **Ben & Jerry's**, **Exxon** is no paragon of socially responsible corporate virtue. However, **Exxon's** management is not entirely to blame. Somehow, we doubt whether **Exxon's** shareholders (unlike those of **Ben & Jerry's**) would want to see their company contributing 7.5% of its pretax profits to charity—which in **Exxon's** case would amount to over $500 million (or nearly 10 times **Ben & Jerry's** total annual revenues). It is also doubtful that **Exxon** would advocate as restrictively egalitarian a compensation policy as **Ben & Jerry's** which could place it at an insurmountable competitive disadvantage vis-à-vis other major integrated oil companies in terms of attracting talented, experienced, and productive personnel.

Still, there are social issues that do matter to **Exxon's** shareholders, and when they do, they have made their will known *explicitly*. An example of such *explicit* direction was the institutional shareholder pressure that was brought to bear against **Exxon** to raise environmental safety to a board level concern. Six of the nation's largest pension funds, who owned millions of **Exxon** shares, threatened to vote against management's slate of directors unless **Exxon** named an environmentalist to its board. **Exxon** did so.

In sum, even if one does not subscribe to Williams' and Burke's contentions that corporations are something more than the private property of their shareholders, it still appears to be ethically defensible that corporations' social responsibilities extend beyond that of maximizing profits for stockholders. Two reasons are:

1. Individuals' *negative* injunctions to do no harm extend to their agents (in this case, managements of the corporations they own). This may justify corporate social responsibility in such areas as pollution control, apartheid, or smoking.

2. Even where no *positive* moral imperative to do good exists, individuals may voluntarily assume such responsibilities. If they do, they may direct the managements of the companies they own to assume such responsibilities as well. This can justify corporate social responsibility in virtually all other areas including employee relations, corporate philanthropy, and the like.

ECONOMIC CONSIDERATIONS

A second objection to corporate social responsibility is more pragmatic: It is self-destructive and leads to corporate suicide. Barry Bluestone of Boston College's Economics Department, while not necessarily subscribing to this argument himself, nevertheless outlined it well:

In the textbook version of free enterprise, competition is so virulent that a firm that does anything but try to maximize profit—

usually by squeezing out excess costs—will face bankruptcy. The philanthropic firm that donates ten dollars to the United Fund is spending precious resources that are crucially necessary to maintain its competitive edge. The firm that offers higher wages or better fringe benefits than its neighbor will face higher costs and therefore will have to charge higher prices. In turn, the higher prices will run the "socially responsible" company right out of business.[8]

In rebuttal, advocates of corporate social responsibility have contended that the by-product benefits of socially responsible policies to the corporation itself may more than offset any costs incurred in pursuing such policies.

For example, "The philanthropic firm that donates ten dollars to the United Fund" may be "spending precious resources," it is true, but that expenditure may not necessarily be wasted—it may purchase more goodwill for the company than would an equivalent expenditure on public relations. Similarly, it is not necessarily true that "The firm that offers higher wages or better fringe benefits than its neighbor will face higher costs and therefore will have to charge higher prices." It is possible that the higher wages or better fringe benefits will result in lower employee turnover, reduced absenteeism, better labor relations, and generally higher employee morale, resulting in productivity increases that more than offset the incremental costs of the improved wages and benefits package. Or, the increased wages and benefits offered by the company might enable it to attract a better qualified work force that would produce a better product for which consumers would be willing to pay higher prices.

In the real world, we already have mentioned **Ben & Jerry's** philanthropic policies and support of social causes as examples of a company's exercise of corporate social responsibility that appear to have paid off for shareholders in the form of very favorable publicity. But there are numerous other examples as well.

E.I. duPont de Nemours (NYSE—DD). The largest chemicals company in the United States, **E.I. duPont de Nemours** boasts annual revenues in excess of $35 billion. Its product line includes oil, natural gas, coal, agricultural, industrial and specialty chemicals, fibers, electronic products, pharmaceuticals, and paints. It is approximately 22% owned by the duPont family and about 23% owned by **Seagram Company Ltd.** (NYSE—VO).

In recent years, **DuPont** has been carving out a major niche for itself in several areas of environmental concern, ranging from water pollution treatment to the development of substitutes for chlorofluorocarbons to the creation of more readily degradable agricultural chemicals and pesticides. (We shall have more to say about these efforts in Chapter 7 on the environment.)

In 1981, **DuPont** acquired **Conoco Inc.**, a major oil producer, through which the company now runs its oil operations. On April 11, 1990, **Conoco** announced that it was ordering two new oil tankers with double hulls and that all its future tankers would be built with double hulls as well in order to reduce the chances of oil spills. That decision could cost the company as much as $20 million extra for the two tankers and tens of millions of dollars more in years to come. That means millions of dollars in reduced profits and/or the necessity to raise prices of a virtually fungible commodity.

Has **DuPont**, via **Conoco**, been acting self-destructively? Will the decision to build new tankers with double hulls put **Conoco** at a considerable cost disadvantage in relation to its competitors? Or, might the decision actually turn out to be good business, reducing **DuPont's** potential liability for oil spills, buying it favorable publicity, and providing it with a jump on its competition before double-hulled vessels are mandated by law? The jury is still out on this one, but somehow we think that **DuPont** may turn out to have done the right thing, both in economic and social terms.

Indeed, whether or not other oil companies follow **Conoco's** lead remains to be seen, but it is far from certain that none will. Lodwrick M. Cook, chief executive of **Atlantic Richfield Company** (NYSE—ARC), for one, previously had indicated his inclination to go to double hulls as well. As he put it: "I think we are going to have to go to double hulls. The American people are saying to me that they will be more comfortable if we have double hulls because there are certain kinds of accidents where they are helpful."[9]

McDonald's Corporation (NYSE—MCD). Operating a chain of over 11,000 fast-food restaurants throughout the world, **McDonald's Corporation** has seen its sales grow at a compounded annual rate of 14% over the past decade, its earnings grow at 15.5% and its dividends grow at 24%. And the company's social record is as impressive as its financial one. In future chapters, we shall have much to say about the important roles the company plays in providing youths with entry-level jobs, in combatting racism in the workplace, and in breaking new ground environmentally.

Suffice it to say at this point that scarcely a week after the **Conoco** announcement, on April 18, 1990, **McDonald's Corporation** made some important news of its own by announcing a new program called *McRecycle USA* to create a $100 million a year market for recycled materials in its restaurants, including construction, renovation, exterior, furnishings, and equipment. That was over and above the millions of dollars it was spending annually for recycled paper products and compared to the expenditure of $5 to $6 million in recycled construction supplies and equipment that it had made in 1989.

Moreover, just as **Conoco's** decision to build all its future vessels with double hulls will cost it tens of millions of dollars, so too, **McDonald's** *McRecycle USA* program could cost it as much as 10% more for recycled construction materials, or as much as an additional $10 million. Thus, **McDonald's** decision might also have been construed as a self-destructive act—but was it really? The fact is, in the long run, it may prove to be a very profitable $10 million investment in public relations, generating considerable positive press and blunting some of the criticism that previously was lodged against the company because of its persistence (until late-1990) in using nonbiodegradable polystyrene packaging.

Even if it is not necessarily economically self-destructive for a corporation to behave with a sense of social responsibility, it is still possible that the process of socially responsible investing itself may produce inferior results for investors (irrespective of the consequences of corporate social responsibility policies on a company's own profitability). This could occur, for instance, if a *passive*[10] investor found that by screening socially *irresponsible* companies from his potential portfolio, his opportunities pool was so reduced in size that he could not structure a sufficiently diversified portfolio to accomplish his objectives.

It could also occur if an *active*[11] investor believed that some socially *irresponsible* companies provided unusual investment opportunities from which he would be precluded if he were to exercise his convictions regarding corporate social responsibility in his own portfolio. He might suffer some pangs of guilt over that but still might not be willing to sacrifice his own potential investment returns because of it.

Finally, since portfolio turnover would rise if investors traded securities not only for economic but also for noneconomic reasons, the structure and maintenance of socially responsible portfolios could entail higher transaction costs than those portfolios managed without such additional constraints.

Several investment experts have made this point in one form or another. For instance, Allan Emkin, vice chairman of **Wilshire Associates**, has stated that "When you limit the number of opportunities, you limit some of the potential for return . . . you're going to forego something."[12]

Not everyone agrees. Doug Salvati, vice president and portfolio manager for **SLH Investment Management**, for one, contends that "Investment performance is not significantly affected by the use of socially responsible investment criteria."[13] Bruce Westcott, senior vice president and portfolio manager for **Lehman Management Company**, has taken a similar position, claiming that "There is no significant performance difference between the portfolios we manage with socially responsible restrictions and similar portfolios that have no such restrictions."[14] And **U.S. Trust Company of Boston**, referring to South African-free funds which it managed, asserted that "Divestment need not impede competitive investment performance to any degree which one would call significant."[15]

U.S. Trust Company reached its conclusion based on a study of the effects of South African divestment which it conducted with **SEI Funds Evaluation, Inc.** for the state of Michigan's multibillion dollar pension plan. Its conclusions were: (1) to set the minds of *passive* investors at ease, South African-free portfolios can be constructed to track the Standard & Poor's 500 or other indices very closely, (2) to reassure *active* investors, limiting the opportunities pool is not necessarily detrimental to performance, and (3) transaction costs are incrementally negligible, amounting to a one-time cost of only 0.35% of the value of stocks, which would not otherwise have been divested, and continuing additional annual costs of only 0.1% of the affected portion of the portfolio.[16]

Other studies have produced similar results, thereby suggesting that while a priori it might appear that limiting the available pool of investment opportunities would reduce potential returns significantly, it hasn't necessarily worked out like that in practice. Or as Marshall Blume, professor of finance at the University of Pennsylvania's Wharton School, has put it: "[B]y restricting your investments in any way, you cannot be better off . . . . [In fact,] you are probably worse off—but the amount may be so trivial that you can ignore it."[17]

Not everyone, however, would agree. Throughout the late 1980s there was some evidence that a South African divestment policy did produce somewhat inferior results to those which might have been achieved through an unrestricted investment policy. From its inception on December 3, 1983 through the third quarter of 1990, the South Africa Free Equity Index of **PanAgora Asset Management** generated a return of only 17.46% compared with 37.41% for the unrestricted Standard & Poor's 500 Stock Index. And, internationally, the South Africa-free FT-Actuaries Europe & Pacific Index declined 11.42% from the first quarter of 1988 through the third quarter of 1990, compared to a drop of only 6.87% in the standard EuroPac index.[18] So perhaps the jury still is out on this one.

However, there are those who would go even further, contending that limiting opportunities by screening for socially responsible criteria does *not* penalize returns, but rather *enhances* them. Their arguments take four forms.

1. Socially *irresponsible* companies are potential problem companies because, over time, they will find themselves in declining businesses such as tobacco or because they will be forced to

pay huge sums to clean up pollution, to recall products, to settle lawsuits, to deal with labor or civil unrest, or to respond to unanticipated changes in government regulations. By screening such companies out of their portfolios to begin with, socially responsible investors can avoid such problems even before they arise.

George Gay, chief operating officer of **First Affirmative Financial Network**, expressed it like this:

> If you don't invest in companies that pollute the environment, you don't get involved in EPA penalties for failing to meet Superfund standards. If you don't invest in nuclear power plants, you don't expose yourself to plant shutdowns for safety violations. If you don't invest in companies with poor labor relations, you're not exposed to big strikes that send companies into bankruptcy like **Eastern Airlines**. . . . Some say you're taking yourself out of opportunities. I say you're taking yourself out of liabilities.[19]

2.   Companies in the forefront on social issues may get a jump on their competition by carving out niches for themselves in emerging growth areas such as child-care centers or alternative energy sources. Corporations involved in cleaning up the environment may be the best example of this.

Indeed, Donavan McKerchar, portfolio manager of **Oppenheimer's Global Environmental Fund**, has opined that "Cleaning up our polluted planet will be the growth industry of the '90's."[20] Jim Craig, portfolio manager of the **Janus Fund**, shared that sentiment, observing that "We're running out of landfill space. So companies that own landfills or help dispose of waste could double in value in three or four years."[21] And Larry Greenberg, portfolio manager of **Fidelity Environmental Services Fund**, is in the same camp, asserting that "We are giving the investor a direct play on the fastest growth industry of the 1990's."[22]

3.   Socially responsible companies often generate very positive publicity and considerable goodwill, frequently translatable into customer loyalty, repeat sales, referrals, premium prices, and rising profits. It has already been noted how this may prove to be the case for **Ben & Jerry's Homemade, DuPont,** and **McDonald's.**

4.   Finally, it is the opinion of a number of institutional investors that a sense of social responsibility may reflect the leadership of an intelligent, thoughtful, and stable management. **Connecticut General Life Insurance Co.**, for instance, believes that "A good environmental or social record is probably indicative of a strong, careful management."[23] **Teachers Insurance Annuity Association—College Retirement Equities Fund** (TIAA—CREF) avers that "The long-run economic interests of its policy holders are best served by socially responsible investment policies."[24] And the **Minnesota State Board of Investment** contends that "In order to comply with its mandate to invest the assets of its funds responsibly and prudently, the social and environmental policies of each corporation must be considered. In order to remain financially stable, a corporation must take the general welfare of society and its members into account."[25]

SOCIETAL CONSIDERATIONS

A third objection to socially responsible investing relates to the consequences of corporate social responsibility for society itself. Here, skeptics contend that such attempts at social engineering won't produce any positive effects at all or that, if they do, they will also produce unintended and offsetting negative effects.

For instance, the company that closes down a widget plant because its operations are polluting the environment will thereby raise the level of unemployment among widget workers. It may also result in a shortage in the supply of widgets and higher prices for those produced elsewhere. The adverse ripple effect on the families of unemployed widget workers, the tradesmen whom they no longer can afford to patronize, suppliers to the widget company, widget consumers, and other companies dependent on widgets in their own manufacturing processes, might well transcend any benefits realized from the reduction in pollution.

This argument actually was made by Adam Smith more than 200 years ago: "By pursuing his own interest, [the individual] frequently promotes that of the society more effectually than when he really intends to promote it. I have never known much good done by those who affected to trade for the public good."[26]

But what happens when the individual pursues his own interest but is enlightened in seeing that interest as transcending short-term profits? As a shareholder, for instance, you do not have to advocate that your company stop polluting the environment only because you are altruistically inclined; rather, you may advocate such a course of action because you are interested in your own good and that of your children and grandchildren. And, if there are enough individuals like you who feel that way, not only will you benefit as individuals, but society will benefit too.

Thus, one need not argue that in today's advanced world, we no longer are helpless in the grasp of Adam Smith's *invisible hand* (although some advocates of corporate social responsibility do take that position). No, it is simply sufficient to point out that, by defining your own individual self-interest in terms of the quality of life for yourself and your descendants, rather than just your financial resources, you will affect the workings of that *invisible hand* to produce the same good for society that you seek for yourself.

Michael Novak distinguished neatly between the anti-capitalist's conception of *selfishness* and *enlightened self-interest* in a column in *Forbes*. In responding to an article by Wesley Granberg-Michaelson of the World Council of Churches in which Granby-Michaelson bemoaned the collapse of Marxism, Novak pointed out that Granby-Michaelson

> misreads Adam Smith when he writes: "Adam Smith, of course, argued that it was precisely the exercise of an individual's selfish pursuits which, when channeled by the 'invisible hand' of the market, led to the well-being of the whole society." Nonsense. Smith didn't say "selfish", he said "self-interest." The self-interest Adam Smith discussed is far from being the same as "selfish pursuits." The interests of the self may be grand, wise, communitarian, selfless, heroic, farseeing, and they may display many other noble qualities; they are not only selfish.[27]

ON THE PRUDENCE AND SOLE AND EXCLUSIVE BENEFIT RULES

There remains but one other potential objection to socially responsible investing by institutions or fiduciaries (although not necessarily by individuals acting on their own behalfs) and that is a legalistic one. This relates to the questions of whether socially responsible investing conforms to the *prudence* and *sole and exclusive benefit* rules of law and whether the inclusion of social, ethical, or political criteria in the investment decision-making process might not violate a fiduciary's responsibilities. As Mark Melcher of **Prudential-Bache Securities** has noted "[some] money managers are incensed by the concept of social investing and tell clients when the subject comes up that applying social criteria to investment strategy is 'stupid.' Then they talk about their 'fiduciary responsibility' to 'maximize return,' etc."[28]

As an individual investor you may, of course, do as you please with your own money, so long as you don't violate the law along the way. You may withhold your investable funds from companies that pollute the environment or trade with South Africa or manufacture cigarettes or provide guns or tanks to the military or generate electricity from nuclear plants. You may do that even if you are convinced that one or more of the companies from which you are withholding your funds will be a big winner in the marketplace. You may do that because it's *your* money.

And you may do that even if, as a consequence, you are left with a very undiversified portfolio of relatively small high risk stocks. You may do all that because it's *your* money.

But suppose it's not your money. Suppose you're managing someone else's money as a *fiduciary* through a public or private pension plan. May you still do that or are you legally held to a different standard?

This is where the problem arises. In general, the law holds that, in such fiduciary situations, you must act *prudently*, which has slightly different meanings under the common law, under the *Employment Retirement Income Security Act of 1974 (ERISA)*, and under the statutes of various states. In all instances, however, it is usually interpreted to mean that you must act as other *reasonable men* would act in a similar situation. (There are nuanced differences as to what would constitute the appropriate class of *reasonable men* against whom you should be compared, with *ERISA* usually interpreted as holding *fiduciaries* to a somewhat higher standard than do the common law or state statutes based on the common law. It is also important to note that, as a federal law, *ERISA* preempts state law, but does not apply to municipal and state plans.)

Whether public plans or private, however, the question still comes down to much the same thing: Is it *prudent* to include social, ethical, or political considerations in the investment process?

A case may be made that it is—so long as those criteria don't take precedence over traditional financial considerations and don't disadvantage beneficiaries. As we have seen, many institutional managers believe that "A good environmental or social record is probably indicative of a strong, careful management" **(Connecticut General Life Insurance Co.)**; or that "The long-run economic interests of its policy holders are best served by socially responsible policies" (TIAA—CREF); or that "To invest the assets of its funds responsibly and prudently, the social and environmental policies of each corporation must be considered" **(Minnesota State Board of Investment)**. In all of these situations, we think that these are the sorts of *reasonable men* against whom you might be judged and that the consideration of social factors, subordinate to financial factors, would be deemed legitimate. So we don't think you'd have much of a problem with the *prudence* rule.

But the common law, *ERISA*, and most state statutes also provide that, as a *fiduciary*, you must invest your client's funds for his *sole and exclusive benefit*. This is somewhat tougher. If, say, you refused to invest in the stocks of companies doing business in South Africa, might you be charged with having violated the *sole and exclusive benefit* rule because you would have invested (or have chosen not to invest), at least in part, for the benefit of South Africa's blacks?

In the case of public plans that are not subject to the provisions of *ERISA* and for which enabling legislation has been written in such a way as to allow social, ethical, or political considerations to enter into the investment decision-making process, the *sole and exclusive benefit* rule is not a problem. Enabling legislation has permitted (and in some cases even mandated) the divestment by some public pension plans of their investments in the securities of companies doing business in South Africa— for ethical, not financial reasons—and where that has occurred, it has not been deemed a violation of the *sole and exclusive benefit* rule. Similarly, when New York City was on the verge of bankruptcy, its pension plans were permitted to assist in the city's bailout.

The answer is not as clear-cut in the case of private plans subject to *ERISA*, however, and for that reason they have not been nearly as prominent in the socially responsible investing movement as have public plans. The Department of Labor, for instance, has taken the position that private plans must always invest for *competitive* returns, not just *reasonable* returns. Thus, private plans of the union construction trades, for instance, have not felt free to make real estate investments at *reasonable*, but less than *competitive*, rates, even to stimulate employment for their own union members; nor have they been able to make low-cost mortgage loans available at *reasonable*, but less than *competitive*, rates to their own members.

Nevertheless, even for private plans, the *sole and exclusive benefit* rule need not be an absolute bar to socially responsible investing, so long as investments are made with the goal of achieving *competitive* returns. That is because the *sole and exclusive benefit* rule has generally been interpreted only as proscribing *positive* acts, such as the purchase of a security for the benefit of a third party, and not merely *negative* ones whereby certain securities or classes of securities are simply avoided in the first place. Moreover, it is usually true that economic considerations will enter into such judgments to some degree anyway (*e.g.*, the avoidance of the financial risk of civil unrest or adverse legislation—sanctions or taxes—affecting one's South African investments).

The bottom line would appear to be that *fiduciaries* may invest in a socially responsible manner, even if they are subject to *ERISA* and notwithstanding the *prudence* and *sole and exclusive benefit* rules, provided that they invest for *competitive* returns and do not subordinate the interests of their clients to those of third parties. And if, in the process of seeking to do well for their clients, which must be their primary goal, they also do good for society—by contributing to a cleaner world, a more peaceful world, a freer world, or a more racially harmonious world—well, could anyone object to that?

———————

Does socially responsible investing make sense for you? We hope so. If it does, how, exactly, are you going to go about it? How will you resolve the inevitable conflicts that will arise? Which specific social or ethical issues might you consider addressing? In the next chapter, we'll begin to deal with these very basic questions.

2

Issues, Strategies, and Conflicts

EXPLORING YOUR OPTIONS

If you've come this far, we assume that socially responsible investing makes sense to you and you want to try it. Before you can start, however, you should first make three basic decisions:

1.   Which social, ethical, or political issue or issues do you wish to address? Apartheid or air pollution or both? Animal rights or tobacco or nuclear power? All of these, or other issues entirely?

2.   What kind of strategy or strategies do you wish to adopt? Would you be most comfortable with an *avoidance* strategy, simply screening *irresponsible* companies out of your portfolio? (This is what most people think of when they hear the term *socially responsible investing*.) Would you prefer an *alternative* strategy, seeking opportunities to invest in ways to do *positive* good rather than avoiding an investment in a company that might cause harm? Or is an *activist* strategy the one for you, engaging the managements of *irresponsible* companies directly as a shareholder in order to try to convince them to change their courses?

3.   Finally, how do you intend to resolve the conflicts that will inevitably arise? What will you do when a company you've invested in or are considering investing in acts *irresponsibly* in

one way but *responsibly* in another? Will you allow as to how the good might offset the bad or will it have to be all or none?

SAMPLING THE ISSUES

At the outset, let's turn our attention to some of the substantive issues themselves. What are they? Which are most important to you?

Shareholder Rights

In one sense, this may be the most important issue of all, the fountainhead from which all other rights, responsibilities, and obligations are derived. Typical of investors' objectives in this area are the receipt of more information on a regular basis regarding corporate affairs; the right to secret balloting; the elimination of excessive management perquisites which might constitute a waste of corporate assets; the curtailment of *golden parachutes, poison pills, greenmail*[1], and other schemes intended to thwart unfriendly takeover attempts; and board representation for institutional investors and other shareholders who control large blocks of stocks.

Consumer Rights and Product Quality

If the issue of shareholders' rights is the most fundamental, the issue of consumer rights is the most all-encompassing. It involves virtually everything the corporation does: the quality of its products, the integrity of its marketing, the services it provides, and so on. Some socially responsible investors emphasize the degree to which a company fulfills its legal obligations; others tend to focus on the quality of a company's goods and services, over and above what legally may be required of it.

The Sin Subjects: Smoking, Drinking, and Gambling

These issues have engaged reformers since the roaring twenties or longer. Over the last three decades, as scientific evidence has mounted implicating tobacco and alcohol in a variety of ailments, socially responsible investors have joined the reformers' ranks in increasing numbers. These investors' objectives include limiting the advertising, promotion, and sale of tobacco (especially to minors), discouraging drinking and gambling and, ultimately, closing gambling casinos and prohibiting the manufacture and sale of tobacco products and alcoholic beverages in their entirety.

Environmentalism

This may turn out to be the biggest issue of the 1990s as many socially responsible investors believe that the very salvation of our planet is at stake if we do not come to grips with our air, water, and solid wastes pollution problems. Specific questions involve smog, acid rain and other air pollution issues, depletion of the ozone layer, the greenhouse effect, recycling, solid waste disposal, the exhaustion of landfill space, toxic and hazardous wastes, incineration, biodegradability claims, pesticides, asbestos removal, strip mining, deforestation, and corporate adoption of the *Valdez Principles*.

Racism and Sexism

Equal employment opportunity, affirmative action, and comparable worth are the major issues addressed by socially responsible investors who are concerned over the twin issues of minority rights and women's rights in our society. However, they are not merely concerned about job opportunities; they are exercised, too, over the issues of corporate support to minority vendors, franchisee opportunities, advancement opportunities within companies, advertising, marketing, and new product development policies as they directly affect women and racial minorities.

Employee Rights

Advocacy of employee rights harks back to the early twentieth century when preliminary efforts were first undertaken in the areas of unionization, child labor laws, workplace safety regulations, and minimum wage laws. Today these issues have been

joined by concerns over equality of employment and advancement opportunities, affirmative action programs, comparable
worth, on-site child-care centers, parental leave programs, priva-
cy rights, retraining programs, and advance notice of plant shut-
downs.

Apartheid and South Africa

Before *environmentalism* leapt to the forefront as the crusade of
the 1990s, the issue of *apartheid* in South Africa was far and away
the biggest concern of socially responsible investors. Even in
1990, there were still more corporate resolutions dealing with
apartheid in South Africa than with any other issue. Moreover,
more investors probably still screen out the stocks of companies
doing business in South Africa than any other class of securities.
Initially, the concern of these investors was that companies in
which they had invested should subscribe to the *Sullivan Principles*. Subsequently, that was not considered sufficient and investors began to press companies to completely withdraw from
South Africa and terminate all their business relationships with
that country instead.

Armaments, Defense, and the Military

Some socially responsible investors seek to avoid investments in
arms manufacturers and major defense contractors (especially
those involved in the production, marketing and sale of biological, chemical, and nuclear weapons). They also seek to convince
companies to terminate military contracts and to convert productive capacity from military goods to civilian needs.

Animal Rights

Advocates seek to limit or prohibit whaling; to mandate or encourage tuna fishing in a manner that does not jeopardize dolphins; to restrict or ban animal testing or experimentation; to end

the trapping or raising of animals to manufacture fur coats; and to breed livestock in a humane manner.

This list is not intended to be exhaustive. For instance, we have not even touched on such issues as corporate philanthropy, nuclear power, energy independence, Northern Ireland, abortion, infant formula, or trade with China. Nor does this list necessarily reflect our personal opinion of what a corporation's social responsibility *should* be. Rather, it is intended merely as a sampling of the kinds of issues on which advocates of corporate social responsibility, in fact, are focusing. In later chapters, these issues will be discussed in greater depth.

INVESTING STRATEGIES

Next, let's look at the different strategies available to socially responsible investors—the three "As" of socially responsible investing:

Avoidance,
Alternative, and
Activist investing.

Avoidance Investing: "First, Do No Harm"

Also sometimes referred to as *exclusionary* or *ethical* investing, this is probably the most common strategy adopted by individuals and institutions and is what we primarily focused on in Chapter 1. It may also be the easiest, or at least the most mechanical, strategy for you to implement since it is mainly a *reactive* rather than a *proactive* one: You simply determine what kinds of activities you consider socially *irresponsible*, you find out which companies engage in such activities, and then you just avoid investing in them.

What simplifies your task is the fact that there are numerous lists available to you as a concerned investor, which enable you to screen out companies from your portfolio for any of a variety of reasons. If, for instance, you are opposed to smoking or drinking, you can readily get a list of tobacco companies or distilling companies from any of a number of standard investment manuals. If you wish to register your opposition to apartheid, there are several options available to you. For example, you can get a list of the signatories to the *Statement of Principles for South Africa* (originally the *Sullivan Principles*) and exclude from your portfolio any company that is not on the list. If you wish to go further, you can get a list of companies with direct investments in South Africa, whether or not they are signatories to the *Statement of Principles*, and exclude them. Or, if you wish to go further still, you not only can screen out companies with direct investments in South Africa, but those with indirect investments there as well.

If your concern is armaments, defense, and the military, you can refer to the U.S. Government's lists of the *100 Companies Receiving the Largest Dollar Volume of Prime Contract Awards* or the *500 Contractors Receiving the Largest Volume of Prime Contract Awards*. If pollution and toxic wastes are your major concern, you can screen out those companies that appear on a list of *The Toxic 500: The 500 Largest Releases of Toxic Chemicals in the U.S. 1987*.

Of course, it won't always be quite that easy. There are only so many lists and the opinions of the list makers may not always conform completely to your own. Sometimes you will have to dig deeper and do some of your own research. You will also need to resolve conflicts in your own mind (e.g., when a company has a splendid record in one area of concern to you but a poor record in another). (We shall have more to say on the question of resolving such conflicts later in this chapter.)

The fact remains, however, that this *avoidance* strategy is easier to implement than the other two which we are about to discuss and that it is the least likely to require tradeoffs against potential returns. (Indeed, remember the point made in Chapter 1 to the effect that screening socially *irresponsible* companies out of portfolios might not penalize returns but actually enhance them.)

Alternative Investing: "If You're Not Part of the Solution, You're Part of the Problem"

Also referred to as *supportive* investing or *inclusionary* investing, this is the flip side of *avoidance* investing. It is a proactive, rather than a reactive strategy and is frequently more difficult to implement. It may also be a riskier strategy and generally is much smaller in scope. Moreover, unlike *avoidance* investing, this approach will sometimes entail a conscious tradeoff of measurable financial returns for a greater psychic, unquantifiable *complete* return. For those who believe that "If you're not part of the solution, you're part of the problem," it may be an even more satisfying investment approach.

Alternative investing entails searching for investment opportunities in companies that are regarded as *responsible* not only because they don't do anything bad, but because they achieve, or seek to achieve, something good in their own right. Such investment opportunities often fall outside the mainstream, such as low- and moderate-income housing or minority owned businesses.

According to Gelvin Stevenson, an advocate of *alternative* investing, "If we are to create a decent and sustainable world, we must develop a way to evaluate investments and measure their complete return. The complete return . . . includes not only the immediate financial reward, but also the financial and physical consequences to other people, the environment and society."[2]

As an example of the kinds of investments to which he is referring, Stevenson cites the purchase of neighborhood housing service partnerships by the Presbyterian Church Foundation. One such loan was to a disabled man and his 87-year-old mother, enabling them to replace their water heater, repair their roof, and insulate their home. The total financial return to the Presbyterian Foundation on this investment was only 4.5% but, in Stevenson's words, "The complete return was much higher."[3]

It may be argued that such *alternative* investing is really not investing at all but simply philanthropy in a different guise, or that it is philanthropy at least in part (to the degree that the *alternative* investor knowingly accepts a return below that which otherwise would have been justified by the market risk characteristics of his investment). But be that as it may, the fact remains: It *is* one form of what is referred to as *alternative* investing.

This kind of investing, however admirable though it may be in a social or ethical sense, is not what most investors necessarily mean when they speak of *alternative* investing. Rather, they use the term to refer to investments in small emerging companies that have a social purpose, such as those researching alternative energy sources (*e.g.*, solar or geothermal), those developing pollution control products, or those attempting to find alternatives to cooling systems that deplete the ozone layer. *Alternative* investments in companies such as these, while generally riskier than traditional investments, may still provide potential returns as commensurate with their risk as those of other venture capital opportunities.

Activist Investing: Changing the Status Quo

Also known as *interventionist* investing, this approach differs from *avoidance* and *alternative* investing in two important respects: (1) It entails investment in *irresponsible* rather than *responsible* companies, with the goal of inducing a change in corporate behavior through stockholder pressure, rather than the support or endorsement of acceptable behavior, and (2) it involves at least some further direct action by the investor after his investment has been made.

Through direct intervention, *activist* investors seek to influence managements to adopt, modify, or rescind corporate policies deemed to have social, ethical, or political consequences. Such intervention may take a variety of forms, including direct communication with managements (either individually or through coordinated telephone or letter writing campaigns), the introduction and support of shareholder resolutions, and the solicitation and voting of proxies to achieve board representation.

In 1990, for example, investors controlling over $450 billion sponsored more than 300 resolutions on social responsibility. These issues included animal rights, corporate governance and political activities, U.S. farm debt and international debt, energy, the environment, equality and employment, housing, infant formula, militarism, Northern Ireland, smoking and tobacco, and South Africa. Included in that number were challenges to more than 100 companies and banks doing business in South Africa, a record 38 resolutions on the environment, and 18 resolutions involving chemical and nuclear weapons. Among the sponsors of these resolutions were a number of Protestant and Roman Catholic organizations, the pension funds of New York City, the Los Angeles Unified School District, the states of Connecticut, Florida, Minnesota, New York, and Wisconsin, **TIAA-CREF, Calvert Social Investment Fund, Franklin Research and Development Corporation**, and **U.S. Trust Company.**

Of course, not all of those resolutions were ultimately brought to a vote. Some were withdrawn by sponsors after negotiations with corporate managements resulted in compromises and the accomplishment of some, even if not all, of their objectives while avoiding rancorous confrontations. Even that represented a kind of victory for socially responsible investors.

Moreover, over the years, there has been a significant trend toward increasing shareholder support for such resolutions. For example, in 1973 only 17.5% of all socially responsible investing resolutions received over 3% of the total shareholder vote (the minimum necessary in order to be able to refile a resolution); in 1989, however, 80% were eligible for resubmission and companies began to sit up and take notice.

As an example of how these different approaches might work in real life, suppose that Andrew (an activist investor), Barbara (an alternative investor), and Carl (an avoidance investor) all share a concern over the adverse consequences of cigarette smoking. Andrew might manifest that concern by investing in **Philip Morris Companies Inc.** (NYSE—MO) and supporting a shareholder resolution aimed at encouraging the company to withdraw from the production and marketing of tobacco by the year 2000. In fact, such a resolution was filed in 1990 and voted on at the company's annual meeting. Similar resolutions were also filed at **American Brands, Inc.** (NYSE—AMB), **Kimberly-Clark Corporation** (NYSE—KMB), and **Loews Corporation** (NYSE—LTR).

Barbara, however, would not invest in **Philip Morris** at all but might consider instead an alternative investment in **Advantage**

Life Products, a small company with less than $6 million in annual revenues which developed CigArrest gum to help smokers kick the habit. Of course, Carl wouldn't invest in **Philip Morris** either, but he wouldn't necessarily seek out an alternative investment in a company contributing to the anti-smoking movement; simply screening tobacco companies out of his portfolio would be sufficient for him.

And yet no one really is all of a piece. Hence, at some point, should it seem to him that his *activist* strategy is producing no tangible results and is unlikely to, Andrew might change his tactics and sell his **Philip Morris** stock, perforce evolving into an *avoidance* investor, at least insofar as that particular security is concerned. Indeed, he might then even reinvest the proceeds of that sale in an *alternative* investment such as **Advantage Life Products**. Sometimes the lines do blur.

DOES ANY OF IT REALLY MATTER?

Do these approaches—*avoidance, alternative*, or *activist*—really have any impact on corporate behavior? We think the answer is yes, although, admittedly, at least in the case of an *avoidance* strategy, that is a difficult conclusion to document.

Proving that *avoidance* investing has a meaningful impact on corporate behavior is especially difficult since most of the companies subjected to this strategy are so large that the decision of an investor, even a major institutional investor, to avoid the stock or sell the shares, will likely have little measurable effect on the stock's marketability or price. Indeed, if *avoidance* investors' decisions to sell stocks or not to buy them in the first place were secret, those decisions probably would have virtually no effect at all. Markets in these issues are so broad and so efficient that even if an *avoidance* investor's action temporarily depressed the price of a stock by some fraction of a point, other investors, unconstrained by considerations of social responsibility, probably would step into the breach quickly in order to take advantage of the selloff as a bargain buying opportunity and the stock would be right back up where it was before very long.

.The fact is, however, that once these decisions are made, they generally are not kept secret, at least not by institutional investors, but are disclosed in ways intended to create maximum adverse publicity for the affected company or companies. When, for instance, Harvard University and New York City's pension plans determined to liquidate their tobacco stock holdings, these actions were heralded as front page news throughout the nation. Thus, just as the main negative effect of a consumer boycott is seldom the actual direct revenues loss but rather is the publicity surrounding the boycott, so too, the principal impact of an *avoidance* strategy on companies subjected to it is often the negative publicity that accompanies it. In many cases, this publicity can be devastating.

In fact, a positive way of looking at this is to note that socially responsible *avoidance* strategies are seldom implemented in vacuo. Rather, they are often adopted in conjunction with other strategies of a political, legal, or economic nature (e.g., consumer boycotts, litigation, legislative lobbying, etc.).

H.J. Heinz Company (NYSE—HNZ). Consider, for example, the tale of **H.J. Heinz Company**, tuna, and the dolphins. **H.J. Heinz** is a major food processor with one of the most extraordinary records of consistent earnings growth in corporate America—its profits have risen every year for 25 consecutive years. Its product line, in addition to *Star-Kist* tuna, includes soups, ketchup, baby foods, *Ore-Ida* frozen potatoes, *9 Lives* cat food, and *Chico-San* rice cakes. It also operates the *Weight Watchers* weight control programs.

Until early in 1990, U.S. tuna companies (including **H.J. Heinz**) regularly purchased tuna from fishermen who caught the fish in a manner that resulted in the death of thousands of dolphins annually. The practice captured the attention of animal rights activists, environmentalists, the press, the general public, and socially responsible investors—all of whom considered it reprehensible. Legislation was proposed in Congress to ban the practice. Consumers mounted a boycott of **Heinz's** products and at least some socially responsible investors liquidated their **Heinz** holdings in protest.

As a result, in April 1990, just two days after **Conoco** announced its decision to build future tankers with double hulls, **H.J. Heinz** disclosed that it had changed its tuna policy and no longer would buy tuna caught in nets that also trap and kill dolphins. It admitted that because of this development it might be forced to raise prices of its tuna fish by a few cents a can to cover its additional costs.

The **Heinz** action drew accolades from consumer activists, socially responsible investors, and the public at large. But was the company making the kind of economic mistake Bluestone was referring to? Would **Heinz's** competitors seek to capitalize on its decision to incur unnecessary incremental costs by undercutting it in price in the marketplace and capturing market share? Was the **Heinz** 25-year earnings growth record in jeopardy?

Apparently not. Here the jury is already in and it is clear that, theory to the contrary notwithstanding, **Heinz's** major competitors did not seek to capitalize on the potential cost advantage **Heinz** gave them. Quite the opposite: Within 24 hours of the **Heinz** announcement, the company's two major competitors, the **Van Kamp Seafood Company**, which markets *Chicken of the Sea Tuna*, and **Bumble Bee Seafoods, Inc.** announced that they, too, would stop buying tuna caught in nets that can trap dolphins. Apparently, both **Van Kamp** and **Bumble Bee** perceived their own long-term interests as best being served by following **Heinz's** lead. By so doing, they, too, might gain goodwill, avoid potentially punishing legislation, and transfer to consumers, via higher prices, the incremental costs of catching tuna in a dolphin-safe manner.

But why did **Heinz** do it? Was it in reaction to the consumer boycott? Apparently not, since, according to the company, the boycott was having no financial effect: Its operating profits from tuna actually increased during the boycott from $115 million in 1987 to $145 million in 1989. Was it due to the adverse publicity? Perhaps, somewhat. According to Ted Smyth, a **Heinz** spokesman, "It was our only brand that had a cloud over it. Why not balance virtue with commerce?"[4]

Or was it due to the threat of federal legislation? Or to the pressures brought by stockholders? Or to the consciences of its own management? We can't know for sure.

But even though it couldn't be proved with certainty one way or the other, it seems reasonable that the pressures brought by socially responsible *avoidance* investors at least contributed to the result—just as it seems reasonable that bad press, the consumer boycott, and the threat of adverse legislation contributed too.

Of course, the question still remains whether **Heinz's** action will or will not result in any net benefit to society—or even dolphins—for that matter. As August Felando, president of the American Tugboat Association, argued in a letter to the editor of *The Wall Street Journal*, the **Heinz** decision could result in more, rather than fewer, tuna being killed. As he explains it:

> U.S. fishermen have pioneered dolphin-safe techniques and technology. America's tuna fleet has a 99.4% dolphin-safety record—three to four times better than foreign fishermen. . . . The canners' decision will put the U.S. at a competitive disadvantage. By forcing us out of the tuna-rich Eastern Tropical Pacific (where tuna traditionally swim with dolphins), the "dolphin-safe" labeling movement invites irresponsible foreign fishermen in—a scenario that . . . will result in greater dolphin mortality.[5]
>
> Whether or not this is the case remains to be seen.

When it comes to *activist* and *alternative* socially responsible investors, however, the evidence is clearer: Both of those strategies *do* have a direct and measurable impact on corporate behavior. In the *activist* arena, for instance, one need only look at a few examples, including **Lockheed Corporation** (NYSE—LK), **Occidental Petroleum Corporation** (NYSE—OXY), **Amoco Corporation** (NYSE—AN), **Foxboro Company** (NYSE—FOX), and **Texaco Inc.** (NYSE—TX) for confirmation.

The very night before its annual meeting in March 1990, **Lockheed's** chairman, Daniel Tellep, anticipating the success of two shareholder resolutions relating to confidential voting and exemption from Delaware's anti-takeover law, announced his support of those resolutions. Even before the vote was counted officially, but it was estimated that the resolutions had carried, Tellep immediately repeated his intention to carry out "the will of the shareholders."[6]

Similarly, the California Public Employees Retirement System (Calpers), the nation's largest public pension plan, agreed to drop its plans to present a resolution at **Occidental Petroleum's** annual meeting calling for the establishment of a shareholders' advisory committee, but only after **Occidental** agreed to have four of its directors meet twice a year with officials of the pension plan to discuss the company's business plans. Likewise, New York City's public employee funds agreed to drop proxy resolutions at **Amoco, Foxboro**, and **Texaco**, in exchange for negotiated agreements on secret balloting procedures at those companies.

The impact of *alternative* socially responsible investing is virtually self-evident. Indeed, many of the businesses invested in on this basis would not even exist if *alternative* investors had not chosen to finance them in the first place.

RESOLVING THE CONFLICTS

Inevitably, having embarked on a socially responsible investment program, you will be confronted by conflicts that only you will be able to resolve. You will find that these conflicts will be of two types and, although only you will be able to mediate them in a manner you'll consider satisfactory, we will try to provide you with some guidance.

First, having decided on the general issues that are important to you, you will have to decide which corporate actions satisfy your requirements. Don't be surprised to discover that your standards differ significantly from your friend's, despite the fact that you both profess to share the same values. For instance, suppose that avoiding companies that support apartheid in South Africa is important to you. Would you invest in companies that do business in South Africa so long as they subscribed to the *Statement of Principles for South Africa?* Or, would you insist that they divest themselves of their operations in South Africa entirely? Would that be enough? Suppose that they sold their assets in South Africa so that they no longer had any offices or plants there, but they continued to trade with companies in that nation or sold goods there or received royalties on business done there by others. Would that eliminate them from consideration as investments in your portfolio?

Suppose the company was in the process of divesting itself of its operations but hadn't totally divested yet. Would you consider holding the stock since the company was in the process of doing the right thing, or would you wait until the divestment was completed? Might your decision depend on whether completion of the divestment was likely to take three months or three years?

There are no right or wrong answers here; it really depends on your own analysis of the specific situation and your personal value system. In this hypothetical situation, for instance, if you believe that the best hope for South African blacks is for an enlightened international corporate presence to be maintained there, then you might choose to own the stocks of companies doing business there, so long as they subscribed to the *Statement of Principles for South Africa*, as Mangosuthu Gatsha Buthelezi, Chief of the Zulus (South Africa's largest ethnic group), has advocated. But, if you believe that the only way that apartheid will ever be brought to an end is for maximum pressure to be brought on South Africa's economy and for the country to be internationally ostracized, then you might choose to avoid the stocks of companies that have anything at all to do with that nation, as Nelson Mandela has asked.

This is a judgment call and, since it's your money that's being invested, you must use your judgment, not someone else's.

Suppose you are a strong supporter of equal employment opportunity. If a company has an unblemished record of being truly color blind in its hiring and advancement practices, would that be enough for you, or would you require that the company have an affirmative action plan in place too? What if management refused, arguing that affirmative action was just another term for quotas and reverse discrimination and reminded you of its impeccable record as an equal opportunity employer. What then?

Again, it's your money. So it's your call.

The second area of potential conflict is even more difficult. It arises when two different principles come into conflict. If you are strongly pro-choice and an avid environmentalist, what do you do about a company like **American Telephone & Telegraph Company** (NYSE—T)? In 1989, the company was nominated by the environmentally progressive Council on Economic Priorities for a *Corporate Conscience Award in Environmental Stewardship* for its paper recycling program; in 1990, it was nominated again for its program to end all use of ozone-depleting chlorofluorocarbons (CFCs) by 1994. Environmentally, you can't get much better than that. And yet in early 1990, the company also announced that it would no longer make annual $50,000 contributions to the Planned Parenthood Federation of America because of that organization's advocacy of abortion rights. Would you still choose to invest in **American Telephone?**

Another example: Suppose you are an animal lover and disapprove of experimentation on animals. Assume further that you have just discovered that one of the companies that you were thinking of investing in experiments on animals in the process of testing its line of cosmetics. You certainly wouldn't invest in that company, would you? That's easy.

Now suppose the company involved wasn't a cosmetics manufacturer but was in the forefront of space exploration and it used animals in its space programs before risking human lives. Maybe you still wouldn't invest, but your decision probably wouldn't be quite as easily made.

Finally, suppose the company were involved in cancer and AIDS research; it was on the verge of a major breakthrough, and it was preparing to test its drugs on animals as the final step in its research process prior to its testing on human volunteers. Might you not reconsider your position on animal experimentation? Maybe you still wouldn't invest, but you must admit that this decision would be even more difficult.

How, then, might you resolve such problems? The following are some suggestions.

First, decide whether the issue which concerns you is, or is not, an *absolute*. By an *absolute*, we mean something as extreme as slavery in the United States before the Civil War or Nazi Germany's "final solution" for the extermination of the Jews. These were such *absolute* evils that there was no room for compromise or mediation where they were concerned.

If a slave plantation in 1860 had been a public corporation, it would not matter whether or not it also contributed generously to charities or had any involvement with the military or was especially enlightened with regard to the environment or animal rights or shareholder rights. The enormity of the evil which is slavery is such that nothing could mitigate it. You simply could not have invested in the company under any circumstances.

Similarly, you could not have invested in **I.G. Farben**, the giant German chemicals company that not only operated a plant at Auschwitz with slave labor but also patented the cyanide crystals that were used to exterminate the Jews at the Nazi death camp. It would be obscene even to ask whether the company, by its activities, also did or did not pollute the environment or what its policy was on corporate philanthropy. None of that could possibly matter in the face of such evil.

Most issues, however, are not absolutes. Shareholder rights, corporate philanthropy, alternative energy sources, employees' working conditions, and so on are all important, no doubt, but none of those issues is of such overriding importance that nothing else would matter. In those cases, we suggest that it would be more appropriate for you to make *situational* judgments, balancing one value against another.

To be sure, not all investors will agree about which issues are *absolutes* and which are *situational*. To some, for instance, apartheid might be an *absolute*, akin to slavery, whereas others, while opposing the practice, might not place it in quite the same class. Similarly, abortion might be equivalent to murder to some investors, while to others, denying a woman the right to an abortion might be tantamount to slavery. For most, however, whether they be pro-life or pro-choice, the abortion issue is not quite as black and white as that; rather, it is *situational*.

Now let's see how this approach might affect your decision in the two examples presented. In the first, **American Telephone**, if you believe that a woman's right to an abortion is an *absolute*, you probably would not buy **American Telephone** stock. In your viewpoint, **American Telephone** has a moral imperative to continue to support Planned Parenthood. By withdrawing that support, the company has violated that imperative and its other policies, in this case environmental ones, wouldn't make a difference to you.

However, even if you favored a woman's right to an abortion but didn't necessarily consider that issue an *absolute*, you probably would make the investment, reasoning that the magnitude of the company's environmental contributions far outweighed its shortfall in withdrawing $50,000 in annual support for Planned Parenthood. (Of course, if you were pro-life, rather than pro-choice, you'd make the investment too; that would be easy.)

Again, in the animal experimentation case, if you believed that animal rights were an *absolute*, you wouldn't make the investment in any of the three cases. If you thought animal rights were important but not an *absolute*, we daresay you'd probably not make the investment if the tradeoff was cosmetics but would make it if a potential cancer or AIDS cure were in the offing.

What if the tradeoff were a contribution to the space exploration program? We'll leave that one to you. After all, we don't have all the answers.

These questions are difficult and different investors will answer them in different ways. In the next chapter, we'll see how four such hypothetical investors—Andrew, Barbara, Carl and Donna— might deal with some of them. We'll also give you a chance to take a short quiz to help you crystalize your own thinking on some of these issues.

3

What's Your SRIQ (Socially Responsible Investing Quotient)?

A TALE OF FOUR FRIENDS

Through four years of college and three years of law school, they were nearly inseparable. They worked together and played together, laughed together and cried together. Day after day, month after month, they shared books, clothing, confidences, meals, rooms, and dreams. They spent untold hours with one another, struggling over the major political and social issues of their day. Civil rights. Apartheid. Feminism. Nuclear power.

They discussed, they argued, they debated, often well into the early hours of the morning, but they did more than just talk—they put their convictions on the line. They marched together, arm in arm, to integrate lunch counters in the South. They prostrated themselves before U.S. Army trucks to protest the transportation of nuclear weapons. They wrote articles for their hometown newspapers, distributed leaflets, formed consciousness-raising groups, petitioned their congressional representatives, and did all in their power at the time to translate their aspirations for a better world into reality.

And then they graduated from law school, passed their bar exams, and entered the real world.

For a while they remained close but, as is often the case with the passage of time, they began to drift apart. Still, they attended each other's weddings and, for the first few years, sent each other long letters and photographs at Christmas, updating one another on the statuses of their families and careers. But eventually, even that stopped.

Andrew, who was always the most radical and militant of the four, relocated to San Francisco. Barbara, who was probably just as idealistic as Andrew, albeit gentler and not as militant, settled in Boston. Carl, the most traditional of them all, remained in Chicago. And Donna, pragmatic Donna, moved to New York.

They continued to "do their thing" but in new ways. Their lifestyles changed. Their priorities changed. While many of their values remained constant, their ways of implementing them often had to be adapted to their changing circumstances.

Andrew, the Activist Investor

When Andrew graduated from law school, he went to work for the Legal Aid Society. Subsequently, he worked for a variety of other public interest legal organizations, representing migrant workers, radical environmental and civil rights groups, and indigent criminal defendants. A lot of his work was pro-bono and he certainly didn't get rich from it. In his free time, Andrew worked at his neighborhood shelter for the homeless. He didn't have much money to contribute to charitable causes, but he did try to give what little he could.

Because of the kinds of cases he accepted and the amount of pro-bono work he did, Andrew earned much less than any of his three classmates and accumulated considerably less wealth—if the term "wealth" should even be applied to his eight-year-old car, spartan furniture, inexpensive and limited wardrobe, and motley collection of folk music tapes and used books. But Andrew had no regrets; he was content with his life and secure in the knowledge that he, at least, had never "sold out."

Not surprisingly, Andrew never invested in the stock market for himself. Indeed, he never had sufficient assets even to consider it. But Andrew did become active in his church and recently was asked to serve on its investment advisory committee. He was flattered to be asked and pleased to do so, but quickly discovered that the job wasn't quite as simple as he'd expected it to be. Several of the other members of the committee focused solely on the investment merits of the securities in which they had invested or were considering investing, to the exclusion of any concern over the social behavior of their issuing corporations. Indeed, many didn't even seem to care whether those companies polluted the environment, conducted business in South Africa, manufactured cigarettes or distilled spirits or armaments or whatever. If a company's margins were wide, if its revenues and profits were rising, if its dividends were secure, the other members of the board were content.

Some of the other members did share Andrew's concerns over corporate social responsibility but even they approached the issue in a different way. A couple thought that the church should only invest in local projects, making below-market interest loans to needy parishioners, minority-owned businesses, and low-income housing projects. Others preferred that the church invest in established well-capitalized companies, but that it screen out of its portfolio the stocks of companies behaving in a socially irresponsible manner—say, by excluding those that did business in South Africa or those that polluted the environment.

Andrew had a different idea entirely. He wanted the church to invest in irresponsible companies, but then to use its clout as a shareholder (through the corporate resolutions process and proxy fights) to encourage those companies to change their ways. By doing this, he argued, the church would truly be a force for good.

Andrew had become the quintessential *activist* investor.

Barbara, the Alternative Investor

Shortly after graduation from law school, Barbara joined a small electronics company in Boston as one of only two lawyers. The company prospered and so did she: today it is a large company and Barbara is a senior vice president and head of the legal department.

Barbara didn't become extremely wealthy along the way but she certainly lives much more comfortably than does Andrew. She trades in her car every two years, has just redecorated her home, and recently began collecting Steuben glass. She volunteers some of her time to charitable causes and a generous amount of her income, and usually feels guilty that she isn't able to contribute more of both. Over the years, she has built up an investment portfolio valued in the low six figures.

Barbara's portfolio is rather unusual and you probably wouldn't recognize most of the names in it. A large chunk is in participations in below market rate loans to community housing developments, worker-owned cooperatives, and minority-owned businesses that Barbara claims generate a very high *complete* return, even if her financial return alone is a little sub-par.

A smaller portion of Barbara's portfolio is invested in some highly speculative private and public ventures which, in Barbara's opinion, serve a social purpose. One such venture is seeking to develop photovoltaic cells as a possible alternative energy source. Another is trying to find a practical substitute for chlorofluorocarbons in refrigeration applications. A third franchises child-care and elder-care centers. The fourth manufactures "cruelty free" cosmetics that are produced without animal testing.

Barbara clearly has evolved into an *alternative* investor.

Carl, the Avoidance Investor

Upon graduating from law school, Carl went to work as a lawyer for the city of Chicago. Over time, he became especially knowledgeable in the legal aspects of pensions and benefits for public employees. Eventually he became responsible, with others, for overseeing the management of the city's employee pension plans. In recent years, Carl has been too busy to contribute much of his time to any charitable volunteer activities but he has tried to make up for that by contributing generously financially.

Carl hasn't exactly become wealthy either but, like Barbara, he has done well enough to live comfortably. He owns his own home (albeit with a large mortgage) and has upward of $200,000 in mutual fund shares and the stocks and bonds of some blue chip companies.

The mutual fund he has invested in is a socially responsible one and the names of the securities in his portfolio, unlike those in Barbara's, are readily recognizable. They are virtually all household names—no venture capital start-ups or private placements in community loans or businesses.

However, you might be struck by what is *not* in Carl's portfolio: you won't find any tobacco or distilling stocks, any companies doing business in South Africa, any major defense contractors, any nuclear utilities or any companies with records of serious violations of environmental or equal employment or workplace safety regulations. Carl has made a very conscious effort to exclude such companies.

In his role overseeing the management of the city's pension fund for public employees, Carl has taken similar positions: He has urged that socially irresponsible companies be screened out. Still, he has not given any encouragement to the idea of investing in the kinds of *alternative* situations that appeal to Barbara, since he feels that his fiduciary responsibility precludes his approving of the fund's investing for sub-par financial returns, no matter what the complete returns might be.

It is apparent that in both his personal and professional lives, Carl is an *avoidance* investor.

Donna, the Traditional Investor

Which brings us to Donna, although it's not immediately clear what she's doing in this exalted company of socially responsible investors. Certainly, she's not an *activist* investor like Andrew. Indeed, she often doesn't even bother to vote the proxies she receives and when she does, it's invariably to support management. Her contention has been that when she owns a company's stock, she won't second-guess management; if she doesn't like the way they're running her company, she'll just sell her stock and go on to something else.

Does this mean that Donna is an *avoidance* investor like Carl?

Not by a long shot. Donna doesn't even pay attention to how the companies she invests in behave on social issues; her sole concern is whether or not those companies represent good investments in strictly financial terms.

Indeed, Donna sees her role as an investor in much the same way that she sees her role as a lawyer, or her husband's role as a doctor. That is, as a lawyer, she wouldn't refuse to represent a client because she disapproved of his politics; nor would her husband, as a doctor, refuse to treat a patient because he deemed him to be socially irresponsible. Similarly, she doesn't think that political or social judgments should enter into the investment decision-making process either.

Obviously, then, Donna wouldn't be an *alternative* investor.

So what is she? That's easy. She's a *traditional* investor, concerned strictly with her financial bottom line. On a straight risk-reward basis, she asks only that a stock (or bond) represent good value. That's it.

Does this mean that Donna, herself, is less socially concerned than Andrew, Barbara, or Carl? Not necessarily. It simply means that Donna distinguishes her role as an individual from her role as an investor in a way that the others do not. Just as she might contribute financially to the pro-choice movement on Monday and defend in court a pro-life advocate accused of having bombed an abortion clinic on Tuesday (because she believes that everyone has a right to a legal defense), so too she might support a recycling program in her neighborhood on Wednesday but invest in a company accused of polluting the environment on Thursday. To Donna, those roles and activities are separable.

Somehow we've gotten ahead of ourselves with Donna. What happened to her when she got out of law school anyway?

Well, she went to New York and joined one of the most prestigious law firms in the city. She performed brilliantly and became the first woman partner in the firm's history. Along the way she earned more money and accumulated more wealth than all three of her friends combined. She has a penthouse apartment in Manhattan, a summer home in the Hamptons, a Mercedez Benz, and a portfolio of stocks and bonds valued at well into seven figures.

Donna has been so busy with her work that she has had no time to volunteer for causes or charities. But she's compensated for that many times over by contributing generously from her accumulated wealth to the causes that she and her friends always supported.

Reunion Revelations and Remonstrances

Last week, Andrew, Barbara, Carl, and Donna met at the 20th dinner reunion of their law school class. It was the first time that they had all been together in nearly 15 years and they were absolutely delighted.

As the evening wore on, they ate together, drank together, danced together, reminisced together. It was like old times. They exchanged addresses and telephone numbers; showed pictures of their families; brought one another up-to-date on what they'd done, where they worked, and how they lived; and promised to keep in touch.

Then somehow they got on the subject of the types of clients they represent and what investments they made and all hell broke out.

When Andrew heard about the corporate clients Donna sometimes represented and how she invested her own money, he accused her in no uncertain terms of having sold out. Was this the same woman he knew in college and law school who marched with him to protest apartheid in South Africa and racial segregation in the United States, the dangers of nuclear holocaust, and the military-industrial complex?

While he was working at his neighborhood shelter for the homeless, what was she doing—preparing legal defenses for corporate polluters and violators of equal employment regulations or reviewing her portfolio of nuclear utilities and racially insensitive war mongers? What had happened to her? Didn't she care any more?

At first, Donna was startled by Andrew's outburst—but then she was quite angry. Why doesn't Andrew grow up? Yes, it's admirable that he ladles out soup at his local shelter for the homeless and that he contributes whatever he can of his time and his limited funds to a variety of other worthwhile causes. But over the last 15 years, she's probably given 20 times as much money as Andrew has to causes of which he would overwhelmingly approve.

Indeed, her contributions to six different homeless centers have enabled them to hire six people to help feed the people at those centers. That had six times the impact of Andrew's personal contribution of his time and provided at least part-time employment to those six people who otherwise might have ended up homeless themselves.

And how was she able to afford that? By working where she worked, representing the clients she represented, and investing in those companies in her portfolio—with her attention always focused on the bottom line. If Andrew *really* cared about his causes and not his precious image of himself as some unwavering and uncompromising do-gooder, he, too, would do whatever was necessary to maximize his income from whatever legitimate sources he could, so that he would have that much more to contribute to his causes.

Barbara and Carl tried not to get involved, but they couldn't help it. Yes, they agreed with Andrew that Donna *seemed* to have sold out by representing the kinds of clients she did and investing in the kinds of companies she did, while Andrew *seemed* to have remained truer to the principles they all espoused in college and law school. And yet, there also *seemed* to be no denying that Donna had accomplished more quantifiable tangible good than any of them by contributing so much more financially to all the causes they cared about.

Perhaps there was some happy medium and perhaps Barbara and Carl had found it.

Certainly Barbara and Carl seemed to have a lot more in common in their senses of socially responsible investing than either of them did with Andrew or Donna or than Andrew and Donna did with each other. Both Barbara and Carl did invest for their own accounts, after all, whereas Andrew did not. Both Barbara and Carl sought out companies that did good (or at least those which did no harm), whereas Andrew looked for those which behaved "badly" so that he might change them. Both

Barbara and Carl cared about the social behavior of the companies in which they invested, whereas Donna didn't care at all.

Yet, Barbara would have preferred it if a little more of Andrew's idealism rubbed off on Carl. And Carl would have liked to see more of Donna's pragmatism influencing Barbara's behavior.

DETERMINING YOUR SRIQ

Where do you fit in? Who are you most like?

Are you most similar to Andrew: *activist*, militant, eager to try to change corporate behavior through direct confrontation? Or are you more like Barbara: thinking globally but acting locally, focusing on those *alternative* investment opportunities where you can make a real difference? Or are you like Carl: the most prevalent sort of socially responsible investor who simply wants to avoid ethically tainted companies in his own portfolio or the portfolios he manages for others? Finally, are you like Donna: a bottom-line-oriented *traditionalist* who separates her investment policies from her social or philanthropic behavior in other areas of her life?

Chances are you fall somewhere in between or share the characteristics of more than one of our hypothetical friends. To help you crystalize your own thinking on that, we've developed the following Socially Responsible Investing Quotient (SRIQ) quiz. It will only take you a few minutes to complete and it may give you greater insight into just what your values are and how you might best implement them.

In the 10 multiple choice questions that follow, accept the premises given in each introductory paragraph. For instance, if it stipulates that you are concerned over animal rights or acid rain, assume that you really are, whether or not those particular issues are genuinely important to you. Then, within that context, select the one answer that best describes how you would act.

Instructions for scoring your results and an evaluation of those results appear at the end of the quiz.

1. You are a staunch animal rights advocate and have just inherited 100 shares of **Bristol Myers-Squibb Company** (NYSE—BMY) from your grandmother. In researching the company, you have discovered that (i) it tests some of its products on animals, (ii) a shareholder resolution, to be voted on in three months at the company's annual meeting and opposed by management, has been filed, urging the company to suspend animal testing, and (iii) from a strictly financial standpoint, the stock appears to be an excellent investment.

   Do you:
   a. Sell the 100 shares and reinvest the proceeds in **Avon Products, Inc.** (NYSE—AVP), which has discontinued animal testing of its cosmetics products and which appears to you also to be an attractive financial commitment in its own right.
   b. Hold the stock so that you may vote your proxy in favor of the shareholder resolution at the annual meeting.
   c. Hold the stock simply because you think it's a good investment, ignoring the shareholder resolution.
   d. Sell the stock and reinvest the proceeds in a speculative venture capital research laboratory that is attempting to develop "cruelty free" computer models and in vitro tissue culture tests as an alternative to animal testing.

2. You are very concerned over the environmental risk of oil spills (especially since the Exxon Valdez) and you strongly support the search for alternative energy sources. You own 1,000 shares of stock in a small oil company which is also on the cutting edge of solar energy research. The stock is selling for $5 a share.

   You have just received a letter from one of the major integrated oil companies that has an especially poor record of oil spills, offering to acquire each share of your stock for $15 worth of its own. It is offering to do this primarily to gain control of your company's oil reserves which adjoin its own and which would greatly strengthen its reserves position. It does not intend to do much with the solar energy research unit.

   If a majority of the shareholders of your company agree, the acquisition will be consummated and you will receive $15,000 worth of the acquiring company's stock in exchange for your own. If not, you'll keep your shares which probably still will be worth about $5,000.

   How would you vote and what would you do if the acquisition were approved?

a. Vote against the acquisition. If it goes through anyway, sell the stock you receive for $15,000 and look to invest the proceeds in another small company that is researching alternative energy sources.

b. Vote in favor of the acquisition. If it goes through, hold the stock you receive in exchange as a good investment in its own right, reflecting the improvement in the acquiring company's reserves position.

c. Vote against the acquisition. If it goes through anyway, hold the stock so that you can introduce shareholder resolutions urging that the acquiring company (i) maintain and expand the solar energy research operation and (ii) improve its environmental record by increasing its safety precautions in its transportation of oil.

d. Vote in favor of the acquisition but with the intention of selling the stock you receive for $15,000 as soon as you get it, so that you don't retain an investment in a company with a bad record of serious oil spills.

3. You are very much opposed to smoking but are strongly in favor of corporate support for the arts. You have received a gift of 100 shares of **Philip Morris Companies, Inc.** (NYSE—MO) and are of the opinion that the stock is an outstanding financial investment, independent of its social characteristics. The company is one of the nation's leading corporate supporters of the arts, having incorporated a branch of the Whitney Museum into its own corporate headquarters, sponsored major art exhibits nationwide, and supported leading dance and ballet troupes. It is, of course, also a major cigarette manufacturer (*Marlboro, Benson and Hedges, Merit, Virginia Slims, etc.*).

At **Philip Morris'** next annual meeting in two months, you will be given an opportunity to vote on a shareholder resolution urging the company to divest itself of its tobacco business before the year 2000. If that were ever to occur, the company's cash flow would be reduced substantially and its programs in support of the arts might have to be curtailed.

Do you:

a. Sell the stock now because you don't want your funds invested in shares of a tobacco company, no matter how good its record of corporate support of the arts. Look for another company that is not in the tobacco business in which to invest your money.

b. Hold the stock so that you can vote your proxy in favor of the company's divesting itself of its tobacco business, even if that would jeopardize its programs in support of the arts.

   c. Hold the stock and vote against the resolution in order to indicate your general support of management's business policies.

   d. Sell the stock and reinvest the proceeds partially in the stock of a small new company that franchises a chain of clinics to help stop smoking and partially in below market rate loans to community cultural activities.

4. You are very involved in the environmental movement in your neighborhood and are going off to college next year, where you intend to major in environmental studies and urban affairs. Your uncle, the president of a major chemicals company with a relatively poor record on environmental issues, has offered you a summer job at his company to help you pay your college tuition.

   He has also offered to let you work during spring and Christmas vacations and in future summers. The money you could earn there probably would be more than you could make elsewhere. As an employee, you would also be eligible to buy the company's stock at a discount and could sell it immediately at a virtually guaranteed profit in the open market.

   Do you:

   a. Politely decline your uncle's offer, explaining that his business philosophy doesn't square with your own. But ask him if he would use his industry contacts to help you find a job, even one paying less, with some other small fringe company involved in seeking a solution to one or more of the industry's environmental problems.

   b. Accept the job and participate in the employee stock purchase program, but avoid getting involved in company affairs (other than to do your job as well as you possibly can). Remain active in environmental activities, not involving your uncle's company, outside of work.

   c. Accept your uncle's offer and, as an employee, try to convince him and your co-workers to become more environmentally responsible. Buy stock in the company through the employee stock purchase plan and vote those shares in favor of shareholder resolutions regarding the company's responsibility to improve its environmental record, assuming that you agree with them, even if those resolutions are opposed by your uncle and his management team.

   d. Turn down your uncle's offer graciously and look for other work outside the chemicals industry.

5. You were active in the civil rights movement in the 1960s and continue to believe strongly in equal employment opportunities for blacks and other ethnic minorities. For several years, you have

owned stock in a socially responsible, well-managed and highly profitable company that has always presented itself as an equal opportunity employer and has never been accused of overtly discriminating in its hiring practices. Moreover, the company has been a long-time supporter of the Urban League, the NAACP, and the United Negro College Fund.

Recently, however, a suit was brought against the company by a group calling itself the Radical Blacks for Affirmative Action, charging that there is a statistical imbalance in the racial configuration of the company's labor force: 80% of its professional staff are white and only 20% are black, whereas 80% of its factory workers are black and only 20% are white. The suit charges that this is prima facie evidence of discrimination and seeks redress through a court-mandated affirmative action program. In support of the suit, two stockholders have also introduced a resolution, to be voted on at the next annual meeting, requesting that the company initiate an affirmative action program on its own.

Management is vigorously defending the suit and is opposing the shareholder resolution, arguing that the success of either would result in quotas and reverse discrimination and that the company opposes discrimination in any form. The company also claims that the alleged racial imbalance simply reflects a similar imbalance in the local labor pool from which it must draw its workers and that it certainly cannot be held responsible for that.

Indeed, management notes that, in actuality, approximately 90% of the applications it receives for factory jobs come from blacks and only 10% from whites, whereas about 90% of the applications it gets for professional positions come from whites and only 10% from blacks. If anything, then, the racial mix of its labor force should be looked on as reflecting an enlightened, rather than discriminatory, employment policy.

Do you:
a. Hold the stock pending disposition of the lawsuit and vote against the shareholder resolution in order to support management's "colorblind" policy. If the court should find the company guilty, sell the stock at that time and reinvest in a company that has not been found guilty of discrimination; otherwise continue to hold the stock.
b. Hold the stock and vote for the shareholder resolution in order to put additional pressure on the company to achieve equality of *results*, rather than merely equality of *opportunity*.
c. Continue to hold the stock regardless of the outcome of the lawsuit since your investment was always predicated on financial, rather than social or ethical, considerations.

    d. Sell the stock and reinvest the proceeds of the sale in minority-owned local businesses.

6. About half of the residents of your neighborhood are members of a community socially responsible investment club. They each contribute $100 a month to the club and decide by majority vote what investments to make. You have been invited to join the club and, before making your decision, you have reviewed the club's records to see what it bought in the past and what it avoided buying. You have also discussed the club's policies with several of your neighbors.

One of the things you have discovered is that it has been club policy not to invest in companies doing business in South Africa, whether or not they subscribed to the *Statement of Principles on South Africa*. Since the release of Nelson Mandela and the legalization of the African National Congress, however, a proposal has been made to revise this policy to permit investments in companies doing business in South Africa, so long as they subscribe to the *Statement of Principles*. You are vehemently opposed to apartheid.

Do you:
a. Decline to join the club lest the proposed policy change be approved because you would not want to invest in any companies doing business in South Africa under any circumstances until the black majority there was totally free and in control of the reins of government. Invest instead in minority-owned businesses in your community.
b. Refuse to join the club because you generally don't agree with the premises of socially responsible investing. But offer to join with your neighbors in other anti-apartheid political action outside the investment arena.
c. Join the club but vote against changing the present policy regarding South African investment because you don't think that international pressure on South Africa should be alleviated at all until the blacks there themselves request it. If the policy is changed anyway, recommend that the club introduce corporate resolutions at the annual meetings of its portfolio companies so that you can try to discourage them from doing business in South Africa.
d. Join the club and vote in favor of the proposed policy change as a way of encouraging the South African Government to continue moving in the right direction. But monitor the situation closely and be prepared to recommend that the change be rescinded if conditions warrant it.

7. You are opposed to apartheid and nuclear energy and are very concerned about environmental degradation. You are also actively involved, through the Chamber of Commerce, in trying to bolster the economy of your community. You have just acceded to a request by the City Council of your community to serve on the city's Public Employees' Pension Fund Management Committee. In that capacity, you will share responsibility with the other committee members for the selection of outside managers to handle portions of the fund, the monitoring of their performance, and the delineation of appropriate investment policies for them to follow.

   Three of the proposals currently before your committee are:

   (i) that the fund not invest in certain areas, including companies doing business in South Africa, companies that pollute the environment, and nuclear utilities;

   (ii) that the fund commit up to 10% of its assets to local investment opportunities that would benefit the city's small businessmen and laborers; and

   (iii) that the fund's managers play an active role in voting proxies to encourage the achievement of social, as well as financial, goals rather than automatically supporting corporate managements.

   In the opinion of the city's legal counsel, there is no legal reason why any or all of these proposals should or should not be approved. That being the case, which of the three would you most like to see approved? (If you are in favor of more than one, select the one which is most important to you.)

   a. Proposal (i).
   b. Proposal (iii).
   c. None of them.
   d. Proposal (ii).

8. You have decided to make an investment in the restaurant industry and have narrowed your choices down to the following three opportunities:

   (i) A nationwide fast-food chain with an outstanding record of employee and community relations and a very generous policy of corporate philanthropy. The company persists, however, in using non-recyclable and non-biodegradable packaging materials.

   (ii) A regional chain with an acceptable but not outstanding record in all areas of concern to socially responsible investors. Its employee and community relations are good, albeit not nearly as good as those of the nationwide chain, and its charitable activities are acceptable but also not nearly as generous as those of the nationwide chain. However, all of the regional chain's packaging is recyclable.

(iii) A local restaurant that is seeking a low interest rate loan to finance a program it wants to initiate providing inexpensive and nutritious food catering for the local senior citizens center, the orphanage, and the shelter for the homeless.

If you were to invest in the national or regional food chains, it would be by purchasing common stock listed on the New York Stock Exchange. In your best judgment, both of those stocks have above average total investment return potential; on that score and in terms of their riskiness, they are roughly equivalent.

If you were to invest in the local restaurant, it would be by lending money at a below market interest rate. In your opinion, on a strictly financial basis, that would be a riskier investment and would provide a lower financial return (but not necessarily lower *complete* return) than either of the other two.

Do you:
a. Make the low interest loan to the local restaurant.
b. Commit half your investable funds to the purchase of stock in the nationwide chain and the other half to the purchase of shares in the regional chain, which would maximize your potential financial return while reducing your risk by providing you with greater diversification than if you were to invest in either one alone.
c. Invest in the nationwide chain with the intention of joining with other investors to introduce a shareholder resolution requesting the company to stop using non-recyclable and non-bio-degradable materials.
d. Invest in the regional chain.

9. You own stock in two local banks: Neighborhood Bank and Community Trust. Both are well-managed, highly profitable, and have exemplary records of socially responsible lending to minority-owned businesses, worker-owned cooperatives, and low-income housing projects.

    Neighborhood Bank has announced that it intends to sell its portfolio of below market rate socially responsible loans to Community Trust and that it will stop making such loans in the future. Community Trust has announced that it will fill the gap that this situation will create by extending additional credit to clients who no longer will be able to borrow from Neighborhood Bank. As a result, Neighborhood Bank is likely to become somewhat more profitable in the future and Community Trust somewhat less profitable.

    Do you:
    a. Sell your shares in Neighborhood Bank and hold your shares in Community Trust. Look for another socially responsible bank in

which to invest the proceeds of that sale (but don't buy any additional shares of Community Trust because you don't want to be overconcentrated in a bank whose future profitability now appears to be somewhat less promising than it had been in the past).

b. Retain your shares in both banks but introduce a shareholder resolution at Neighborhood Bank urging it to reconsider its decision to discontinue socially responsible lending.

c. Sell your stock in Community Trust and reinvest the proceeds of that sale in Neighborhood Bank in order to maximize your profit potential.

d. Sell your stock in Neighborhood Bank and reinvest the proceeds of that sale in Community Trust to show your support of Community's expanded socially responsible lending policy.

10. You own shares of a well-managed international conglomerate that has diverse interests in foods, pharmaceuticals, entertainment, and military hardware (all of which are profitable). It also owns a nationwide chain of child-care centers catering to working mothers in low-income-minority-neighborhoods (which, to date, has been unprofitable). Except for its involvement in the manufacture of military hardware (which, incidentally, is its most profitable division), the company has an impeccable record in all areas of concern to socially responsible investors.

Management has just announced its intention to sell the unprofitable child-care centers to stockholders through a rights offering and to invest the proceeds of that sale in an expansion of the military hardware division. Without the backing of the parent company, there is a risk that the chain of child-care centers may not survive. For the parent company itself, however, overall profitability will be enhanced.

Do you:

a. Exercise your rights to buy shares of the chain of child-care centers. Sell your stock in the parent and use the proceeds of that sale to purchase additional shares in the child-care centers in the open market since they will require your financial support now more than ever.

b. Sell your rights and reinvest the proceeds of that sale in additional shares of the parent company in order to maximize your own profit potential.

c. Sell your rights and contribute the proceeds of that sale to a group lobbying for world disarmament. Retain your shares in the parent company but introduce a shareholder resolution urging management to use the proceeds of the sale of rights for some purpose other than an expansion of the military hardware division—preferably to expand one of its other life-supporting businesses.

d. Sell your shares in the parent because you disapprove of the decisions to sell the child-care centers and expand the military hardware division. Sell the rights, too, because the economic viability of that business is now in question. Look for some other well-capitalized, financially sound, socially responsible company in which to invest the proceeds of both sales.

HOW TO SCORE YOUR SRIQ QUIZ

For all odd-numbered questions—1,3,5,7, and 9—score 3 points for each (a) answer, 1 point for each (b) answer, 4 points for each (c) answer, and 2 points for each (d) answer.

For all even-numbered questions—2,4,6,8, and 10—score 2 points for each (a) answer, 4 points for each (b) answer, 1 point for each (c) answer, and 3 points for each (d) answer.

Add up your total score. If your total score is:

10–16. You appear to be most like Andrew—an *activist* investor eager to engage management directly on those socially responsible issues which concern you. You don't believe that socially responsible investing is limited just to the buy and sell decision-making process but that it entails dialogue, involvement, and confrontation between shareholders and management on a continuing basis. You place considerable emphasis on the benefits to be gained through the shareholder resolution and proxy processes.

17–24. You seem to be most similar to Barbara—an *alternative* investor who believes in *thinking globally but acting locally* and who insists that *if you aren't part of the solution, you're part of the problem.* You prefer to make specific investments that could produce identifiable, tangible results, and you are sometimes willing to accept somewhat lower financial returns or greater risks in order to generate what you consider to be higher *complete* returns. You don't think it's enough to just avoid the bad, but try to seek out the good as well.

25–32. You appear to most resemble Carl—an *avoidance* investor who thinks that one may invest in good conscience in a socially responsible manner without sacrificing returns. Unlike Andrew, you believe that if you disapprove of a company's behavior, the most effective message you can send its management is to sell the stock—you'd be uncomfortable holding it anyway (even as part of an *activist* policy of corporate engagement). Unlike Barbara, you are unwilling to sacrifice returns to accomplish specific goods through the investment process, although you certainly are willing to forgo opportunities in areas that are distasteful to you and might be prepared to make charitable contributions to accomplish some ends that are similar to hers. More socially responsible investors are like you than either of the other two types.

33–40. Like Donna, you don't really appear to be a socially responsible investor at all. When you invest, it is with an eye toward maximizing your own risk-adjusted returns, not as a means to accomplish social goals. That is not to say, however, that you might not be socially responsible in your personal life. Indeed, you may be as socially responsible or even more so than the others, contributing as much or more in time and/or money to socially responsible causes. And it may be the very success of your traditional investing approach that provides you with the wherewithal to do so.

With that, we conclude the first part of this book. So much for the history and philosophical underpinnings of the socially responsible investing movement; the arguments for and against it; the strategies and conflicts with which socially responsible investors are concerned; and, perhaps most important, some thoughts on how and where you might fit in. In the next part, we will begin to look at some of the substantive issues with which socially responsible investors actually are concerned. For starters: shareholder rights.

ISSUES

4

Shareholder Rights: Companies' Responsibilities to Their Stockholders

THE FOUNTAINHEAD OF CORPORATE RESPONSIBILITY

Most of those who consider themselves to be socially responsible investors would disagree with Milton Friedman's contention that "There is one and only one social responsibility of business—to use its resources and engage in activities designed to increase its profits so long as it stays within the rules of the game, which is to say, engages in open and free competition, without deception or fraud." But what is it exactly with which they would disagree? Surely not with the ethical legitimacy of a corporation's desire to increase its profits, but only with the *exclusivity* of that goal as expressed in the phrase "one and only one." Indeed, change Friedman's statement to read "There is [a] social responsibility of business to use its resources and engage in activities designed to increase its proftis . . ."[1] and, we daresay, no one would disagree.

The generation of profits for stockholders is, after all, a corporation's very raison d'etre and, even if one accepts that a company may have several legitimate objectives, surely the generation of profits must be one among them. But if the generation of profits for stockholders is a corporate responsibility, then corporate managements must have corollary responsibilities to stockholders as well.

They must, for instance, act in such a way as not to squander corporate assets on unnecessary corporate perquisites or golden parachutes. They must place the financial interests of stockholders above their own and gracefully withdraw if stockholders opt to replace them with new managements of their own choosing that they think will do a better job for them. And they must not pay greenmail or engage in poison pill defenses that could prevent shareholders from realizing substantial returns on their investments from unfriendly takeovers, just so they might hang on to their own jobs.

In other words, corporations have responsibilities to their stockholders which are inherent in the very nature of shareholding or corporate ownership. That, in itself, is fundamentally different from the derivation of a corporation's responsibilities (if any) to whatever other constituencies it might have (now sometimes referred to as *stakeholders*), whether those constituencies are employees or potential employees (equal employment opportunity, affirmative action, comparable worth, workplace safety), the community or nation at large (support for the arts, charitable contributions), South African blacks (opposition to apartheid), or even our entire generation and generations yet unborn (protection of the environment). For notwithstanding the arguments of those who perceive corporations as something other than the property of their shareholders and belonging somehow to society, it is our contention that in none of those *stakeholder* instances do corporate responsibilities obtain simply by virtue of the constituency's existence. Rather, such responsibilities only derive from the inherent responsibilities or voluntary direction of stockholders themselves (the owners of corporations in the first place).

However, if that is how responsibilities to other *stakeholders* develop, then corporate managements must be obligated at least to listen to what their shareholders have to say and to keep them informed as to their actions. This engenders another array of responsibilities to shareholders themselves—including the moral obligation to implement shareholder resolutions supported by a majority of stockholders, to provide board representation to shareholders with large equity positions, and to maintain frequent and open communications with all stockholders.

Unfortunately, many corporations have often come up short in fulfilling these responsibilities, three of the most egregious examples having been **Avon Products, Inc.** (NYSE—AVP), **Time Warner, Inc.** (NYSE—TWX), and **Armstrong World Industries, Inc.** (NYSE—ACK).

Avon Products, Inc. (NYSE—AVP). Avon Products is the world's largest manufacturer of cosmetics and toiletries, with annual revenues in excess of $3 billion. In an attempt to prevent a hostile takeover, even if that would be in the best financial interest of its shareholders, the company's management adopted a poison pill defense. Shareholders objected and introduced corporate resolutions at the company's 1990 annual meeting to cancel the plan or submit it to a shareholder vote. More than 60% of the votes cast at that meeting endorsed both proposals.

And what was management's response? Merely to aver that **Avon's** board would take the votes into consideration but that it would not consider them binding. A clear denial of management's responsibility to heed the will of stockholders.

Time Warner, Inc. (NYSE—TWX). In 1989, **Paramount Communications Inc.** offered to acquire **Time, Inc.** for $200 a share. With support from the Delaware courts, **Time's** management succeeded in blocking the acquisition and merged with **Warner Communications** instead, thereby creating the world's largest media and entertainment company.

More telling from the point of view of stockholders, however, a year later, shareholders owned a stock selling below $100 a share—or less than half what they would have got if the **Paramount Communications** acquisition had been permitted to go through. To paraphrase the lyrics of a popular country-western song: "Management kept the gold mine; shareholders got the shaft."

Armstrong World Industries, Inc. (NYSE—ACK).

Armstrong World Industries is a leading manufacturer of furnishings, including flooring, tiling, and furniture. Its annual revenues exceed $21.5 billion. In July 1989, Canada's Belzberg family acquired about 10% of the company's stock through its New York merchant bank, and announced that it might seek to buy the firm. Two months later, the Belzbergs unsuccessfully sought board representation and, in January 1990, announced their intention to wage a proxy fight to achieve such representation.

Armstrong's response was outrageous. It joined with a number of other Pennsylvania-based corporations to prevail upon the State of Pennsylvania to pass the nation's toughest anti-takeover statute. The law was written in a kind of Orwellian "Newspeak," suggesting that it would be a boon for socially responsible investors. Among other things, it redefined the fiduciary duty of corporate directors to allow them to base their decisions not only on the interests of stockholders but also on the interests of employees, customers, and other *stakeholders*.

Superficially, at least, that might seem consonant with the position of socially responsible investors who often argue for consideration of the impact of corporate actions on ethnic minorities, the environment, South African blacks, and the like. Indeed, isn't the consideration of the interests of *stakeholders* other than shareholders the very height of corporate responsibility? Unfortunately, *no*. On the contrary, upon deeper analysis the Pennsylvania statute is not only inconsistent with the concept of enlightened socially responsible investing, but actually undermines the very foundation of that concept.

As expressed in Chapter 1 and again earlier in this chapter, corporate responsibilities to do anything other than maximize profits for shareholders may be justified under certain circumstances, but only if they derive initially from the duties or will of shareholders themselves. For example, the obligations to stop polluting the environment, to withdraw from South Africa, or to make generous charitable contributions (in the absence of legislation mandating such actions) may be justified, but only in response to the implicit or explicit direction of shareholders. It is still shareholders who own their corporations, after all and, in the long run, it is they—not their temporarily hired managers—who must have the right to determine their corporations' directions and the disposition of their assets.

It is this fundamental right which the Pennsylvania law has overturned.

On the surface, it may seem desirable to socially responsible investors that corporate managements consider the interests of constituencies other than shareholders, but this is a pernicious concept which cuts both ways.

Suppose, for instance, that shareholders urged management to get out of the tobacco business and management refused, on the grounds that such a move would not be in the interest of their *customers stakeholders* who, as smokers, prefer that they continue to manufacture cigarettes. What if shareholders pressed management to withdraw from South Africa and management refused, on the grounds that its South African *suppliers stakeholders* preferred that they remain? Or if shareholders requested management to shut down plants that polluted the environment and management refused, on the grounds that its *employee stakeholders* or *community stakeholders* objected because of the adverse effect that would have on employment and the area's economy.

In fact, over time, the Pennsylvania law will do more social harm than good, and not just to stockholders. In its four major provisions, the Pennsylvania statute has mandated that:

1. Shareholders who have owned stock in a Pennsylvania corporation for less than two years and then sell it within 18 months after a failed attempt to control the company through a proxy fight or buyout must "disgorge" their profits to the target company.

2. Shareholders controlling 20% or more of a company's stock may not exercise their voting rights to change corporate control without the approval of the remaining "disinterested" shareholders.

3. Labor contracts and severance pay are guaranteed in the event of a takeover.

4. Finally, as noted above, directors are allowed to base their decisions on the interests of *stakeholders* (i.e., employees, customers, suppliers, or the community), not just those of shareholders. And should they do so, directors would be insulated from lawsuits by any group, including stockholders, which claimed its interests were ignored.

Thirty-nine other states, including Indiana, Delaware, New York, Massachusetts, Mississippi, and Ohio, have passed some kind of anti-takeover law and most are frightening in their implications. Most preclude holders of one-fifth or more of a company's stock from voting on mergers. Massachusetts requires that board members serve staggered terms and that they can only be removed for very limited reasons, not including mismanagement or incompetence. It also mandates substantial severance pay for employees fired within one year after a hostile proxy fight. Mississippi requires the purchasers of 20% stakes in companies to run newspaper advertisements announcing it.

Wayne Marr, finance professor at Clemson University, has studied the effect of these laws and concluded that "It seems that while Eastern Europe is trying to become more like the U.S., we're trying to become more like Eastern Europe."[2] In a 1987 study by the Securities and Exchange Commission, it was estimated that Ohio's 1986 anti-takeover legislation had reduced the market value of 36 companies in the state by more than $1 billion.

While several states now have laws of this sort, Pennsylvania's is the most far-reaching and the most odious. *The Economist* has noted that "One of its targets is the basic principle of capitalism, that managers are accountable to shareholders" and blasted it as forming "part of a growing contempt for shareholders. . . ."[3] Richard Breeden, chairman of the Securities and Exchange Commission, condemned the bill because, in his words, it would leave incompetent managers "free to run a company into the ground."[4]

Ronald Gilson, professor at Stanford Law School, said that

investors in Pennsylvania's public companies should react to this law "the same way you'd react to a rattlesnake curled up on your pillow."[5] Roland Machold, director of the New Jersey State Investment Division, has said that, in light of the passage of this legislation, "I can't see myself buying the stock of any Pennsylvania company coming to market now."[6]

Henry J. Goldschmid, professor at Columbia Law School, referred to the disgorgement provision of the law as "clearly one of the most significant and least wise provisions passed by any state legislature."[7] Senator Vincent Fumo, ranking Democrat of the Pennsylvania Senate Appropriations Committee, viewed the law as designed to assist "hacks trying to protect their fat-cat jobs."[8] And, Kenneth Mertz, head of Pennsylvania's own State Employees Retirement Fund, said that if the law were passed, he would stop investing in all companies incorporated in the state because of his fiduciary obligations to the fund's beneficiaries.[9]

Nevertheless, the law did pass overwhelmingly, resulting in another variable with which investors must contend. It will no longer be enough for them to ask what a company's financials (e.g., book value, growth rate, cash flow) look like, or even what its social policies are (vis-à-vis the environment, South Africa, or affirmative action). In the future, it will also be necessary for them to determine where the company is incorporated.

And there are many public companies incorporated in Pennsylvania—more than 300, in fact—including about 4% of all those listed on the New York Stock Exchange. In addition to **Armstrong World Industries** they include **Aluminum Company of America** (NYSE—AA), **H.J. Heinz Company** (NYSE—HNZ), **Mellon Bank Corporation** (NYSE—MEL), **Sun Company, Inc.** (NYSE—SUN), **Scott Paper Company** (NYSE—SPP), **Westinghouse Electric Corporation** (NYSE—WX), **Consolidated Rail Corporation** (NYSE—CRR), **VF Corporation** (NYSE—VFC), **AMP Incorporated** (NYSE—AMP), **PPG Industries Inc.** (NYSE—PPG), **Allegheny Ludlum Corporation** (NYSE—ALS), **Quaker Chemical Corporation** (OTC—QCHM), **PNC Financial Corporation** (NYSE—PNC), and **Rorer Group Inc.** (NYSE—ROR).

But even here, some distinctions need be made. While **Armstrong World Industries, Scott Paper, Consolidated Rail, Aluminum Company of America, Rorer Group, AMP,** and **PPG Industries** were supporters of Pennsylvania's anti-takeover bill, **Westinghouse Electric**, although not opposing the bill, did work to get opt-out provisions included in it so that companies could choose not to be subjected to it, if they wished. And **VF Corporation** was especially enlightened and outspoken in its opposition. In a letter to Governor Robert P. Casey, exhorting him not to sign the bill (which he did anyway), Lawrence R. Pugh, chairman and chief executive officer of **VF Corporation**, wrote: "I agree that corporations should be given proper time to respond to raiders [but] I do not agree that there should be legislation that protects weak management from shareholders."[10]

Ironically, when push finally came to shove and the law was passed, several companies, including some of its original supporters, opted not to be subject to one or more of its provisions. Many did this as a result of pressure from institutional investors who owned shares in their companies. For example, both Flint, Michigan's pension fund and Houston, Texas' firemen's pension fund stated that they would divest themselves of the stocks of companies in Pennsylvania that did not choose to be exempted from the law.

Others opted out because they believed, on their own, that the law was not in their shareholders' interests. As John M. Mazur, head of investor realtions at **Heinz**, expressed it: "The anti-takeover provisions of the law weren't necessarily for **Heinz** and not helpful with respect to our long-term objective of enhancing shareholder value."[11] According to James Schmitt, a **Westinghouse** spokesman, "a best offense against takeover is a well-run company. We want to be judged on our ability to increase shareholder value and, by opting out, **Westinghouse** puts itself in the best position to be judged on our merits."[12]

As a consequence, by the end of July 1990, more than 65 of Pennsylvania's public corporations (constituting about one-fifth of those in the state and including a majority of the Fortune 500 firms domiciled there) chose not to be covered by at least some portion of the statute. These included **Westinghouse Electric,**

H.J. Heinz, Sun Company, Mellon Bank, Consolidated Rail, Allegheny Ludlum, Quaker Chemical, PNC Financial, and **Rorer Group**.

However, not only **Armstrong World Industries**, but also **Scott Paper, PPG Industries**, and **Aluminum Company of America** still chose to remain subject to all the provisions of the law. Socially responsible investors ought keep those latter names in mind when considering which companies they might want to exclude from their portfolios for being least responsive to their own stockholders.

Lockheed Corporation (NYSE—LK). Turning from the Pennsylvania situation, let's take a look at another company: **Lockheed Corporation**. This is an illustrative example of a company that acted in a singularly irresponsible manner toward its own shareholders for years but which, under pressure from a dissident investor group and the institutional investment community, subsequently changed its ways (mostly).

Lockheed Corporation is one of the largest U.S. defense contractors, with annual revenues approximating $10 billion. In the late 1980s, the company had a dismal record: Its backlogs shrank, its earnings deteriorated, and its return to shareholders was negative. Nonetheless, the company's directors not only continued to tolerate management but even acted to further entrench it: They re-incorporated the company in Delaware, a more protective state than California; they voted a poison pill plan into effect; and they adopted several charter revisions intended to repel takeovers. In effect, according to Howard D. Sherman, director of the proxy advisory service at **Institutional Shareholder Services Inc.**, "They removed all accountability of the management to shareholders."[13]

Not surprisingly, this created a climate within which a dissident stockholder challenge to management was all but inevitable. When it finally did occur, it came in the form of a proxy fight by Harold C. Simmons through **NL Industries**, the company he controlled which owned approximately 19% of **Lockheed**.

In seeking to take control of **Lockheed** by running his own slate of directors in opposition to management's choices, Sim-

mons predicated his challenge on two grounds: (1) the company's
poor economic performance and (2) its cavalier attitude toward
shareholders. In pressing this second point, he supported four
shareholder initiatives:

1. To implement confidential shareholder voting;
2. To exempt the company voluntarily from the anti-
   takeover provisions of Delaware law;
3. To abolish the practice of greenmail; and
4. To rescind the company's poison pill plan.

Simmons enlisted the support of the institutional investment community in his crusade, but when all the votes were in, management's slate of directors still prevailed. Nevertheless, Simmons
and his cohorts did achieve a substantial victory for shareholders'
rights. The existing board remained in place but management
agreed to add three more directors to represent the interests of
institutional shareholders; the four shareholder resolutions all
passed; and, with the exception of the rescision of the poison pill
plan, management agreed to abide by the results. (Rescision of
the poison pill plan was passed as a nonbinding measure and
management only agreed to reassess its position on the issue in
light of it.)

THE TIP OF THE ICEBERG

This certainly was a step in the right direction but it was not the
only one. For instance, in March 1990, **Occidental Petroleum
Corporation** (NYSE—OXY), under pressure from its institutional shareholders, agreed to allow four of its directors to meet twice
a year with officials of the California Public Employees Retirement System (Calpers) to discuss corporate business plans. In
return, Calpers agreed not to introduce a resolution at **Occidental's** annual meeting seeking the creation of a shareholders' advisory committee. And the directors of **Texaco Inc.** (NYSE—TX),
Amoco   Corporation   (NYSE—AN),   **Foxboro   Company**

(NYSE—FOX) and **Borden, Inc.** (NYSE—BN), among others, all have agreed to allow secret ballots for proxy voting.

But even this is only the beginning. As of March 1990, more than 40 shareholder resolutions had been filed seeking to mandate confidential shareholder voting. Targets included **USAir Group Inc.** (NYSE—U), **Coca Cola Company** (NYSE—KO), **Figgie International, Inc.** (OTC—FIGI), and **K Mart Corporation** (NYSE—KM), among others. These resolutions were supported by 16.3% of votes cast at **Coca-Cola** and 18.6% at **Figgie**. Forty resolutions were filed to repeal staggered terms for members of boards of directors (which tend to entrench managements) at **USX Corporation** (NYSE—X), **Chase Manhattan Corporation** (NYSE—CMB), **General Host Corp.** (NYSE—GH), and others. Nearly three dozen companies, including **Consolidated Freightways, Inc.** (NYSE—CNF) and **Kerr-McGee Corporation** (NYSE—KMG) were asked to repeal their poison pill plans. Eleven companies, including **Bethlehem Steel Corporation** (NYSE—BS) and **Santa Fe Pacific Corp.** (NYSE—SFX), were urged to opt out of state anti-takeover laws. In addition, several corporations, including **Transamerica Corporation** (NYSE—TA) and **Ryder System Inc.** (NYSE—R), were confronted by proposals to eliminate golden parachutes.

In the forefront of the movement advocating greater corporate responsibility to shareholders themselves is Dale Hanson, chief executive of Calpers, who, as much as anyone, was responsible for forcing **Lockheed** to name representatives of the institutional investment community to its board and for persuading **Occidental** to meet regularly with Calpers officials. It was Hanson, too, who convinced **Honeywell Inc.** (NYSE—HON) to repeal its two anti-takeover provisions.

Nor is Hanson letting up. He has developed an organized approach to the evaluation of companies in the Standard & Poor's 500 Stock Index, using the services of two shareholder research groups (**Institutional Shareholder Services** and **Analysis Group Inc.**) with an eye toward discovering violations of shareholders' rights such as the use of poison pills or golden parachutes. When such violations are discovered, Hanson approaches the companies involved in the hopes of resolving the issues amicably and cooperatively; as a final resort, he might draw up proxy resolutions to be presented to shareholders.

Calpers has been joined by the United Shareholders Association in its efforts to democratize corporations. The United Stockholders Association is a group of 60,000 small investors. Together, they have urged the Securities and Exchange Commission to consider major changes in the proxy process, specifically including the mandating of confidential voting in order to prevent corporate managements from selectively re-polling stockholders in order to urge them to alter their votes. As James E. Heard, managing director of the **Analysis Group**, has said: "The whole proxy system is enormously tilted against shareholders. We would never tolerate in the political system the kind of voting we have in the corporate world."[14]

In sum, the shareholders' rights movement is but one aspect of the broader socially responsible investing movement but, at least for *activists*, it very well may be the most important for two reasons:

1. It is the fountainhead of rights from which all other rights derive. It is only the will of shareholders which lends legitimacy to the overall socially responsible investing movement in the first place. If the claims of shareholders may be dismissed out of hand, then the socially responsible investing movement would have no justification.

2. As a practical matter, it is only through the exercise of their rights as stockholders—by, for example, communicating with managements (and being listened to), by passing binding resolutions, by replacing managements through the proxy process, or by being allowed to accept takeover offers—that *activist* socially responsible investors can succeed in achieving their goals. If those rights may be thwarted with impunity, what hope is there for anyone else?

Shareholders are the owners of corporations; as such, they have first claim on their corporations' assets, earnings, and social re-

sponsibilities. After all, within our capitalist system, if there were no shareholders, there would be no corporations to have responsibilities to begin with.

But what about customers? Without them, there would be no corporations either—or, if there were, they certainly would be short lived. If any constituency other than shareholders, themselves, might lay claim to being the legitimate recipient of corporate social responsibilities, surely it would have to be consumers. We'll talk about them in the next chapter.

5

The Customer Always Comes First—or at Least Second

THE CASE FOR THE CONSUMER

No secret has been made of the fact that, in our opinion, the primary constituency to which a corporation's management is beholden is its own shareholders. However, not everyone agrees with that thought. There are those (including many environmental activists) who grant primacy in the hierarchy of corporate responsibilities to all mankind, including generations yet unborn. There are others of a more parochial bent (including those in the isolationist and protectionist political camps) who give priority to the nation, or even the community. There are even some (often within the labor or union movements) who put the interests of a company's employees above all else.

Perhaps the largest number contends that the constituency to which a corporation owes its primary allegiance, even before its own shareholders, is its customers or clientele. As **H.B. Fuller Co.** (OTC—FULL) expresses it: "Customers are first, employees second, shareholders third, and the community fourth."[1]

There is some merit to this position, both logically (or economically) and humanistically (or ethically). For while a company's raison d'etre may be to generate profits for its stockholders, the way in which it does that is by providing goods or services to its customers for which it is paid a sum sufficient to cover its costs and generate those profits.

The entire process entails contractual relationships (implicit or explicit) between the company and its customers. Goods and services are warranted to be what they appear to be. And a whole host of contextual assumptions regarding the quality of goods offered, the correlation between quality and price, the truth of advertising claims, and so on, are subsumed in the relationship between the corporation and its customers.

THE MINIMAL CASE: HONESTY AND INTEGRITY

It is unimaginable that even the most fervent critics of the concepts of corporate social responsibility and socially responsible investing would have any difficulty subscribing to the notion of corporate responsibility to customers in this most limited sense. Thus, Milton Friedman, when he asserted that "there is one and only one social responsibility of business—to use its resources and engage in activities designed to increase its profits" added the important qualifying clause "as long as it stays within the rules of the game, which is to say, engages in open and free competition, without deception or fraud."[2]

It is that qualification, "without deception or fraud," which mandates that the corporation act responsibly vis-à-vis its customers and clients. The company must not lie to its customers or cheat them. It must live up to its promises. It must also provide goods and services that in reality are what they seem.

Most companies, of course, do behave in a socially reponsible manner to their customers, at least in this minimal sense. If they did not, the legal system, or the marketplace, or both would take their toll and companies violating the basic ethical precepts of our society would not remain in business for long.

When companies do violate these ethical imperatives, customers and potential customers are made aware of it quickly. Newspaper and television investigative reporters, chambers of commerce, better business bureaus, government agencies, consumer advocacy groups, the judicial system and, most important of all, consumer word-of-mouth all act to ostracize or penalize such outlaw companies, forcing them to change their behavior or go out of business.

AN EVEN HIGHER STANDARD: QUALITY AND EXTRA SERVICE

Most socially responsible investors mean more than this when they demand that companies act responsibly toward their customers. More often what they ask is not simply that a company live up to the negative injunctions not to behave fraudulently or deceptively but that it also fulfill certain positive obligations as well (i.e., to provide healthier or even higher quality products than customers might demand or that it deliver extra or premium services).

Lands' End, Inc. (NYSE—LE). A sterling example of a company that has always given high priority to its customers' interests and delivered more than what normally might be expected of it is **Lands' End, Inc.**, a mail-order catalog vendor of classic-styled clothing. Founded in 1963 by Gary Comer, the company acquired an exceptional following by providing high-quality goods at reasonable prices coupled with extraordinary service.

Quality and price competitiveness were maintained by eliminating high overhead (the company prides itself on having "no fancy emporiums" and boasts that its main location is "in the middle of a cornfield in rural Wisconsin") and through eliminating middlemen by eschewing branded merchandise and only selling products made to its own specifications. As Comer puts it: "We don't go two streets over because it's a nickel cheaper. If a manufacturer meets our standards, we'll stick with him. Otherwise we move on."[3]

But it is when it comes to service that **Lands' End** really shines. Over 200 company volunteers, including the company's founder and its chief executive officer, Richard Anderson, personally respond to the approximately 50,000 letters received annually from customers. Telephone orders are answered within three rings. Shipments go out the very next day after orders are received. And, perhaps most impressive of all, the company guarantees its products unequivocally; it accepts returns for any reason, at any time, no questions asked.

This approach enabled **Lands' End** to achieve an exceptional record—at least until 1989. Revenues more than doubled from $172.2 million in fiscal 1984 (pro-forma ended January 31, 1985) to $455.8 million in fiscal 1988 (ended January 31, 1989); earnings per share grew nearly fourfold from 37 cents to $1.61.

Still, the best of social intentions and consumer relations don't guarantee continued success and in 1989, the company ran into its first problems. Increased competition from other mail-order discounters, deep discounts at retail stores, its own "tired" merchandise, and excess inventory combined to result in its experiencing the first year-to-year earnings decline in its history. Although revenues climbed again, this time to $545.2 million, earnings per share slipped for the first time to $1.45.

Earnings declined again in the first nine months of fiscal 1990 and a loss actually was incurred in the second quarter—the company's first loss since having gone public in 1986. Concurrently, the company launched a major effort to introduce new children's and traditional merchandise lines and to reduce excess inventory and catalog costs. It remains to be seen whether or not the company will be able to restore its lagging profitability, without jeopardizing its exemplary record of providing superior customer service and quality goods at outstanding prices.

H.B. Fuller (OTC—FULL). The world's largest publicly owned adhesives company, **H.B. Fuller**, manufactures sealants, coatings, and glues for use in everything from diapers to cigarettes to automobiles. From its outset, the company made it clear that it put the interests of its customers first. According to Anthony L. Andersen, chief executive officer, "When we went public in 1968, I said I wasn't going to run this company for short term investors"—and he hasn't.[4]

The company's initial success was achieved by locating its

offices and plants near customers and delivering goods promptly when needed. In 1982, however, it embarked on a phase of international expansion and, in the process, allowed things to slip domestically. That was subsequently corrected with the reassignment of hundreds of research, technical and sales personnel so that the company has since regained its reputation of really knowing its customers' needs and catering to them.

Despite this, however, the company remains cyclically dependent on several industries, including automobiles and construction, which were a drag on domestic earnings in 1988 and 1989. Internationally, the company was also hurt by currency devaluations in Brazil and Argentina, with the net result that profits, after hitting a record high of $2.69 per share in 1987, declined to $2.20 in 1988 and only $1.64 in 1989. Restoration of the 1987 level of profitability may have to await the next cyclical economic upturn.

H.J. Heinz Company (NYSE—HNZ). Another company that achieved an outstanding operating record but then stumbled over the issue of product quality was **H.J. Heinz** (which we discussed briefly in Chapter 2 in relation to its decision to discontinue the marketing of tuna caught in a manner which threatened dolphins). For more than 20 consecutive years, **Heinz** increased its operating margins by cutting costs, reducing payroll, closing plants, and speeding up production lines. But the company paid a price for that: at its *Ore-Ida* potato processing operations, for instance, the taste of **Heinz's** *Tater Tots* was actually adversely affected. New slicing machines produced the food more quickly but also cut the potatoes too fine; as a result, the *Tater Tots* came out mushier than customers liked and sales declined.

J. Wray Connolly, a senior vice president at **Heinz**, admitted that for a while "the focus [at the company] was not on quality."[5] But **Heinz** learned its lesson. It slowed down production lines at *Ore-Ida*, placing considerations of product quality above shorter term quantitative production goals. It worked: sales of *Tater Tots* increased, more than offsetting the incremental cost of slowing down the line. **Heinz** took similar actions at other divisions, including *Star-Kist*, where production lines were also slowed and labor costs increased, again with a net improvement both in quality and profits to the company.

Merck & Co., Inc. (NYSE—MRK). One of the nation's leading pharmaceutical companies, with annual revenues approximating $7 billion, **Merck & Co.** has achieved an outstanding record of earnings growth and the reputation to accompany it. Earnings have compounded at a 15.5% average annual rate over the past 10 years, having increased annually since 1981. In addition, in *Fortune's* 1990 annual survey to determine the most admired corporations in the country, **Merck** again ranked first out of 305 companies (it has held this position since 1986), placing first in four out of eight categories (ability to attract, develop, and keep talented people; innovativeness; financial soundness; and quality of products or services), second in three (community and environmental responsibility; use of corporate assets; and value as a long-term investment), and third in one (quality of management).[6]

An example of the kind of action that has earned **Merck** these accolades and has endeared it to consumer advocates and socially responsible investors was the company's announcement in April 1990 that it would reduce the prices of its prescription drugs to Medicaid patients, making them available to them at the lowest prices it charges its volume purchasers. Senator David Pryor, who had been drafting legislation to reduce drug costs for Medicaid and Medicare recipients reacted enthusiastically stating that "**Merck** has taken an important step away from the policies of greed and unfairness that unfortunately characterize today's drug companies."[7]

But the **Merck** plan was good business, too. It was made contingent on the states not restricting access to any **Merck** drugs so that the company could end up with even higher sales as a result. And it could put even more pressure on **Merck's** competitors, whose pricing policies differ from its own.

Rubbermaid Inc. (NYSE—RBD). Despite the very prosaic nature of its business, manufacturing a variety of mundane resin-based products such as dish drain boards, wheelbarrows, trash containers, and patio furniture, **Rubbermaid** has managed to achieve an exceptional financial record. Its annual revenues now approximate $1.5 billion and its earnings have risen annually since 1980, compounding since then at a 15.5% average annual rate.

Rubbermaid accomplished this by emphasizing the quality of its products and putting the needs and interests of its customers first. (The company ranked third overall and second for the quality of its products in *Fortune's* 1990 survey.) For instance, **Rubbermaid** adds anti-static chemicals to its plastics so that its products won't attract dust. And it redesigned a dustpan simply because its chief executive officer, Stanley C. Gault, was convinced by a doorman that the lip where the dustpan met the ground was too thick, leaving a line of dirt.

More and more companies have come to recognize that putting the interests of their consumers first is not just socially responsible behavior, it is also good business. According to Roger A. Enrico, president of **Pepsico Worldwide Beverages**, for instance, "If you are totally customer-focused and you deliver the services your customers want, everything else will follow."[8] And they're not just saying it; they're doing it.

Marriott Corporation (NYSE—MHS), a diversified lodging and food services company that operates over 450 hotels throughout the United States, for instance, instituted a 15-minute delivery guarantee for breakfast in 1985 and saw its breakfast business rise 25%. In 1983, **Deluxe Corp.** (NYSE—DLX) achieved its goal of two-day turnaround time on check printing 95.6% of the time with 99.1% accuracy. By 1989, the company's turnaround time goal had been cut to one day. At **Xerox Corp.** (NYSE-XRX), the leading U.S. manufacturer of copying machines, executives devote one day a month to taking complaints from customers so that they might better comprehend their needs.

In reviewing the history of corporate responsibility to customers in the United States, one inevitably is drawn to the automobile industry—and then to the Japanese. In the early days of the automobile industry, **Ford Motor Company** (NYSE—F), the second largest automobile company in the world, focused almost entirely on the production side of the business, with the attitude that customers would accept what it gave them and like it. That, of course, created an opportunity for **General Motors** (NYSE— GM), the world's largest automobile manufacturer, to cater more to the consumer, which it did with great success, eventually coming to dominate the industry.

Over time, however, **General Motors** also began to take its customers increasingly for granted, which created a new opportunity for the Japanese to enter the U.S. market in the postwar period. Their car companies offered higher quality products and better ser·ice than anything offered by the American companies, namely **General Motors, Ford**, or **Chrysler** (NYSE—C). This just didn't happen in the automobile industry: The same sort of thing occurred throughout various sectors of the American economy (especially in the high technology areas). The Japanese stepped in with superior quality and service and managed to fill the gaps left by those U.S. companies which failed to exhibit a Japanese-like sense of social responsibility to consumers.

The results were inevitable. The Japanese gained a major foothold in the American economy, largely by catering to customers in ways that their U.S. counterparts had neglected for years. But American companies finally got wise: They began to see that recognizing their corporate social responsibilities to customers just might make good business sense.

When this is the case—when the business interests of corporations coincide with their social responsibilities to their customers—there is no problem. When **Lands' End** got more customers by providing better service, everybody was happy. When **Heinz** sold more *Tater Tots* by slowing down production lines, not only its customers, but its employees and stockholders benefited as well. The same was true for **Marriott, Xerox, Ford**, and **General Motors**: when, by providing higher quality goods or better service, they also increased their profits, everybody gained. Under such circumstances, behaving in a socially responsible manner toward customers wasn't just altruistic, it was good business.

SOCIAL RESPONSIBILITY VS. FREEDOM
OF CHOICE

However, it is only in storybooks that the world *always* works like that. Sometimes, providing a superior product or service to customers *may not* be economically beneficial to a corporation. Sometimes, it may be too costly. Sometimes, it may not be what the customer wants, and sometimes it may not even be in the customer's overall own best interest. What then?

It is easy enough to commend **Lands' End** for its exemplary service to customers or **Heinz** for producing a superior potato product or **Marriott** for delivering breakfasts promptly when these companies were compensated (through higher sales and profits) for their actions. What if their costs for performing these tasks were *not* recapturable?

Suppose, for instance, that customers deserted **Lands' End** for a competitor whose prices were lower but whose service was inferior, while indicating that they would have been more than willing to forgo **Lands' End** service if only it had met its competitors' prices. Or suppose that consumers rejected *Tater Tots* for a cheaper, albeit mushier, alternative, while readily admitting that they preferred the taste of the original (but not enough to pay the higher price). Under such circumstances, should **Lands' End** or **Heinz** still have persisted in offering their superior but uneconomic service or product anyway, knowing that by so doing they would end up with fewer customers, lower sales, and reduced profits?

Most conservatives would say no. Their contention would be that consumers have the right to trade off quality for price if they wish. Also, there is nothing socially responsible about a company's stubborn persistence in attempting to impose its will on consumers, especially when it is contrary to the demands consumers have expressed in the marketplace and goes against the company's own economic interests.

But now suppose that the issue is more serious than **Lands' End's** unconditional guarantees or the promptness of **Marriott's** breakfast deliveries or the texture of **Heinz's** *Tater Tots*. Suppose it is a question of health or safety or even life itself.

NUTRITION, CHOICE, AND FAST FOODS

This issue of social responsibility versus freedom of choice has been most evident in the pressures brought to bear on fast-food restaurants (e.g., **McDonald's Corp.** [NYSE—MCD], **Burger King Corp.**, a subsidiary of **Grand Metropolitan PLC, Wendy's International, Inc.** [NYSE—WEN], and **Hardee's Food Systems Inc.**, a subsidiary of **Imasco, Ltd.** [TSE—IMS.TO] to upgrade the nutritional quality of their menu offerings, whether or not that was what their customers wanted and independent of the cost consequences of doing so to the companies themselves. Often, those demands came from pressure groups such as The National Heart Savers Association which, at one point, accused **McDonald's** of participating in "the poisoning of America," and were reinforced by government agencies such as the U.S. Department of Agriculture (USDA). According to Karen Bunch, a USDA spokesperson, "The trend toward eating more fast food reduces the variety in our diets and may increase the risk of nutritional deficiency. A typical fast food meal contains half the recommended daily allowances of calories and protein, but only a third of the RDA of vitamin C, thiamin, and niacin, and lesser amounts of iron, calcium and vitamin A."[9]

Specifically, many of these groups demanded that healthier menu items be introduced such as chicken, salads, baked potatoes (instead of french fries), leaner hamburgers, and french fries that were not cooked in saturated fat. Over time, the industry capitulated. In 1985, **Wendy's** introduced a *Light Menu*, including a salad bar that proved to be a marketing success. Other chains, including **Burger King** and **Arby's Inc.**, a subsidiary of **DWG Corporation** (ASE—DWG), followed suit. **McDonald's** introduced its *Chicken McNuggets* alongside its *Big Macs* and **Burger King** introduced its flame-broiled chicken alongside its *Whoppers*. Baked potatoes, low-fat milk shakes, apple bran muffins, and frozen yogurt began to appear on fast-food menus too.

In 1990, the industry took two other major steps. First, **Hardee's** introduced a new hamburger called *The Lean 1*, which has only 18 grams of total fat—30% less than its standard quarter pounder and only half as much as **Burger King's** *Whopper*. Second, **Burger King, McDonald's**, and **Wendy's** all followed **Hardee's** lead and decided to cook their french fries in vegetable oil, thereby eliminating cholesterol and reducing saturated fat.

Do these restaurant chains deserve kudos for changing their menus and their cooking methods in order to provide more nutritional meals for customers? Not necessarily—and they would be among the first to admit it. Their motivation was not to be socially responsible in providing what they or some self-selected experts considered healthier food, but rather simply to give their customers what they wanted—and their customers indicated that what they wanted were more nutritious meals.

Thus, Melissa Oakley, a spokesperson for **McDonald's** on nutritional issues, stated that

> Our menu has been changing over the years, but not because of pressure from outside organizations. Our menu changes because what people want to eat changes. When Ray Kroc opened the first **McDonald's** 35 years ago all we served was hamburgers, french fries and milk shakes, because that's what people ate. As people's eating habits changed, so did our menu. Our business is to give customers what they want."[10]

John Merritt, senior vice president of public affairs for **Hardee's**, had a similar comment on his company's introduction of *The Lean 1*. He said:

> Our strategy is not necessarily to move towards healthier items. Our strategy is to move towards more choice. We found ourselves in a situation where one in three people was on some kind of diet, which meant that every time a party of three came in there was one who wanted a different choice. Our salad bars are a great success, and the light burger seemed like a natural progression."[11]

Perhaps this is really what corporate social responsibility in this sphere is all about—providing the customer with what *he* wants, not with what the company thinks might be best for him. In other words, trusting in the ability of others to make rational decisions concerning their own self-interest. After all, isn't that what the free market is all about?

McDonald's has taken this a step further by voluntarily posting nutritional information in its restaurants, developing a number of nutrition education programs (e.g., *Eating Right, Feeling Fit*, a package for elementary school children, and a *Nutrition Information Center* for answering health and nutrition questions that particularly pertain to the company's own foods).

SEATBELTS, AIRBAGS, AND AUTOMOBILE SAFETY

At least as important as the question of the nutritional value of fast foods is the issue of automobile safety. Currently, federal law requires that automobile manufacturers install some form of passive restraint in new cars, but that may be in the form of airbags or automatic seatbelts that do not have to be buckled manually.

Airbags are much more expensive than automatic seatbelts, costing about $1,000 each to install and adding that much to a car's cost. In addition, research has shown that they are only marginally effective and still should be used in conjunction with seat belts. The question then becomes: Absent legislation mandating it, should an automobile manufacturer be deemed to have a social responsibility to include airbags as standard safety equipment in all its models even if consumers don't demand it and even if it would be uneconomic for it to do so?

Many conservatives would say no, contending that it still should be left up to the consumer, in voluntarily contracting with the manufacturer (or up to the government through legislation) to decide what products and services are bought and sold. Perhaps paying extra for airbags, which they would willingly forgo if given the option, will force many automobile buyers to do without some other desired good—such as medical care or more nutritious food—with the net result being that their overall health, safety, or life expectancy would be reduced, rather than enhanced.

Liberals, however, would tend to affirm the corporation's responsibility to provide airbags, even when they are not required by law, even when there is no overwhelming consumer clamor for them (or even when there appears to be a consumer disinclination to purchase them), and even when their provision would be uneconomic for automobile manufacturers. In support of that position, they marshall several arguments, including the principal (and a somewhat patronizing one) that consumers often don't know what's best for them (although, presumably, consumer activists always do).

The other major liberal argument on this subject relates to the external costs resulting from driving without airbags. If, in fact, that results in more highway deaths, it is not just deceased drivers themselves who are affected, but all of society in the form of higher automobile insurance rates, greater alternative expenditures by the state on highway safety, additional welfare benefits to survivors, lost productivity, and so on.

Where does this leave you as a socially responsible investor? Well, if you subscribe to the liberal philosophy in this instance, you have no problem. If you are an *activist*, you enthusiastically will have attempted to convince those automobile companies of which you are a shareholder to include airbags in all their models. And so far you will have met with considerable success.

Chrysler led the industry by making airbags standard on all its American-made automobiles in 1989 and most other automobile manufacturers have since followed suit—or announced that they will. **General Motors** said that it will install driver-side air bags on all its American-made cars beginning in late 1995 and some for front-seat passengers by 1992. **Ford** already installs airbags on the driver-side in about 50% of its cars and plans to have airbags for all drivers and front-seat passengers by the mid-1990s. **Nissan** plans to have driver-side and passenger-side airbags in its light trucks and most of its cars by 1995. **Toyota** intends to put airbags in all its cars as it redesigns them over the next few years. And **Honda** will make driver-side and passenger-side airbags standard in virtually all *Honda* and *Acura* models sold in the United States by 1993.

If you're an *alternative* investor, you might also seek out companies like **TRW Incorporated** (NYSE—TRW) or **Morton**

International, Inc. (NYSE—MII) the primary manufacturers of airbags, or a smaller company like **OEA, Inc.** (ASE—OEA), which manufactures the explosive mechanism that triggers the inflation of an airbag when a car crashes. Both **TRW Incorporated** and **Morton International** are billion dollar conglomerates for which airbags constitute only a small percentage of their total business, but with the rapid growth envisioned for this market, it should still make a meaningful contribution to both companies' earnings over the next few years. For **OEA Inc.**, a much smaller company with annual revenues of less than $100 million and 70% of the market for airbag initiators, however, the potential leveraged impact of the growth of this market is considerably greater.

If you are a socially responsible investor and a conservative, your problem is more difficult. You may decide that the most responsible thing an automobile company can do is provide its customers with an array of choices, rather than attempting to impose its will on them and, in that case, you might decide that the right course for you to take is to invest in companies that offer airbags optionally but do not feature them as standard equipment on all their models.

But suppose you are a conservative, a socially responsible investor, and a believer in the net value of airbags. What should you do?

The answer is easy: You should do exactly what your liberal counterpart is doing and be proud of it, although you'll reach the same conclusion as he by an entirely different route. As a conservative, you may defend the right of the consumer to buy cars with or without airbags, but *you* don't have to sell him the cars without airbags through *your* company if you don't want to. Remember, as a stockholder, it is *your* company, not that of any other *stakeholders*, such as suppliers, employees, or customers.

This, incidentally, is a good example of the point we attempted to make in Chapter 4 to the effect that the concept of corporate *stakeholders* other than shareholders, as reflected in Pennsylvania's anti-takeover statute, while superficially supportive of the idea of corporate social responsibility, is really a pernicious concept that can work the other way around. Under ordinary circumstances, even conservative socially responsible investors who strongly favor the use of airbags may try to convince their automobile companies' managements to include them in all models without regard to the wishes of employees, customers, or anyone else. Under terms of the Pennsylvania statute, however, managements could thwart the will of their own shareholders with impunity by arguing, for instance, that customers-*stakeholders* preferred cars without airbags.

SOCIAL RESPONSIBILITY AND CORPORATE SURVIVAL

Finally, there are those socially responsible investors who contend that a corporation has at least a minimal responsibility to its customers not to produce goods that are inherently dangerous (e.g., cigarettes or alcoholic beverages) even if suspending production of such goods would cause the very survival of the corporation itself to be at stake. Others contend that companies have no such paternalistic responsibility and that, so long as their products are legal, so long as they spell out the risks inherent in those products, and so long as those risks are voluntarily assumed by their customers, they are doing nothing wrong.

This is a variation on the automobiles issue discussed earlier, but with two important differences. First, here we are dealing with a question of the acceptability of a company's basic product (tobacco, for instance, or alcohol), not just with a question of whether or not that product should or should not be modified (e.g., by including airbags in automobiles). This, of course, gets us into the treacherous philosophical territory of line drawing and categorizing: One might argue, for instance, that automobiles, too, are inherently dangerous (because there are 50,000 driving-related fatalities annually or because of the air pollution they cause) and that, therefore, they should be opposed by socially responsible investors too, but that argument is seldom made.

The second difference is that, since we are dealing with the question of whether or not a company's basic product should or should not be produced, the corporation's very survival may be at stake. It is one thing to suggest that a company modify its product or service, even at a substantial cost to the company, and quite another to ask that it stop manufacturing its product altogether and go out of business. This is clearly a difference of kind, not of degree.

The resolution, however, is the same as that which we proposed in the last section. The question of a company's responsibility, if any, to its customers, once it has spelled out honestly the risks inherent in its products, is a fundamental ethical issue that you must resolve for yourself—and it is not an easy one.

As a liberal you might argue that smokers or drinkers really don't know what's best for themselves and that they and/or society pay too high a price for their ignorance. As such, you might try to do all you can as a socially responsible investor to get those products off the market, even in the face of consumer opposition and even if it costs the life of the corporation itself.

As a conservative, however, you might consider the provision of legal goods in response to consumer demand to be the most responsible thing a company can do—so long as it did it honestly and fairly. As such, you might choose not to ask your company's management to get out of the tobacco or alcohol business, even if you personally disapproved of those products, so long as you were convinced that that was what your company's customers wanted.

But remember, when it is *your* company, there is no reason why *you* have to go along with its producing goods of which *you* disapprove. Thus, you still might try to encourage your company to leave those businesses or you might avoid investing in them in the first place. If others choose to do so, you don't have to try to stop them, but you need not personally be a part of endeavors of which you disapprove.

————————

Tobacco and alcohol are, of course, two of the major specific issues confronting socially responsible investors. Indeed, they may have been the first issues that socially responsible investors dealt with more than 70 years ago. In the next chapter, we will discuss these issues (as well as gambling) in somewhat greater detail.

6

Selected Sins: Smoking, Drinking, and Gambling

THE CASE AGAINST TOBACCO

There are three interrelated but distinguishable arguments that may be made against smoking and, collaterally, against investing in tobacco companies:

1. *Tobacco is hazardous to a smoker's health.* According to the Surgeon General, smoking causes lung cancer, emphysema, and heart disease and accounts for approximately 400,000 deaths annually in the United States alone. Worldwide, according to the American Medical Association's Council on Scientific Affairs, tobacco use is responsible for almost 2.5 million deaths annually. Or, as Timothy Smith, executive director of the Interfaith Center on Corporate Responsibility, put it: "Philip Morris, American Brands and Loews produce lethal weapons, which cause the deaths of more people than heroin, cocaine, alcohol, AIDS, fire, homicide, suicide and automobile accidents combined."[1]

This argument continues: The nicotine in tobacco is highly addictive—even more so than drugs such as marijuana and cocaine, which are illegal. Consequently, tobacco should also be banned or, if it is not, its use should be discouraged (for instance, by prohibiting sales to minors who purchase an estimated 947 million packs of cigarettes valued at over $1.2 billion annually, by banning sales through vending machines, by restricting media advertising, and by limiting smoking to specified areas).

The argument concludes: Individuals who smoke either don't realize what is good for them or, because of their addiction, don't have the willpower to act on their knowledge. In either case, the government or society—or socially responsible investors—should try to protect them from themselves, by passing legislation that prohibits smoking or, at least, by attempting to influence corporations to get out of the tobacco business.

2. *Tobacco is directly hazardous to the health of others.* The inhalation of secondhand, passive, or sidestream smoke is dangerous to persons who do not choose to smoke themselves. The Environmental Protection Agency has estimated that passive smoke causes 3,800 lung cancer deaths annually, which includes 2,500 adults who never smoked and 1,300 former smokers. Also, according to Dr. Stanton A. Glantz of the University of California, "Passive smoking [i.e., being in the presence of smokers and subjected to their smoke exhalations] causes heart disease and the number of deaths due to heart disease is 10 times the number due to cancer."[2] Indeed, Dr. Glantz has estimated that non-smokers living with smokers have a 20 to 30% higher risk of dying from heart disease than do other non-smokers and that as many as 50,000 Americans may die annually as a result of inhaling such sidestream smoke (with two-thirds of those dying from heart disease).

Smokers, this argument continues, must be prevented by the government or society from imposing those toxic substances on innocent bystanders. Socially responsible investors should attempt to influence companies to get out of the tobacco business or, at least, restrict their advertising and marketing efforts in order to help protect those innocent victims of secondhand smoke.

3. *Tobacco is indirectly hazardous to society.* The death or disability of smokers (or those affected by secondhand smoke) takes its toll on all of us in the form of lost productivity, increased insurance premiums, higher welfare benefits to survivors, and so forth. In California alone, according to Dr. Kenneth Kizer, the state's health director, "The cost of tobacco use is staggering . . .

smoking costs the citizens of [California] more than $7.1 billion in health care and lost productivity."[3] Similar studies in New York state by the Health Department suggest that the cost to New York approaches $5 billion annually.

This argument concludes that the government and society have a vested interest in mitigating those indirect costs. And that socially responsible investors can help.

Liberal socially responsible investors tend to agree with all three arguments. Since their inclinations frequently are to focus more on people in their roles as members of society than as individuals in their own right, to argue that it is the responsibility of the state (rather than the individual) to determine what is in the individual's own best interest, and to place the well-being of society above considerations of personal liberty, they seldom have difficulty with arguments restricting smokers' rights (or restricting the rights of corporations to cater to them).

Conservative socially responsible investors, however, tend to have a problem with the first of these arguments. It is not that they deny that smoking is hazardous to one's health; indeed, they readily admit that it has been well-established that smoking is the leading preventable cause of death, contributing to the onset of lung cancer, emphysema, and heart disease. However, they argue that it does not necessarily follow that individuals shouldn't have the right to act contrary to the interests of their own health, so long as they are adults and understand the implications of their actions. Why should they be prevented from voluntarily trading off their health or one or more years of life for the temporal pleasures they derive from smoking?

Such tradeoffs may seem foolish to those of us who are not smokers but it is, after all, their lives, not ours. Mountain climbing may seem foolish, too, to those who don't choose to climb mountains; race car driving may seem stupid to those who don't drive race cars; even playing football may seem dumb to those who don't play football. Yet, we allow people to climb mountains, drive race cars, play football, or engage in all sorts of other hazardous activities if that's what they choose to do because we recognize that it is their right, not ours, to decide what risks to take with their health and their lives.

Indeed, even driving a car is risky, with over 50,000 people dying annually in automobile accidents, but no one proposes legislating automobiles out of existence. Why should cigarettes be treated any differently?

Libertarians generally share the *conservative* attitude toward the first of the three arguments. In addition, they have just as little patience with the third argument. Society, they argue, has neither a claim on the productivity of individuals nor an obligation to compensate them for the consequences of self-assumed risks; hence, if individuals choose to jeopardize their health or their lives by smoking, that is their business.

If others, acting collectively through the government or as society, choose to alleviate that suffering through welfare programs, that may be kind and humane of them, but it does not impose obligations on the beneficiaries of such largesse. It is illegitimate to force the smoker to live by society's standards simply because society prefers not to incur the costs that it is under no obligation to incur in the first place.

The second argument, however, is another matter entirely. This argument is convincing across the entire political spectrum. If secondhand smoke does cause harm to others, and it is reasonably certain now that it does, then certainly it is legitimate for the government, society, or individuals to act to prevent smokers from imposing that hazard upon others. After all, one of the core values of many political philosophies is that no one may initiate the use of force or fraud nor do gratuitous harm to another. If secondhand smoke causes such gratuitous harm, then it is justifiable for the state to prohibit or restrict it. And, even absent governmental action, it still is legitimate for socially responsible investors to avoid investments in tobacco companies, to seek out alternative investments, or actively to try to convince managements to leave the tobacco business.

Thus, while any or all of the three arguments could justify anti-tobacco socially responsible investing practices on the part of most *liberals*, and both the second and third arguments might justify it for most *conservatives*, only the second argument would satisfy it for virtually everyone.

In addition, any investor, (whatever his political inclinations) is always free to oppose the use of his own assets for purposes that he diasapproves of, whatever the reason. And the shares of a corporation which he owns *are* his own assets.

Thus, even if there were no secondhand smoke issue, any socially responsible investor, no matter what his politics, *could* still object to his funds being used to produce cigarettes. Under those circumstances, some might favor and others might oppose legislation restricting the right to smoke or a company's right to manufacture tobacco products, but all could still refuse to allow their *own* money to be used to fund those activities.

Avoidance Investors and Tobacco Companies

Pioneer Fund is an unusual mutual fund. Although it does not commit itself in its prospectus to the use of socially responsible criteria, it may well be the oldest mutual fund in the country that has consciously avoided investments in tobacco stocks since 1928.

Today, **Pioneer** no longer stands alone among mutual funds in avoiding tobacco stocks. Two newer funds in the **Pioneer** group (**Pioneer II** and **Pioneer III**) also avoid investments in tobacco, as do at least two other socially responsible funds: **Pax World Fund** and the **Parnassus Fund**. Even with this, for a long time, the rejection of tobacco stocks by socially responsible investors was limited to just a handful of mutual funds, a number of churches, and individual investors.

To be sure, in 1981 (16 years after the federal government first required warning labels on cigarette packages and advertising and 11 years after tobacco advertising was banned on radio and television), the American Medical Association did decide to divest itself of the tobacco stocks in its own investment portfolio. Six years later it asked medical schools and their parent universities to do the same, but that appeal fell on deaf ears.

Then, in 1990 things began to change. In March, **Teachers Insurance Annuity Association—College Retirement Equities Fund** (TIAA-CREF), the nationwide pension system for college and university employees, introduced a *Social Choice Account* which would not invest in tobacco companies. The same month, the *Tobacco Divestment Project* was formed in Boston to pressure institutional investors to divest themselves of their tobacco holdings.

In May, Derek Bok, president of Harvard University, revealed that Harvard had eliminated all tobacco stocks from its investment portfolios. In disclosing that action, he stated in a letter to three students at Harvard's public health school that the decision "was motivated by a desire not to be associated as a shareholder with companies engaged in significant sales of products that create a substantial and unjustified risk of harm to other human beings."[4]

In the same month, the City University of New York announced that it, too, intended to divest itself of its tobacco holdings. Edith Everett, vice chairman of the board of trustees at City University and a long-time opponent of the tobacco industry, was also on the board of trustees of the *Tobacco Divestment Project*. It is she who was credited with having persuaded the City University board to vote as they did to divest their tobacco stocks.

As of mid-1990, the Harvard and City University of New York divestitures were the biggest anti-tobacco victories that had been achieved by socially responsible *avoidance* investors, but it is unlikely that they will remain the only ones. Both the Rockefeller Family Fund and the Kaiser Foundation have also indicated that they have sold their cigarette stocks. And, flush with its victories at Harvard and City University, the *Tobacco Divestment Project* quickly targetted three Hartford insurance companies— **Aetna Life & Casualty Company** (NYSE—AET), **Travelers Corporation** (NYSE—TIC), and **Cigna Corporation** (NYSE—CI)— as well as several hospitals and universities and the Connecticut state pension fund.

Almost concurrently, a bill was introduced in the Massachusetts state legislature to require the state to divest itself of all its tobacco stocks. Independent of that bill, Governor Michael S. Dukakis announced that he favored divestment, too, and that he would attempt to accomplish that by executive order. Two weeks later, Governor Mario M. Cuomo of New York, indicated that he, too, favored divestment of tobacco stocks by New York state, describing the idea as one with "incredible appeal."[5]

Still, not everyone agrees with the idea of institutional divestment of tobacco stocks. In Connecticut, for instance, the state treasurer, Francisco L. Borges, has said that he was certain his state would *not* divest itself of tobacco stocks since his principal responsibility was to get the best possible return on the state's investments.

In New York, State Comptroller Edward V. Regan, the sole trustee of the state's pension fund, took a similar position in continuing to oppose forced divestment of tobacco stocks on the grounds that it would violate his fiduciary responsibility and could cost the fund as much as 1% in transaction fees. As Regan put it:

> While the motives may be noble, these proposals impose new nonfiduciary restrictions on the pension fund at a time when it can least afford to handle them. At this time, it is incumbent on the state to allow us broader investment discretion rather than arbitrarily restricting and narrowing our investment opportunities.[6]

Where does this leave you if you are a socially responsible *avoidance* investor and are opposed to tobacco? Well, among the securities you might consider excluding from your portfolio are the stocks and bonds of the following companies:

American Brands, Inc. (NYSE—AMB). The nation's fifth largest cigarette manufacturer, **American Brands** derives approximately 65% of its operating income from cigarettes. It manufactures *American, Carlton, Lucky Strike, Malibu, Misty, Montclair, Pall Mall,* and *Tareyton* cigarettes domestically, *Benson and Hedges, Berkeley,* and *Silk Cut* cigarettes in Great Britain (through its **Gallaher Ltd.** subsidiary which is the largest tobacco company in the United Kingdom), and *Benson and Hedges* and *Hamlet* cigars, and *Condor* pipe tobacco. **American Brands** is also in the life insurance and distilling businesses.

B.A.T. Industries PLC (ASE—BTI). The world's largest tobacco company, **B.A.T. Industries** generates 52% of its operating income from cigarettes through its **Brown & Williamson** and **British American Tobacco** subsidiaries. Its leading cigarette brands include *Kool* and *Richland 20's.* It also owns 40% of **Imasco Ltd.**

Brooke Group Ltd. (NYSE—BGL). Smallest of the six cigarette manufacturers in the United States with about a 3% market
share, **Brooke Group Ltd.** (formerly **Liggett Group Inc.**) derives
most of its operating income from cigarettes, including *Chester-
field*, *L&M*, *Lark*, and *Pyramid*.

Culbro Corp. (NYSE—CUC). A diversified consumer products company, **Culbro Corp.** manufactures *Garcia y Vega*, *Tip-
arillo*, and *White Owl* cigars as well as other tobacco products,
candy, health and beauty aids, plastic components, and packaging and labeling systems.

Dibrell Brothers, Inc. (OTC—DBRL). One of the leading
tobacco dealers in the United States, **Dibrell Brothers** is engaged
in the purchasing and processing of leaf tobacco for sale to
cigarette manufacturers.

Imasco Ltd. (TSE—IMS.TO). A diversified Canadian company, **Imasco Ltd.** controls more than half of the Canadian cigarette
market with *duMaurier* and *Players* brands; the company also
operates the Hardee's fast-food chain and Peoples drug stores in
the United States as well as Shoppers Drug Mart in Canada.

Kimberly-Clark Corporation (NYSE—KMB). One of the
country's largest paper companies, **Kimberly-Clark** manufactures
Kleenex, *Huggies* disposable diapers, paper towels, newsprint,
and *Kotex* feminine napkins, but it is also a leading manufacturer
of cigarette papers.

Loews Corporation (NYSE—LTR). Through its wholly owned
Lorillard Inc. subsidiary, **Loews** generates more than a third of its
operating income from the sale of *Kent*, *Newport*, and *True*
cigarettes. The company also owns 83% of **CNA Financial Corp.**,
a multiple-line insurance company, 97% of **Bulova Corp.**, and
25% of **CBS Incorporated** (NYSE—CBS) and owns and/or operates 16 hotels.

Philip Morris Companies Inc. (NYSE—MO). A leading consumer products company, **Philip Morris** derives over 65% of its

operating income from cigarettes, including *Benson & Hedges, Marlboro, Merit, Parliament,* and *Virginia Slims.* The company also manufactures coffee, cereals, packaged foods, and beer through its **General Foods**, **Kraft**, and **Miller Brewing** subsidiaries.

RJR Nabisco, Inc. Through its **R.J. Reynolds Tobacco Company** subsidiary, **RJR Nabisco** generates 73% of its operating income from the sale of cigarettes. Its principal brands include *Camel, Century, Doral, More, Now, Ritz, Salem, Vantage,* and *Winston.* The company's **Nabisco** subsidiary is also one of the largest packaged food companies in the world.

Standard Commercial Corp. (NYSE—STW). The world's second-largest tobacco leaf importer and exporter, **Standard Commercial** is also one of the world's 10-largest wool merchants.

Universal Corp. (NYSE—UVV). The largest leaf tobacco importer and exporter in the world, **Universal Corp.** also owns **Lawyers Title Insurance Corp.**

UST Inc. (NYSE-UST). The leading United States producer of chewing tobaccos, with 85% of the market, **UST Inc.**'s brands include *Copenhagen, Skoal,* and *Skoal Long Cut.* The company is also a manufacturer of cigarette papers, pipe tobacco, and wines.

Alternative Investors and Tobacco Companies

There are not a lot of options available to *alternative* socially responsible investors who wish to invest in a manner that will register their disapproval of tobacco and smoking. One thing that anti-tobacco socially responsible investors might do is seek out as potential investments those companies that totally ban or severely restrict smoking in their own workplaces. Included in this group would be **Goodyear Tire & Rubber Company** (NYSE—GT), **Ford Motor Company** (NYSE—F), **Kansas Gas & Electric Company** (NYSE—KGE), **US West Inc.** (NYSE—USW), **Boeing Company** (NYSE—BA), **Adolph Coors Company** (OTC—ACCOB), and **Deluxe Corporation** (NYSE—DLX).

Banning smoking by employees, incidentally, might not just be socially responsible; it might also make good business and investment sense. Some statistical studies have shown that smokers have higher rates of absenteeism, lower productivity, and higher medical claims for themselves and their families than do non-smokers. Thus, this may be just another example of how *doing good* can lead to *doing well* too.

Activist Investors and Tobacco Companies

When it comes to tobacco, it is as *activists* that socially responsible investors finally have come into their own. For years, the Securities and Exchange Commission refused to allow shareholder resolutions opposing tobacco product manufacturing and advertising. In 1990, however, Paul Neuhauser, attorney for a group of churches that sought to introduce such resolutions, convinced the SEC to reverse its position.

Neuhauser, professor of law at the University of Iowa, argued successfully that tobacco product manufacturing no longer could be considered a routine business matter "when you read the daily obituaries and one out of every six deaths in the United States is attributable to smoking."[7] Seizing on that reversal in the SEC's position, several religious investors, who are members of the *Interfaith Center on Corporate Responsibility*, introduced anti-tobacco resolutions at four companies during the 1990 proxy season.

Resolutions were introduced at **Philip Morris**, **American Brands**, and **Loews Corp.**, proposing that those companies stop manufacturing or marketing tobacco products anywhere in the world after 1999. A second resolution was also introduced at **Philip Morris**, asking that company to report on the effect of its advertising and promotional activities on children's decisions to smoke. And a third resolution was introduced at **Kimberly-Clark**, asking that it stop manufacturing cigarette papers.

All of these resolutions were strongly opposed by management and all failed. Indeed, none received as much as 4% of the votes cast. But that really was not the point; no one expected them to pass. The real purpose behind their introduction was to call more attention to the tobacco issue, to keep it in the public eye, and to maintain continuing pressure on the tobacco companies. All of that was certainly accomplished.

THE CASE AGAINST ALCOHOL

The arguments against alcohol and against investing in the stocks of brewers, distillers, and wineries are similar to those against tobacco and investing in tobacco companies. One's acceptance or rejection of those arguments will also likely depend on one's personal philosophical or political orientation:

1. *Alcohol is hazardous to a drinker's health.* This fact is well-established but the reasoning behind it is, at the same time, both sharper and fuzzier than in the case of tobacco. On the one hand, while the tobacco industry persists in disputing the case against tobacco (which rests primarily on statistical evidence linking cigarette smoking to cancer, heart disease, and higher mortality rates), no one, even within the alcohol industry, denies that drinking alcohol gets people drunk and that drunkeness can lead to accidents and death. That much is clear cut.

On the other hand, when we speak of tobacco's being hazardous to a smoker's health, we are referring simply to the fact that the inhalation of tobacco smoke, per se, has been proven to be a direct cause of lung cancer, emphysema, and heart disease. However, when we speak of alcohol's being hazardous to a drinker's health, we generally mean something more than that.

In that latter situation, we don't just mean that alcohol may cause cirrhosis of the liver or that it has been implicated in mouth cancer or respiratory tuberculosis. Those claims may be true but, in addition, we mean that alcohol has also been implicated in the deaths of tens of thousands of individuals in automobile and other accidents. That is a less clear-cut linkage since it requires the *abuse* or *overuse* of alcohol, not merely its use as intended (which is sufficient for the indictment of tobacco).

Thus, when the National Centers for Disease Control reported that more than 100,000 Americans died from injuries or diseases linked to alcohol in 1987, they didn't only include the nearly

20,000 people who died of digestive diseases (including cirrhosis of the liver). They also included more than 30,000 people who died of injuries, chiefly resulting from automobile accidents involving drunken drivers.

2. *Alcohol is hazardous to the health of others.* No one dies from inhaling the alcohol fumes exhaled by drinkers, as some may from the inhalation of secondhand smoke. Still, it is estimated that 9 out of 10 teenage automobile accidents involve alcohol and the number of innocent non-drinkers who die in automobile accidents caused by drunken drivers runs into the tens of thousands annually. Furthermore, injuries and deaths from child abuse, wife abuse, and barroom brawls that result from drunken behavior add to the toll. While the linkage between drinking and these deaths and injuries may not be as direct as between smoking and the deaths it causes, the consequences are just as dire.

Additonally, fetal alcohol syndrome is one of the three leading causes of birth defects and the only one that is preventable. Thus, drinking during pregnancy can be a direct cause of injury to an innocent party—the unborn child.

3. *Alcohol is indirectly hazardous to society.* Just as smoking costs the nation billions of dollars in lost productivity, higher welfare payments to survivors, and bigger insurance premiums, so does drinking. Indeed, according to the Department of Health and Human Services, the annual cost to the country of alcohol abuse and alcoholism is about $135 billion—and that figure is projected to rise to $150 billion by 1995.

We need not recap the kind of reasoning that leads some to accept all three of these arguments and others to subscribe to only one or two of them; suffice it to say that they do. The need to balance individual rights against the well-being of society again comes to the fore and, depending on one's philosophical and political predilections, different conclusions will be reached by different investors.

As far as you are personally concerned, however, through it all remember that it's *your* money, so that if *you* don't want to invest in companies that manufacture alcoholic beverages, it's *your* right to refuse to do so. No matter *what* your reason.

Socially Responsible Investing and Alcohol Companies

There are just a handful of socially responsible mutual funds, including the funds of the **Pioneer Group**, the **Pax World Fund**, and the **Parnassus Fund**, which refuse to invest in alcohol companies, just as they exclude tobacco stocks from their portfolios. (Some churches won't invest in the manufacturers of alcoholic beverages either.) In general, the opposition of socially responsible investors to alcohol is not even close to the level of their opposition to tobacco. There is, for example, no concerted movement comparable to the *Tobacco Divestment Project* under way to convince public pension plans and other institutions to divest themselves of their alcohol, as well as their tobacco stocks. However, if you are a socially responsible *avoidance* investor who is opposed to alcohol you might consider excluding the following companies from your portfolio.

American Brands, Inc. (NYSE—AMB). In addition to its tobacco operations commented on earlier, **American Brands** produces *Jim Beam* and *Old Crow* bourbons, *Windsor Canadian Supreme Whisky*, *DeKuyper* cordials, *Gilbey's* gin and vodka, and *Kamchatka* vodka.

Anheuser-Busch Companies, Inc. (NYSE—BUD). The nation's largest brewer with 43% of the U.S. market, **Anheuser-Busch** manufactures *Bud Light, Budweiser, Busch, Classic Dark, Michelob, Michelob Dry, Michelob Light*, and *Natural Light* beers. The company also manufactures baked goods, frozen foods, and snack foods through its **Campbell Taggart** and **Eagle Foods** subsidiaries.

Brown-Forman Corp. (ASE—BFB). A major producer and importer of wine and distilled spirits, **Brown-Forman's** principal brands include *Bolla, California Cooler, Canadian Mist, Early Times, Jack Daniel's, Korbel*, and *Southern Comfort*. The company also manufactures and markets *Lenox* china and crystal and *Hartmann* luggage.

Adolph Coors Company (OTC—ACCOB). The fourth largest brewer in the United States, **Adolph Coors** manufactures *Coors, Coors Light, Extra Gold, Herman Joseph's, Keystone*, and *Keystone Light* beers. The company also operates an aluminum recycling plant and owns over 400,000 acres of oil and gas leases in Colorado.

Grand Metropolitan PLC. A major international conglomerate whose interests range from fast foods **(Burger King)** and packaged foods **(Pillsbury)** to wines and distilled spirits **(Heublein Holding, Paddington, Valkyrie Three)**, **Grand Metropolitan's** leading brands of wines and distilled spirits include: *Popov, Relska*, and *Smirnoff* vodkas; *Black Velvet* Canadian whisky; *Jose Cuervo* tequila; *Christian Brothers* brandy; *Club* cocktails; *Arrow* cordials; *Inglenook* and *Almaden* wines; *J & B* scotch; *Bailey's* cordial; *Beaulieu* wines, *Bombay* gin; and *Cinzano*.

Guiness PLC. A multinational brewing and distilling company, **Guiness PLC** produces and distributes wines and distilled spirits through various subsidiaries including **Schenley Industries Inc.** Its leading brands include *Gordon's* vodka and gin, *Tanqueray* gin, *Dewar's* scotch, *Sonoma Vineyards*, and *Dubonnet*.

John Labatt Ltd. (TSE—LBT.TO). Canada's largest brewer with 41% of the market, **John Labatt** markets *Labatt's 50, Labatt's Blue, Labatt's Lite*, and *Rolling Rock* beers. The company also produces dairy products, fruit juices, grain products, and frozen foods and owns 45% of the *Toronto Blue Jays* baseball team.

Molson Companies Ltd. (TSE—MOLA.TO). A diversified Canadian company, **Molson Companies** is engaged in specialty chemicals, retail merchandising, and brewing (*Molson* beer). It is the third-largest exporter of beers to the United States and owner of the *Montreal Canadiens* hockey team.

Philip Morris Companies Inc. (NYSE—MO). In addition to manufacturing tobacco and other products (see above), **Philip**

Morris brews *Lowenbrau, Meister Brau, Miller High Life, Miller Lite*, and *Milwaukee's Best* beers through its **Miller Brewing Co.** subsidiary.

Seagram Company Ltd. (NYSE—VO). The largest wine and distilled spirits company in the world, **Seagram Company's** major brands include *7 Crown, Crown Royal, Lord Calvert*, and *V.O.* Canadian whiskies, *Chivas Regal* scotch, *Seagram's* gin, *Wolfschmidt* vodka, *Leroux* cordials, *Ronrico* rum, *Mumm, Glenlivet*, and *Martell*. **Seagram** also owns **Tropicana**, the leading U.S. juice producer, and 24% of **E.I. duPont de Nemours**, the largest U.S. chemicals company.

UST Inc. (NYSE—UST). In addition to manufacturing tobacco products (see above), **UST Inc.** produces *Chateau Ste. Michelle, Columbia Crest, Conn Creek*, and *Villa Mt. Eden* wines.

However, if you are not unalterably opposed to the use of alcohol under any circumstances but simply feel that the manufacturers and marketers of alcoholic beverages have social responsibilites, say, not to market to children or to educate people as to the risks of drinking and driving, then you might be interested in knowing which, if any, of these companies, have been making socially responsible efforts in those areas. In fact, several have.

More than 50 years ago, **Seagram Company** first began to campaign through advertising against drunk driving. More recently, the company produced a handbook and audiotape educational program called *Talking About Alcohol*, which was designed to advise parents on how to communicate with their children on the differences between responsible alcohol consumption and alcohol abuse. In addition, **Adolph Coors Company** developed a program called *Alcohol, Drugs, Driving and You*, which provides high school students with information on the effects of alcohol and drugs.

Philip Morris, through its **Miller** division, developed a corporate advertising campaign around the theme *Think When You*

Drink. The company has also provided financial support to the *Health Education Foundation* and the *Alcohol Policy Council*. And it has developed two programs called *TIPS* (Training for Intervention Procedures by Servers of Alcohol) and *AIM* (Alcohol Information from Miller). The former is a training program for bartenders and waiters about responsible drinking and the handling of customers who drink to excess. The latter is directed at distributors, providing them with the information necessary to instruct others about responsible drinking.

Anheuser-Busch's efforts may be the biggest and most visible. The company's corporate advertising centers around a *Know When to Say When* theme. It has distributed 200,000 copies of its kit entitled *How to Talk to Your Kids About Drinking . . .*, and it has worked closely with *Students Against Drunk Driving (SADD)* through 20,000 high schools nationwide, reaching an estimated four million children.

According to Bill Stolberg, senior vice president at **Fleishman-Hillard** which works both for **Anheuser-Busch** and *The Beer Institute* trade association of which **Anheuser-Busch** is the largest member,

> We have consulted with the *American Council on Alcoholism . . .* on education and medical issues. We have been the biggest funder of *Students Against Drunk Driving. . . .* **Anheuser-Busch** has put into education campaigns in the past few years . . . more than they spend promoting most of their brands. Only *Bud* itself had a bigger budget. We are very serious about addressing this issue.[8]

To date, activists have not been very involved in the proxy resolution process at brewing or distilling companies. Indeed, according to the *Interfaith Center on Corporate Responsibility*, in the 1990 proxy season, none of the 219 resolutions filed at 157 companies bore on issues relating to the production, marketing, or distribution of alcoholic beverages.

SRI AND THE GAMBLING INDUSTRY

Over the years, social reformers have tended to include gambling with smoking and drinking as one of the three *sins* that should be prohibited by law or, at least, strongly discouraged. Yet, what, if anything, does gambling have in common with smoking or drinking?

Certainly, gambling is not directly hazardous to the health of a gambler or that of his neighbors in the sense that smoking and drinking are. Smoking, after all, has been proven to be directly hazardous to the health of smokers (and even non-smokers, through passive smoke). Drinking is directly hazardous to drinkers as a cause of cirrhosis of the liver, it has been implicated in cases of respiratory tuberculosis and mouth cancer, and it has resulted in the deaths of thousands of drunken drivers; it is also hazardous to non-drinkers, including unborn children (fetal alcohol syndrome) and the innocent victims of automobile and other accidents resulting from drunken behavior. Both smoking and drinking can affect society by taking a toll on productivity, increasing insurance premiums, necessitating greater government expenditures for survivors' welfare, and so on.

But what has that got to do with gambling?

Surely, no one develops an illness or dies as a result of placing a bet at a race track or playing roulette, craps, slot machines, or blackjack at a casino. No spouse, neighbor, or friend suffers a physical ailment or dies as a direct result of one's gambling. Or do they?

The argument against gambling is much more tenuous than that against either smoking or drinking, since there is no direct adverse physical consequence which results from making a wager. One might even benefit by winning! So what's the problem?

To some, the answer is that man is more that just his body— he has also a spirit or a soul—and gambling can be as destructive to the spirit or soul as smoking or drinking are to the body. That is because gambling is a non-productive, irresponsible and, ultimately, parasitic activity. In the Judeo-Christian tradition, man is responsible for his own life, productivity is a positive value, and it is considered better to contribute to society than to take from it. Since the gambler produces nothing, he is in the inevitable position of parasitically taking from society, never giving back. That is true whether he wins or loses.

Most of those who oppose gambling, however, don't object to it on transcendent religious or moral grounds but rather on the practical grounds that, in fact, gambling can, and often does, lead to irresponsible behavior toward one's family and others to whom one is obligated. It results in excessive indebtedness, family dissolutions, violence, white collar crime (especially embezzlement), lost productivity, and so forth.

Inevitably, most gamblers lose. If their gambling becomes obsessive, as it often does, they then sacrifice other goods in order to have a stake to wager in attempting to recover what they lost. They neglect to purchase food, clothing, or needed medical care for themselves and their dependents. They fail to pay their debts. They might steal from friends or employers. Their families and society in general suffer. And of course, at the extreme, if everyone were to substitute gambling for productive labor, the entire race would perish, for nothing would be produced and then there'd be nothing to gamble for!

In light of these considerations, *liberals*, concerned with the good of society and the state's right and responsibility to protect individuals from the consequences of their own voluntary actions, if that is deemed to be in their best interest, generally have no abstract problem with legislating against gambling or discouraging it through socially responsible investing practices. And, most *conservatives*, so attuned as they are to the value of productivity, the sanctity of property rights, and the importance of honoring contracts including debts, often agree with the *liberals* on this one. But *libertarians*, with their emphasis on individual liberty, as a rule are not exercised by the gambling issue.

It is not that *libertarians* respect or glorify gamblers; on the contrary, the very idea of gambling, rather than producing, is generally repugnant to them. But *libertarians* bend over backward to allow maximum freedom to individuals so that they can run their own lives as they see fit—so long as they do not use force or fraud or cause gratuitous harm to others in the process. And there really is nothing inherently wrong about gambling on that score.

While smoking has been implicated directly in the sufferings of others against their will through the inhalation of secondhand smoke, and drinking has similarly been implicated directly, at least in fetal alcohol syndrome, there is no comparable absolute necessity that gambling causes harm to others. So there is some reluctance on the part of *libertarians* to see this as a socially responsible investing issue.

Still it is *your* money we are talking about and if *you* are opposed to gambling for whatever reason, there probably are a number of stocks you'll want to avoid. These might include:

Aztar Corp. (OTC—AZTR). A hotel and casino operator, **Aztar Corp.** runs three gambling entertainment facilities, the *Las Vegas Tropicana*, the *Ramada Express*, and the *TropWorld Casino and Entertainment Resort*.

Bally Manufacturing Corp. (NYSE—BLY). A manufacturer of slot machines, lottery ticket machines, and exercise equipment, **Bally Manufacturing** owns and operates four gambling casinos-hotels, *Bally's Las Vegas*, *Bally's Park Place*, *Grand*, and *Reno*. The company also owns 315 *Jack LaLanne* fitness centers and *Six Flags* theme parks.

Caesars World, Inc. (NYSE—CAW). A resort, hotel, and casino operator, **Caesars World** owns three gambling casinos-hotels, *Caesars Atlantic City* (New Jersey), *Caesars Palace* (Las Vegas, Nevada), and *Caesars Tahoe* (Stateline, Nevada) as well as four resorts in the Pocono Mountains of Pennsylvania.

Circus Circus Enterprises, Inc. (NYSE—CIR). The owner and operator of two gambling casinos-hotels and two other walk-in casinos in Las Vegas, **Circus Circus Enterprises** also owns a casino/hotel in Reno and another in Laughlin, Nevada.

Golden Nugget, Inc. (NYSE—GNG). Golden Nugget owns and operates two casinos-hotels in Las Vegas (the *Golden Nugget* and the *Mirage*) and another casino, the *Nevada Club*, in Laughlin, Nevada.

Hilton Hotels Corp. (NYSE—HLY). One of the leading hotel chains in the United States, **Hilton Hotels** owns or manages 271 hotels thoroughout the country, including three casinos-hotels, the *Flamingo Hilton*, the *Flamingo Hilton-Reno*, and the *Las*

Vegas Hilton in Nevada. Through its *Conrad International* subsidiary, **Hilton Hotels** also operates other hotel and gaming properties outside the United States.

International Game Technology (OTC—IGAM). The world's leading manufacturer of casino gambling machines, **International Game Technology** also operates slot machines throughout Nevada.

Jackpot Enterprises, Inc. (NYSE—J). **Jackpot Enterprises** owns and operates over 2,000 gambling machines, including video poker and slot machines, throughout Nevada.

Showboat, Inc. (NYSE—SBO). **Showboat Inc.** owns and operates two casinos-hotels, one in Las Vegas and the other in Atlantic City.

A principal reason underlying the opposition of socially responsible investors to tobacco companies relates to the unintended consequences of passive smoke on the health of innocent parties. Imagine, then, the attitude of such investors toward those companies responsible for the production of smog, acid rain, oil spills, toxic wastes, and other forms of environmental pollution, all of which may also have severe adverse effects on the health and lives of innocent persons. We shall discuss this in the next chapter.

Environmentalism: The Crusade of the 1990s

WHAT DID YOU DO ON EARTH DAY, DADDY?

April 22, 1990. Earth Day. An estimated 200 million people in 140 countries around the world participate in the largest grass-roots demonstration in history. And what a demonstration it is.

In the United States, more than 3,600 communities commemorate the 20th anniversary of the first Earth Day in 1970 by engaging in marches, rallies, street fairs, and festivals, by planting trees, by picking up trash, and by staging workshops on everything from wildlife and endangered species to recycling. In New York City, an estimated three-quarters of a million people gather for a concert in Central Park. Elsewhere in the city, 42 astronauts from 14 countries meet at the United Nations to address the problems of deforestation and oil spills as depicted in photographs they had taken from outer space. In Washington, DC, over 100,000 celebrate the day by listening to environmental activists on the Capitol Mall.

Japan celebrates with an *Ecofair* on a landfill island reclaimed from Tokyo's garbage. In Antarctica, there is a trash pickup—

115

and another on a trek by U.S., Soviet, and Chinese climbers up Mt. Everest in Nepal. Participants form a 300-mile human chain across France while 5,000 people lie down on the road in Italy to protest car fumes. Trees are planted throughout the world: 10,000 along the site of the Berlin Wall which had separated East and West Germany; more in Kenya; even more along the banks of the Mississippi and Missouri rivers in the United States; and on Vancouver Island in Canada.

All in all, it is quite a day.

For some people, of course, it is just a big party or happening—the place to be so that they might tell their children or grandchildren about it. But to others, it is a symbol of what they perceive to be the most important issue of our time: the very survival of our planet.

FORERUNNERS OF TODAY'S ENVIRONMENTALISTS

In its broadest sense, the environmental movement goes back a long time—at least to the 1800s and early 1900s and to Henry David Thoreau, John James Audobon, George Perkins Marsh, John Muir, Aldo Leopold, Theodore Roosevelt, and a host of others who exhibited a passion for nature, wildlife, and the wilderness. But the environmental movement as we know it today has changed mightily since then; what began as a conservation movement out of an esthetic love of nature has evolved into nothing less than a full-blown crusade to save the planet.

In the 1960s and 1970s, this transition began to take place. In 1962, Rachel Carson wrote *Silent Spring*, focusing attention on the risks inherent in the overuse of pesticides. In the same year, Gaylord Nelson, today a counselor of the Wilderness Society, was elected U.S. Senator from Wisconsin; eight years later, Nelson fathered the nation's first Earth Day.

In 1969, the Santa Barbara oil spill galvanized Congress to write the country's first major environmental legislation: the *National Environmental Protection Act*. And in 1970, William D. Ruckelshaus, now chief executive officer of **Browning-Ferris In-**

dustries, Inc. (NYSE—BFI), was named the first head of the newly created Environmental Protection Agency.

Other major environmental legislation followed in short order: the *Endangered Species Act*, the *Clean Air Act*, the *Clean Water Act*, and the *Resource Conservation and Recovery Act*. In the 1980s, the trend continued and accelerated to such a degree that, by 1989, it took the *Environmental Law Reporter* 3,500 pages to summarize federal environmental law; in 1971, it had been able to accomplish that in just 33 pages.

The environmental movement reached a crescendo in 1989 and 1990. The Coalition for Environmentally Responsible Economies (CERES) created the *Valdez Principles* (fashioned after the *Sullivan Principles*) in 1989. A record 38 shareholder resolutions on the environment were filed with corporations in 1990. The far-reaching *Clean Air Act of 1990*, with a potential price tag of anywhere from $25 billion to $100 billion was passed (although environmental propositions on the ballot in several states, including California's *Big Green* initiative, were rejected by voters as part of an across-the-board rejection of government in general at the polls that year). And of course, there was Earth Day.

As Jay Hair, president of the National Wildlife Federation, the largest environmental organization in the United States, put it: "To be an environmentalist now, it is no longer enough to enjoy or study nature passively. We are activists engaged in promoting the wiser use and protection of global natural resources."[1]

Thus, while today's environmentalists remain exercised, for example, over the future of Brazil's rain forests, their concern is now part of a much larger agenda. It is not that the rain forests themselves are inherently so important, as last century's conservationists might have proclaimed, but rather that their preservation has come to be looked on as essential to maintaining the world's ecological balance and thereby allowing the Earth itself to survive. Consequently, the main thrust of today's environmental movement relates more to such issues as air and water pollution, solid waste disposal, acid rain, recycling, biodegradability, depletion of the ozone layer, and the greenhouse effect. In that sense, today's environmental movement is no more than 20- or 30-years old.

GAIA WORSHIPERS, EARTH FIRST!ERS, AND DEEP ECOLOGISTS

Environmentalists come in all shapes and sizes. In the mainstream are those who care about the environmental quality of the life we lead today and about the sustainability of that quality of life for our children and grandchildren. At the extreme, though, are those who sometimes seem to forget that the Earth exists for man and not the other way around. We ought to comment on them briefly, if only to get them out of the way so that we might get on with more serious stuff.

The Gaia hypothesis is a *scientific* theory, originally propounded in the 1700s by James Hutton, to the effect that the Earth is a single *superorganism*. Hutton compared the flow of nutrients from the soil to plants and animals and back again and the flow of water from sea to rain to land to sea as analogous to blood circulation. His ideas were picked up again from time to time by other scientists but never attracted much of a following until James E. Lovelock resurrected them in the 1960s.

In Lovelocks's incarnation, the Earth as a whole was perceived of as a self-correcting mechanism—the sum of all organisms that can adjust and sustain its own optimum environment. The salinity and temperature of the oceans, the chemical composition of the atmosphere, the population balance among different species sharing territories were all regulated through the natural flow of causes and compensating effects. An increase in the population of a predator species, for instance, resulted in a decline in the population of the species on which it subsisted; the decline in the food source then resulted in a decline in the predator species. Eventually equilibrium was restored.

Whether or not there is any scientific merit to the Gaia hypothesis, it was not intended to have any religious ramifications. The Gaia hypothesis views the Earth as a system or mechanism, but not as a rational, thinking, conscious being. Be that as it may, however, there are always those who either misunderstand or whose psychological or emotional needs are such that they choose to imbue inanimate objects with consciousness, intelligence, wisdom, or even godlike attributes.

On the fringes that has happened with the Gaia hypothesis. For some, it was but a small step to go from viewing the Earth as an organism to viewing it as a goddess, deserving of worship in her own right. Thus, Gaia worshipers within the environmental movement do not advocate environmental measures because that is a way to improve the quality of life for themselves and their descendants, but rather because that is what they perceive as being in the interests of the Earth itself.

Akin to the Gaia worshipers are the Earth First!ers, the most radical and angriest arm of the environmental movement. According to Earth First!ers, humans exist for the sake of the Earth and not the other way around. In an Earth First! publication, AIDS once was described as "a welcome development in the inevitable reduction of human population."[2] And at an Earth First! meeting in the Adirondacks, one speaker, when asked what he thought the optimum human population of the Earth should be, responded "Zero."[3]

Earth First!ers have taken much of their philosophy from the idea of *deep ecology*, the notion that humans aren't any more nor less important than plants, animals, or even viruses. In 1985, Bill Devall and George Sessions, advocating a decrease in human population and a change in policies of "human interference with the non-human world" wrote in *Deep Ecology* that "human and non-human life on Earth have value in themselves. . . . These values are independent of the usefulness of the non-human world for human purposes."[4]

Of course, very few environmentalists explicitly endorse such outlandish notions. But people don't always think through the consequences of superficially appealing romantic or idealistic concepts. And so we find that many environmental activists often act as if they believed that man exists for the Earth and not the Earth for man.

It was in response to such attitudes that John Cardinal O'Connor took the occasion of Earth Day to deliver a homily at St. Patrick's Cathedral in which he asserted that "The earth exists for the human person and not vice versa." Cardinal O'Connor further urged that we focus on "the sacredness of the human person" and not on "snails and whales."[5]

U.S. Budget Director Richard G. Darman has taken a similar position, noting that "Americans did not fight and win the wars of the twentieth century to make the world safe for green vegetables." Along the same vein, he added that "If we were to regulate houses with the same principles we now apply to our food and air . . . we would all have to live in single-story homes—for fear of falling downstairs."[6]

A RESPONSIBLE APPROACH TO ENVIRONMENTALISM

If the Gaia worshipers, Earth First!ers, and deep ecologists are as far out as all that, does it follow that the entire environmental movement is without merit? Not at all. Environmental concerns are legitimate—when those concerns are for the quality of life for ourselves and our descendants and not for some Gaia-like abstraction.

The fact is that we *do* have serious environmental problems: by some counts, for example, 4,000 lakes in the United States and 164,000 in Canada are acidified or threatened as a result of acid rain. Half of all Americans live in counties that violated Federal air standards at some time in 1988. Many fish in the Great Lakes carry toxic chemicals making them dangerous to eat.

Garbage produced per person per day in the United States rose from 2.5 pounds in 1960 to 3.6 pounds in 1986 and we're rapidly running out of landfill space in which to dump it. Atmospheric concentrations of two of the most ozone-damaging chlorofluorocarbons rose 85% between 1975 and 1985. And global warming may be a real risk, although the jury is still out on this.

Indeed, there are legitimate, serious environmental issues about which we ought to be concerned. But the operative word here is *concern*, not *panic*: We should be concerned to the point of analyzing, evaluating, and acting as necessary, but we must be careful not to act mindlessly or precipitously. For as noted earlier, there are always tradeoffs and actions that might appear essential, but might not even prove to be desirable when all of their ramifications are taken into account.

This point was made abstractly in regard to a hypothetical widget factory in Chapter 1, but the point need not be abstract or hypothetical at all. In a more concrete example, it is true that we can control acid rain with scrubbers that remove 95% of the sulfur dioxide that otherwise would occur with the burning of coal by electric utilities. But doing so produces millions of pounds of waste annually at each plant where they're used. It also consumes about 5% of the energy produced, thereby necessitating an increase in total coal consumption, raising carbon dioxide emissions, and aggravating the buildup of gases that may cause global warming.

Similarly, banning the logging of ancient trees in the Pacific Northwest would protect the spotted owls which live among them, but it could also cost 10,000 loggers' jobs. Would the tradeoff be worth it?

President George Bush summarized this issue neatly when he stated,

> I reject those who would ignore the economic consequences of the spotted owl decision. The jobs of many thousands of Oregonians and whole communities are at stake. But I also think that we ought to reject those who do not recognize their obligation to protect our delicate ecosystem. . . . Common sense tells us to find a needed balance.[7]

Unfortunately, however, people don't always do cost-benefit analyses when asked emotionally charged questions. When, for example, in March-April 1990, a *New York Times/CBS News Poll* asked a random sample of 1,515 Americans whether they agreed that "protecting the environment is so important that requirements and standards cannot be too high, and continuing environmental improvements must be made regardless of cost," 74% replied *yes*. (In 1981, 45% replied affirmatively.)[8]

On its very face, this is an absurd response. If true, it means that 74% of Americans would be willing to sacrifice national defense, government support for education, medical research, Social Security, employment, stable prices, and any and all other values at whatever level to generate continuing environmental improvements. All this to avoid risk to individuals at the rate of one in a billion or one in a trillion. This is just plain silly.

When Americans are presented with the need to make trade-offs, however, they turn out not to be quite so foolish after all, although they do continue to exhibit a considerable concern for the environment. Thus, in the same poll, when Americans specifically were asked whether they would be willing to trade off jobs in their communities for the sake of the environment, a still substantial but somewhat lower number of 56% said *yes*.[9]

A *Wall Street Journal/NBC News Poll* held at about the same time produced similar results: 93% of respondents said that they would agree to require people to separate garbage and solid wastes for recycling and 68% said that they would agree to require pollution control equipment in automobiles even if that would add $600 to the cost of a new car. But not quite half said that they would agree to pay an additional 20 cents per gallon for cleaner burning gasoline and only 33% said that they would agree to close pollution-producing factories if that would result in a loss of jobs.[10]

Indeed, even William K. Reilly, head of the Environmental Protection Agency and former president of World Wildlife Fund—United States, an individual with impeccable environmental credentials, allowed that if he had been asked the *New York Times/CBS News Poll* question, he would have answered no, because some environmental tradeoffs would be too extreme even for him.[11] Reilly, while an avowed environmentalist, recognizes just how important cost-benefit analysis can be.

And you, as an investor, must do your own cost-benefit analysis when considering most of the environmental issues which we are about to discuss. That kind of analysis is, after all, at the very heart of the investment decision-making process and ought not be abdicated simply because the issues it deals with in these instances are complex and emotionally charged ones.

SOLID WASTE DISPOSAL

The United States is not the most populous nation in the world but it certainly is the most affluent. And it ranks first in the production of garbage, generating approximately 3.6 pounds per day or 1,300 pounds per year for every man, woman, and child in the country. Included in that annual total is enough wood and paper to heat 10 million homes for a century; more than 32 billion aluminum cans or enough aluminum to rebuild the American fleet 70 times over; approximately 16 billion disposable diapers; and more than 35 billion glass bottles.

This waste is more than an eyesore. It is not just that it is visually and aromatically unpleasant for the nation to be dotted with junkyards and garbage dumps that look unsightly and smell worse. No, it goes well beyond that. Much of this garbage (including medical wastes, toxic chemicals, and nuclear wastes) is also hazardous, directly threatening the health and lives of 250 million Americans.

And there is an economic problem, too. All this garbage must go somewhere. That requires resources and costs money.

There only are four ways to get rid of this mountain of solid waste:

1. bury it,
2. burn it,
3. recycle it, or
4. don't produce it in the first place.

Bury It: The Landfill Solution

To date, the overwhelmingly favored approach has been to bury it. Indeed, today approximately 160 million tons of municipal solid waste, or about 80% of U.S. garbage, is being stored in landfills annually. But there are two serious problems with this approach.

First, many landfills lack proper pollution control systems, resulting in ground and water contamination, the emission of noxious gases and potential explosions. Rainwater can seep in, leaching toxic materials into the ground water, thereby contaminating the drinking supply. Decomposing garbage may produce potentially explosive methane gas. Moreover, much of our solid waste garbage is not biodegradable even if in principle it might be, since it is packed so tightly and exposed to so little light that natural decomposition resulting from exposure to light, air, and moisture is severely delayed.

Second, we are simply running out of available landfill space. Between 1978 and 1990, the number of available U.S. landfills declined by more than two-thirds from 20,000 to 6,500. Over the next five years, the Environmental Protection Agency (EPA) estimates that another 2,000 to 3,000 will close.

Moreover, according to the EPA, its new regulations to improve landfill standards are expected to increase the annual cost of operating landfills by $880 million. These new regulations will require new landfills to have one or two liners to separate leachate from groundwater and plumbing systems to treat it. Methane gas would have to be collected and either burned off or used as fuel to generate electricity.

Other regulations could require recycling and composting operations at landfills, too. **Waste Management, Inc.** (NYSE—WMX) has estimated that, as a result, acquiring the land and permits for a 100-acre landfill, constructing required systems, and maintaining the site for 30 years after it is closed could cost as much as $32 to $55 million.[12] With these regulations in effect, it will become increasingly difficult to replace closed landfills economically.

In approaching this issue of solid waste pollution, a good starting point for socially responsible investors may well be the companies that have invested in landfills, including **Waste Management Inc., Browning-Ferris Industries, Chambers Development Co., Inc.** (ASE—CDVA), and **Laidlaw Inc.** (OTC—LDMFB). Many investors believe that companies such as these will prove to be big winners in the financial marketplace in the years ahead because they will be controlling limited resources (landfills) for which there inevitably will be growing demand.

Barry Mannis, an analyst with **Shearson Lehman Hutton**, noted that "landfill space, a commodity that is already rare, will become rarer still after Subtitle D [of the Resources Conservation and Recovery Act goes into effect, establishing tougher new EPA standards]. That makes it more valuable."[13] Indeed, it is even possible that waste disposal companies may ultimately be valued on the basis of their landfill reserves as oil companies are valued on the basis of their oil reserves.

Not all analysts are quite so optimistic. Some point out that the new regulations are a two-edged sword. Michael Hoffman of **Salomon Brothers**, a subsidiary of **Salomon Inc.** (NYSE—SB) for instance, has noted that "The costs of [landfill] operation have been rising faster than free cash flow . . . [so that these companies] are not going to be the great cash cows some people once thought."[14]

Waste Management, Inc. (NYSE—WMX).

Largest of the landfill companies, both in terms of revenues and land reserves, is **Waste Management, Inc.** with annual revenues in 1989 of nearly $4.5 billion. Servicing over eight million customers in 600 North American communities, the company also has operations in Europe, Australia, South America, and the Middle East. Earnings per share have increased annually since 1975.

In addition to its basic solid waste systems operations, **Waste Management** is also a major factor in the collection and disposal of chemical, nuclear, and medical wastes. It owns 79% of highly profitable **Chemical Waste Management** (NYSE—CHW), the largest hazardous waste company in the United States.

At least two environmentally concerned mutual funds have major positions in **Waste Management**: As of January 31, 1990, **Freedom Environmental Fund** owned 1,328,400 shares, making that the third-largest position in the fund's portfolio. As of October 31, 1989, **Waste Management** was also the second-largest position in **Fidelity Select Environmental Fund's** portfolio, accounting for nearly 8% of that fund's value.

But **Waste Management** is not everybody's darling. Peter Camejo, president of **Progressive Asset Management Inc.**, for instance, is negative on the company because of its record of EPA violations. However, according to David Beckwith, the **Freedom Environmental Fund's** portfolio manager, **Waste Management** "[runs] the cleanest landfill dumps in the business and [has] received a lot of violations because [it's] easy to target."[15]

Browning-Ferris Industries, Inc. (NYSE—BFI).

Browning-Ferris Industries, Inc. is the second-largest waste management company in the United States, with revenues in fiscal 1989 (ended September 30, 1989) in excess of $2.5 billion. In fiscal 1990,

revenues are expected to exceed $3 billion. The company operates in over 400 locations and owns more than 100 landfills. It is
expanding rapidly in the medical waste, recycling, waste-to-
energy, and solid waste markets. Excluding non-recurring losses
from discontinued operations, the company's earnings per share
have increased annually since 1976.

The company did have disasterous experiences in the hazardous waste area for a decade. Its **Cecos International Inc.**
hazardous waste subsidiary was plagued with regulatory problems
and generated returns that were much lower than those of
Browning-Ferris' other operations. Indeed, Cecos suffered operating losses from late 1988 until 1990 while accounting for only
2% of **Browning-Ferris'** total revenues.

In early April 1990, the company finally decided to bite the
bullet. William D. Ruckelshaus, chairman and chief executive
officer and formerly the highly regarded head of the EPA, announced that the company would leave the hazardous waste
business. In so doing, it incurred a one-time charge of $295
million or $1.93 a share.

In the wake of **Browning-Ferris'** decision to withdraw from
the hazardous waste business, Wall Street analysts' opinions of
the stock's investment merits were mixed. On the one hand,
Vishnu Swarup of **Prudential Bache Securities** said that "It's now
the best stock in the waste-handling group" and Douglas Augenthaler of **Oppenheimer & Company** said "It was a good buy
before but now it's better."[16]

On the other hand, Richard Rossi of **Dean Witter Reynolds**
expressed concern lest the reserves established by the company to
cover the costs of closing **Cecos'** operations and cleaning up its
sites prove inadequate. Moreover, Scott Jay Williams of **Tucker,
Anthony Inc.** averred that **Browning-Ferris'** decision to "[abandon] the business that will provide the greatest economic opportunity in the environmental field over the next 20 or 30 years . . .
shows their inability to diversify and general management problems."[17]

As of January 31, 1990, **Freedom Environmental Fund** owned
28,600 shares of **Browning-Ferris**. As of October 31, 1989, **Fidelity Select Environmental Fund** had also committed about 5% of
its assets to this stock.

Laidlaw Inc. (OTC—LDMFB). Laidlaw Inc., the largest school bus operator in North America, also owns the second-largest solid and chemical waste management company on the continent. In fiscal 1989 (ended August 1989), **Laidlaw's** revenues exceeded $1.4 billion. More than half of that came from its waste management business. Earnings have compounded at a 30% average annual rate over the past 10 years.

Laidlaw is another favorite of the environmentally oriented funds. It was the single largest position in **Fidelity Select Environmental Fund's** portfolio, accounting for nearly 10% of that fund's total value, as of October 31, 1989. As of January 1, 1990, **Freedom Environmental Fund** also owned over a million shares, marking it as the fourth-largest position in that fund's portfolio.

Chambers Development Co., Inc. (ASE—CDVA). Chambers Development is in both the solid waste management and security and investigative services businesses. It collects and disposes of solid wastes for commercial, industrial, and residential customers in 11 states.

Chambers Development is much smaller than **Waste Management, Browning-Ferris**, or **Laidlaw**, with revenues in 1989 having amounted to less than $200 million. But the company is growing rapidly by expanding existing landfills, opening new ones, and acquiring other companies. Both **Freedom Environmental Fund** and **Fidelity Select Environmental Fund** have positions in **Chambers Development**.

Burn It: The Waste-to-Energy Solution

Currently, about 9% of our solid wastes are burned (or incinerated) but this solution is not perfect either. Household garbage contains substances which, when burned, pollute the air as heavy metals, acid gases, or dioxins. Thus, the solid waste problem is simply transformed into an air pollution problem. Moreover, after burning, some toxic ash still remains to be buried.

However, we are rapidly running out of landfill space and a NIMBY ("not in my backyard") attitude is spreading rapidly. Thus, incinerating our garbage no longer may be ignored as a viable option. Indeed, by 1994, the EPA has estimated that 15 to

20% of our municipal waste will be incinerated. To that end, 166 incineration plants were in operation in 1990 and another 52 were under construction or on the drawing boards.

An ideal solution to our solid waste disposal problem would be to burn or incinerate our garbage, if we thereby could convert it into energy. If we could do that extensively, we'd kill two birds with one stone. And there are companies doing just this.

Ogden Projects, Inc. (NYSE—OPI). **Ogden Projects** was created as a wholly owned subsidiary of **Ogden Corporation** in 1984 to be the exclusive U.S. licensee of the *Martin* system of waste-to-energy technology which was developed in West Germany 30 years ago. In May 1989, the company also acquired **Ogden Environmental Services** from **Ogden Corporation**. **Ogden Environmental** provides on-site remediation services for sites contaminated by hazardous wastes.

In August 1989, **Ogden Projects** sold 11% of its stock to the public. **Ogden Corp.** continues to own the remaining 89%.

Ogden Projects contracts with municipalities for the design, financing, construction, operation, and, usually, ownership of plants that burn municipal solid waste to provide energy. Typically, these plants accept unsorted garbage that is incinerated to produce steam or electrical energy and reduced to 5 to 10% of its original volume. Thus, garbage is disposed of less expensively than through landfills and an alternative energy source is created.

Ogden Projects has had an explosive growth record, virtually doubling its revenues annually since 1985: from $24 million in 1985 to $49 million in 1986, $72 million in 1987, $154 million in 1988, and $335 million in 1989. An annual growth rate of 100% is, of course, not sustainable but revenues are still expected to exceed $450 million in 1990.

In 1990, **Ogden Projects** had 20 incineration plants, with total daily capacity of nearly 20,000 tons, operating or under construction. Six more plants with a total daily capacity of more than 7,000 tons were awaiting construction pending regulatory approval. All told, the company accounted for approximately 18% of total U.S. incineration capacity.

Wheelabrator Technologies Inc. (NYSE—WTI). Another major factor in the waste-to-energy sector of the environmental industry is **Wheelabrator Technologies**. It is currently building or operating 14 waste-to-energy facilities, with total daily capacity of nearly 22,000 tons, in 7 states. In addition to constructing and operating such plants, the company also operates small co-generation power plants, water purification and air pollution control systems, and manufactures materials cleaning equipment. The company's revenues approximate $1.5 billion annually. It is 55%-owned by **Waste Management**.

The other leading companies in the field include **American Ref-Fuel**, a joint venture of **Air Products & Chemicals Inc.** (NYSE—APD), and **Browning-Ferris Industries Inc.** (NYSE—BFI); **Asea Brown Boveri Inc.; Westinghouse Electric Corporation** (NYSE—WX); and **Foster Wheeler Corporation** (NYSE—FWC). Together with **Ogden Projects** and **Wheelabrator Technologies**, these companies account for more than 50% of total U.S. incineration capacity.

Recycle It: Use It Again and Again and . . .

Only about 11% of our garbage is currently being recycled. This is a promising approach but in order for it to be implemented on a very large scale, we will have to see major changes on the part of industry in the manufacturing process (to produce recyclable rather than disposable products) and the creation of conveniently located recycling centers.

In particular, it will require major advances in our ability to recycle plastics. At present, more than 50% of aluminum cans are being recycled, about 35% of newspapers and 12% of glass containers, but only 1% of plastics. Yet plastics now constitute 7% of U.S. garbage by weight (and 20% by volume) and those figures are expected to double by the end of the century.

Fortunately, progress is being made. In 1988, for instance, only three New Jersey towns recycled plastics. Two years later, that number increased to 300. In 1990, the first government approval was granted to use recycled polystyrene in food packaging (egg cartons) and, before the year was out, both **Coca-Cola**

Company (NYSE—KO) and **PepsiCo, Inc.** (NYSE—PEP) announced their intention to introduce bottles made from recycled plastic in 1991. That, in turn, could constitute a major break-through for the recycling movement: according to Jackie Prince, a staff scientist with the Environmental Defense Fund, it "could set a precedent for the fact that there may be technologies that can eliminate contaminants and enable a resin to be reused in a food application."[18] Indeed, by the mid- to late-1990s, approximately 25% of plastics are expected to be recycled.

One reason this approach is so promising is that most Americans believe they could recycle much more than they now do and they would be very willing to do so, if only recycling programs and facilities were made available. According to the results of a poll by the National Solid Waste Management Association released in May 1990, 74% of Americans thought they could double the amount of waste they recycle (up from 40% in July 1989). The public's attitude is also reflected in several states' recycling goals: California and Iowa intend to recycle 50% of their wastes by the year 2000; New York expects to get there three years earlier; Washington will try to make it by 1995; and Maine hopes to accomplish that by 1994.[19]

The major stumbling block at present is that there are not sufficient products or markets to absorb the rising quantity of recycled items. But the public is pressing for more such products and has indicated that it would be willing to pay a premium for them. In one survey, 78% of consumers said they would pay more for a product made of recyclable or biodegradable materials and 53% indicated that they actually had not bought some product because of environmental concerns.[20] And in our free market society, that is just what it will take for this approach to become a genuine solution.

The companies on which we have commented so far in regard to the issues of solid wastes—**Waste Management, Browning-Ferris, Chambers Development**, and **Laidlaw**—are among those within the environmental industry that are dealing directly with these problems. **Waste Management**, for instance, has entered into a joint venture with **E.I. duPont de Nemours & Company** (NYSE—DD) to form Plastics Recycling Alliance in order to recycle plastic bottles for molding into park benches and highway traffic barricades; by 1994, they expect to be recycling 1.6 billion bottles (100,000 tons) annually. But there are other companies, too, in a variety of other industries, that have been seeking ways to mitigate these problems, at least by making sure that their own products are recyclable. Socially responsible investors ought to know about them.

And, of course, there are those companies which, by marketing and distributing non-recyclable products, are a big part of the problem. *Avoidance* and *activist* investors, in particular, should know about them.

Many environmentalists agree that polystyrene packaging material has several undesirable characteristics: It does not degrade easily in landfills; it is not extensively recyclable; it is a petrochemical whose manufacture utilizes non-renewable energy resources; and, in some instances, its manufacture requires the use of chlorofluorocarbons (CFCs) which contribute to depletion of the ozone layer. In light of this, several companies, including **Burger King Corp.** (a subsidiary of **Grand Metropolitan PLC)**, **Denny's**, and **Champion International Corporation** (NYSE—CHA)—long ago completely eliminated the use of polystyrene in their own operations. Many of these companies replaced polystyrene with biodegradable packaging materials such as paper and cardboard.

But not all companies made the change. **McDonald's Corp.** (NYSE—MCD), for instance, for a long time continued to use polystyrene packaging for its fast foods, which prompted three *activist* church groups to sponsor a resolution in 1990 (subsequently withdrawn) calling on the company to eliminate its use of polystyrene and replace it with biodegradable packaging materials. In addition, **McDonald's** came under attack because the bottom of the paperboard containers in which it served its hashbrown potatoes was stamped "Recyclable Paper," even though the package was not made of recycled paper, wasn't being recycled at the time, and might not even have been recyclable because of promotional labels glued to its back.

Does this mean that **McDonald's** was clearly one of the *socially irresponsible* bad guys? Before you jump to that conclusion, recall that this was also the same company which, in April 1990, launched project *McRecycle USA* to create a $100 million a year market for recycled materials for its restaurants.

The company explained that what had happened with the hash-brown potatoes packaging was an oversight and that from then on the recycling logo would only appear on products that were actually being recycled. Indeed, according to Shelby Yastrow, **McDonald's** senior vice president for environmental affairs, the mislabeling only occurred because **McDonald's** originally used the label to accommodate environmental groups that urged the company to use it to educate consumers to the fact that paper products could be recycled.

Finally, **McDonald's** claimed that its polystyrene packaging was actually friendlier to the environment than paper (which ultimately would require cutting down trees) and that polystyrene *was* potentially recyclable. To that end, **McDonald's** began a recycling program in New England[21] and in late 1990 was on the verge of taking that recycling program national to all 8,500 of its restaurants in the United States.

Suddenly, however, **McDonald's** changed its mind and decided to phase out its polystyrene packaging entirely (beginning with its ubiquitous hamburger "clamshell" box) and to switch to paper packaging instead. That decision was made in part because of an unusual agreement which the company had entered into with the Environmental Defense Fund in August 1990 to jointly examine the company's solid wastes problems. Under considerable pressure from the Alliance, from the general public and from *activist* investors, **McDonald's** management ultimately determined that even if polystyrene packaging *was* environmentally sound (and in the company's opinion it was), it still would be politic of the company to abandon it. As Edward H. Rensi, president of **McDonald's U.S.A.**, put it: "our customers just don't feel good about it. So we're changing."[22]

So maybe **McDonald's** turned out to be one of the really good guys after all. Could it be?

The real point of this, of course, is that issues are often not as black and white as they might initially seem, that sometimes companies do change their policies for the better, and that the socially responsible investor must answer some tough questions for himself before leaping to investment conclusions. Consider some of the following:

1. *What does recycled mean and how important is it?* This term is frequently applied to paper and paper products, the implication being that no trees were cut down to produce them. Rather, it is implied that those products were manufactured from waste paper previously used by consumers, paper from which ink had been removed.

There are two problems with this. First, there is no agreement as to how much of such used paper actually must be included in the recycling process for paper to be labeled *recycled*. In fact, today wastes (including paper spoiled in the mill, cuttings and overruns) are reused throughout the paper production process and, by some definitions, paper produced in that way may be considered *recycled*. Indeed, some government agencies allow paper made solely from mill waste to be labeled *recycled*, although others have required a minimum percentage of fibers from which ink has been removed.

The second problem is that some paper products, such as toilet tissue, are almost all made from recycled paper now. Thus, for a particular manufacturer to label its toilet tissue *recycled* might suggest that it was something out of the ordinary when it really was not.

The term *recycled* can also refer to products other than paper, including metals, glass, and plastics. For example, **Proctor & Gamble Company** (NYSE—PG) has begun packaging its *Cheer, Era*, and *Tide* liquid laundry detergents and liquid *Downy* fabric softener in bottles manufactured partially from recycled plastic. As Robert Viney, an advertising manager for **Proctor & Gamble** expressed it: "We believe that recycled plastic won't cost any more than virgin plastic, and the consumer wants it. So we are trying to jump-start recycling and hope others will follow."[23] **Colgate-Palmolive Company** (NYSE—CL) has done the same thing with its *Palmolive* dishwashing liquid. And **Unilever** is testing recycled plastic in bottles designed for its *Snuggle* liquid fabric softener and *Wisk* liquid laundry detergent.

2. *What does recyclable mean and how important is it?* If the

technical expertise exists to recycle a product but there are no facilities actually available to do so, is the product *really* recyclable? (If a tree falls in a forest and there's no one there to hear it fall, does it make a sound?) For instance, if a polystyrene container is labeled *recyclable* but the closest polystyrene recycling plant is hundreds of miles away, should that product really be considered *recyclable* in practice?

As an example **Amoco Corporation's** (NYSE—AN) consumer products division produces polystyrene cups that are labeled *recyclable*. However, as of early 1990, there was only one plant capable of recycling these cups and it was located in New York. How *recyclable* were they to consumers in Detroit?

Similarly, **H.J. Heinz Company** (NYSE—HNZ) announced in April 1990 that it would introduce a new *recyclable* ketchup bottle in 1991. Officials of the Natural Resources Defense Council, however, immediately challenged the company's depiction of the product as *recyclable*, on the grounds that facilities didn't 'exist to accomplish the actual recycling. In response, David Ruder, **Heinz'** vice president for consumer affairs, explained that the company intended to use the year before the new bottle actually was introduced to start recycling programs and educate the public on how to recycle plastics.

Several other companies deserve special mention for their recycling efforts, including **Reynolds Metals Company** (NYSE—RLM), **Mobil Corp.** (NYSE—MOB), and **Sonoco Products Company** (OTC—SONO). One of the leading aluminum producers in the country, **Reynolds Metals** runs 722 recycling centers nationwide where it purchases cans and other types of aluminum from the public. In 1989, **Reynolds Metals** was responsible for the recycling of nearly 10 billion aluminum cans.

Mobil Corp., after having had to back down from its biodegradability claim for its *Hefty* trash bags, launched a much more credible recycling campaign for the plastic grocery bags that it produces for supermarkets and which have been the bane of many environmentalists' existence. More than 12 billion of these bags are used by grocery store chains annually and **Mobil**, as the country's second-largest manufacturer, produces more than five billion of them.

These bags account for 60% of all bags used in supermarkets (compared to as little as 5% in 1982). They have been a godsend for storeowners because they cost only half as much as paper bags and occupy 70% less storage space. Still, environmentalists have objected to them on the grounds that they are not biodegradable and consumers have begun requesting paper bags, which are at least theoretically biodegradable, instead. (We say *"at least theoretically"* since, when tightly packed in landfills, many products, even paper bags, may prove to be not nearly as biodegradable as one might have assumed.)

Enter **Mobil**. In May 1990, the company announced a national recycling effort for these plastic bags beginning at 244 **Safeway** stores in California, Nevada, and Hawaii. The company admitted that its goal was to create an environmentally acceptable product as an important marketing tool. Along the way, recycling would also provide **Mobil** with free plastic to convert into more plastic bags.

Prior to the introduction of the recycling program, between 15 and 40% of **Mobil's** bags were already being made out of recycled plastic but **Mobil** had to buy that plastic from other companies. In one pilot program, **Mobil** discovered that 20 to 25% of its bags were returned; if that percentage holds up nationally, more than a billion of **Mobil's** bags would be recycled annually. So at least in this case, the exercise of corporate social responsibility would turn out to be good business, too.

Mobil promoted this program as the first national effort to recycle plastic supermarket bags, but **Sonoco Products Company**, the largest manufacturer of such bags in the country, challenged that claim, averring that it had already initiated bag recycling programs at 1,500 locations nationwide, although it had not previously made any announcement to that effect. **Sonoco's** program, though, was not geared to converting old bags into new ones as **Mobil's** was; rather, **Sonoco** sells the bags it collects to another company which makes plastic tubing from them.

3. *What does biodegradable really mean and how important is it?* Before launching its plastic bag recycling program, **Mobil Oil**, for instance, developed allegedly *degradable Hefty* trash bags. The bags contained a chemical additive so that they would

break down after exposure to sunlight and the elements. **Dow Chemical Company** (NYSE—DOW) did the same thing with its *Handi-Wrap* plastic wrap. **American Enviro Products Inc.** marketed its *Bunnies* diapers as biodegradable, too, because they included a cornstarch additive, produced by **Archer-Daniels-Midland Company** (NYSE—ADM), that accelerated the break-up of the plastic in the diapers.

But if all of these products end up tightly packed in landfills where they are not exposed to sunlight, how degradable will they be after all? Maybe not very.

Indeed, **Proctor & Gamble**, which manufactures *Luvs* and *Pampers* disposable diapers, claims in its own advertising that "There is no such thing as a biodegradable diaper." According to Steve Collier, a **Proctor & Gamble** spokesman, "Biodegradability is really a myth . . . and we are trying to squelch that."[23]

Initially, Robert Chickering, president of **American Enviro Products, Inc.**, insisted that *Bunnies* diapers were biodegradable while admitting that it could take quite a while for this to happen, with the span ranging from 18 months in moist situations to anywhere from 12 to 15 years in a dry landfill in the middle of Death Valley.[24] Eventually, however, under continued pressure from a task force of 10 state attorney generals, who argued that those claims were, at the very least, misleading, the company agreed to refrain from making such claims on packaging and in advertising.

In October 1990, the company began distributing a new diaper which was 28% smaller than its original and which utilized cotton instead of wood pulp, permitting it to degrade in composting facilities that allow in air and light. But the company agreed that its packaging and advertising will indicate that such composting facilities are "generally unavailable" in the United States.

Under similar pressure, both **Mobil Oil** and **Dow Chemical** also withdrew their claims of biodegradability for *Hefty* trash bags and *Handi-Wrap* plastic wrap. Thus, just as *recyclable* may be a fair description if facilities are readily available to accomplish the actual recycling, but a misleading one if they are not, so too may *biodegradable* be a legitimate appelation if, upon disposal, a product is likely to be exposed to sunlight and the elements, but a misleading one if it is more probable that it will end up in a densely packed landfill.

4. *Are the objectives of* biodegradability *and* recyclability *at odds with one another?* In some ways, yes. Additives that help plastics break down (biodegradably) can weaken products made from recycled materials. Thus, some architects who used construction panels made from recycled plastics found that the products fell apart after only a few months because they contained some biodegradable residues. Does this mean we should discourage the recycling of biodegradable products?

5. *How much of a tradeoff is acceptable between the environmental goals of biodegradability or recyclability and other goals in the areas of esthetics, convenience, health, or economics?* The fact remains, tradeoffs are required and there is still no such thing as a free lunch.

The need for such tradeoffs may be nowhere so evident as in the area of diapers—at least to those parents who are being urged to substitute recyclable cloth diapers for the disposables to which they have become accustomed. In 1961, when **Proctor & Gamble** introduced *Pampers*, disposable diapers accounted for only 1% of the diaper market; today, diapers are a $3.5 billion industry and disposables account for 85% of that.

Disposable diapers obviously are more convenient than cloth diapers but cloth diapers have two other advantages: (a) they are somewhat cheaper and (b) they are recyclable whereas disposables are not. Disposable diapers now account for about 2% of solid wastes in landfills with about 16 billion ending up there annually; and the biodegradability of newly introduced disposable diapers that have cornstarch in their plastic linings remains debatable.

Most parents easily made the decision to trade off the economic advantage of cloth diapers for the convenience of disposables. Now they are being called on to decide on another tradeoff: convenience versus the environment. And that may not be such an easy one.

For on closer analysis it develops that cloth diapers are not totally environmentally cost-free either. To be sure, even **Proctor**

& Gamble has admitted that, according to the results of an Arthur D. Little study which it sponsored, disposable diapers consume seven times as much raw material in their manufacture as do cloth diapers and produce nearly 100 times as much solid waste. But the balance is not completely one-sided when all things are considered, including the obvious need to launder cloth diapers. According to the same Arthur D. Little study, when those considerations are also factored in, it develops that cloth diapers consume up to six times as much water and nearly four times as much energy as disposables and that they create nearly 10 times as much air and water pollution.[26] So the jury may still be out. Again, things are not always quite what they seem and there is still no such thing as a free lunch.

But the tradeoffs won't necessarily end there. Those who do decide to switch back to cloth diapers may find that, as a result, they not only sacrifice convenience, but also health, for the sake of the environment. That is, the American Academy of Pediatrics and the American Public Health Association strongly recommend disposable rather than cloth diapers in out-of-home childcare programs on the grounds that there would be a public health problem of infectious diseases if infants in day-care centers were to wear cloth rather than disposable diapers. **Kinder-Care Learning Centers Inc.** has adopted this position in its own business, requiring the children in its centers to use disposable diapers on the grounds that "disposable diapers can be dealt with more sanitarily."[27]

Nor are such tradeoffs only limited to diapers. **Wendy's International, Inc.** (NYSE—WEN), for instance, tried to replace its non-biodegradable foam plates with flimsier paper plates but consumers would have no part of it. **PepsiCo, Inc.** (NYSE—PEP) tried to sell soda in plastic three-liter bottles but consumers didn't go for that either: although the larger bottles cut down on trash, they didn't fit easily into refrigerators. And, in one of the most ironic examples of the need to make tradeoffs, the *Sierra Club*, a bulwark of environmentalism, decided not to print its highly admired calendars on recycled paper because virgin paper reproduces photographs better. At least two of its own membership groups refused to sell the calendars as a result.

More significantly, financial or economic risk-return tradeoffs must be calculated when companies commit to major environmental expenditures not mandated by law. Will **McDonald's** be able to recoup the incremental costs it will incur by creating a $100 million market for recycled materials? Will **Heinz** be able to raise ketchup prices enough to recoup the costs it will incur in creating a recyclable bottle or will it gain enough market share to recoup those costs? These are the kinds of questions you must ask as an investor, for a socially responsible investor is still, after all, an investor.

Don't Produce It: Source Reduction

The fourth solution, not producing in the first place, has some merit, if it is simply taken to mean eliminating unnecessary packaging materials. The facts are that packaging materials *do* account for about 30% of all solid waste by weight and 34% by volume and that some packages do incorporate separate layers of paper, metal foil, and plastic, making them too complex to be recycled or composted.

But if "not producing" or "source reduction" is intended in a neo-Luddite sense to mean forgoing some of the material benefits of our affluent society and doing without some goods in order to return to an Eden that never was, then it really is not a sensible proposal at all. For, in fact, it is the same advanced technology and free market capitalist system that allow us to produce and consume more than any other nation, which ultimately provides solutions to our environmental problems (such as the development of new products and markets to justify increased recycling and the manufacture of technologically advanced pollution control equipment).

Evidence that this is the case is apparent in even a cursory comparison between the environmental picture in the capitalist United States and that of the historically socialist Eastern Europe. Bleak as the environmental picture may be in the United States, it is nowhere near as horrifying as it is in Eastern Europe. At least environmental progress is being made here, whereas in

Eastern Europe, prior to the collapse of the communist bloc, conditions continued to deteriorate.

Consider this: In the United States, utilities are burning twice as much coal for electricity today as they did 20 years ago, but they are producing 15% less sulfur dioxide (the cause of acid rain). New cars emit 96% less carbon monoxide and hydrocarbons and 76% less nitrogen oxides than older cars. In New York City, the water contains more oxygen today than it did 80 years ago. This is not to say that we don't still have problems, for we surely do. But we are dealing with them and making progress.

Now contrast that with Eastern Europe. The situation there is only beginning to become apparant to us with the collapse of the communist bloc and the exposure of what really has occurred environmentally. Toxic wastes, sewage, and polluted air have taken a toll beyond anything even imaginable in the United States or Western Europe.

It is estimated, for example, that 80% of East Germany's rivers are contaminated and that some of that country's air is polluted 50 times above safe limits. Pollution in East Germany is estimated to cost $18 billion annually. In the industrial cities of Leipzig, Halle, Dresden, and Karl-Marx-Stadt, death rates from cancer and lung and heart disease are 15 to 25% higher than in Berlin.

In Bulgaria, 80% of farmland is threatened by erosion and one-quarter of animal and plant species are endangered. In Poland, the World Bank has estimated that 10% of the gross national product has been lost as a result of environmentally caused illness and because much of the nation's water is contaminated and can't be used industrially; in Poland's Kalowice area, 41% of the children under six years of age have serious health problems caused by pollution. In Czechoslovakia, one out of three men in the industrial center of Northern Bohemia has cancer.

This environmental disparity between the United States and Eastern Europe did not occur *despite* the difference in politico-economic systems. Rather, it occurred *because* of it. In Eastern Europe, *command* economies that are ruled by dictated production targets created no incentives to deal with environmental problems. But in the relatively free market economy of the

United States, those problems prompted consumer demands, the creation of a whole new pollution control industry, market solutions, and environmental progress.

E.I. duPont de Nemours & Company (NYSE—DD). One of the best examples of a company that has succeeded in translating problems and vulnerabilities into business opportunties is **E.I. duPont de Nemours**, the largest chemicals company in the United States. Confronted by the threat of adverse legislation, lawsuits, and cleanup bills in virtually all areas of its business (the company generates $36 billion annually in revenues from chemicals, plastics, petroleum, coal, and fibers), **DuPont** determined to convert itself from a company with environmental problems to one of the world's largest environmental services firms.

It spent $1 billion on pollution control equipment, $800 million annually to operate it, another $1 billion to develop substitutes for chlorofluorocarbons, and $500 million to clean up its own old environmental problems. Finally, it is all beginning to pay off.

The company's scientists have developed a line of herbicides that break down quickly, posing less of a threat to our groundwater. It is recycling a billion pounds of its own polymers in waste reduction programs. It has entered into a joint venture with **Waste Management Inc.** to recycle plastic bottles into **DuPont** products. It is cleaning up hazardous wastes and runs the largest waste water treatment operation in the country. And, through its **Conoco** subsidiary, **DuPont** was the first company to announce that it would build all its future oil tankers with double hulls to reduce the risk of oil spills.

However, **DuPont** still has a long way to go before it can claim to be environmentally perfect or even close to it. In 1988, it was the nation's biggest emitter of toxic chemicals, having released 338.4 million pounds into the air, water, and ground. It ranked sixth that year in the release of chemicals linked to birth defects and tenth in emissions of chemicals thought to cause cancer, according to EPA data compiled by Citizen Action.

The company does not deny this. Indeed, it is confronting its own problems head-on and assuming responsibility for them.

According to Edgar S. Woolard, Jr., **DuPont's** chairman and chief executive officer, the company will have to reduce its toxic air emissions by 60% by 1993 from the 1987 level, and it is attempting to do just that. As he expressed it: "The environmental groups cannot solve any of these problems. Governments can't do it. Corporations have to do it."[28]

In recognition of the environmental efforts Woolard is leading at **DuPont**, Jay D. Hair, president of the National Wildlife Federation, has said: "I cannot think of a single corporate leader at the level of Ed Woolard who has spoken as consistently on these issues as he has. He understands that in today's public climate, companies have to conduct their affairs in ways that are environmentally acceptable."[29]

In short, **DuPont** has functioned like a textbook case in a course on capitalist solutions to environmental problems. It's the way the system is supposed to work and will if it is allowed to.

Julian Simon, professor of business administration at the University of Maryland, has made the point succinctly:

> Some environmentalists say affluence causes the deterioration of the environment. And while it is true that very poor people do not produce much trash, affluence is what cleans up the environment. This is true in part because the affluent can afford better services, but also because waste and pollution present opportunities. . . . [T]he economic system is responsive: every shortage is an opportunity for someone to fill a need.[30]

HAZARDOUS WASTE MANAGEMENT

Hazardous wastes may be handled through temporary on-site containment measures or through permanent remedial technologies. The latter, obviously, are preferable and fall into three categories:

1. *Destruction technologies* are remedies that irreversibly destroy or detoxify all or most of the hazardous wastes in question to acceptable cleanup levels. Treated materials

leave no residue containing unacceptable levels of hazardous contaminants.

2. *Separation treatments* are remedies that separate hazardous contaminants from waste material, leaving a residual stream with acceptable levels of contaminants and a concentrated waste stream with high levels of contaminants. Wherever possible, the concentrated waste stream then is destroyed or detoxified.

3. *Solidification-chemical fixations* are remedies that reduce the mobility of inorganic hazardous wastes by mixing contaminated wastes with binding materials such as cement or fly ash. This creates a solidified mass that immobolizes the contaminants.

Chemical Waste Management, Inc. (NYSE—CHW). While **Browning-Ferris** has withdrawn from the hazardous waste business, several other companies remain active in it, perhaps agreeing with Scott Wollins that this is "the business that will provide the greatest earnings opportunity in the environmental field over the next 20 or 30 years."[31] Foremost among these is **Chemical Waste Management, Inc.**, originally a wholly owned subsidiary of **Waste Management** and now a publicly owned company in its own right (although still 79%-owned by **Waste Management**).

Largest of the hazardous waste companies in the country, **Chemical Waste Management** provides a variety of chemical and low-level radiation waste management services, including transportation, treatment, and disposal to commercial, industrial, and other waste management companies. The company's revenues more than doubled from $418 million in 1986 to $892 million in 1989 and are estimated at more than $1 billion in 1990. Net profits nearly tripled over the same period from $52 million, or 28 cents a share, in 1986 to $144 million, or 72 cents a share, in 1989.

Rollins Environmental Services, Incorporated (NYSE— REN). **Rollins Environmental Services** is involved in the business of hazardous waste treatment and disposal through a variety of methods including land disposal, biological degradation, chemical treatment, and incineration. Most promising of these are its incineration operations which, as hazardous landfill space grows increasingly scarce, may become the favored route.

The company is in the process of substantially increasing its incineration capacity by building *Rotary Reactors* (its patented incinerators that can process up to 90% solids compared with the typical 60% solids—40% liquids mix at other incinerators). **Rollins** is also constructing additional landfill cells for its own ash disposal needs. Revenues approximated $163 million in fiscal 1989 (ended September 30, 1989) and are expected to exceed $200 million in fiscal 1990.

EA Engineering, Science & Technology Inc. A small firm in the field with revenues in fiscal 1989 (ended August 31, 1989) of less than $40 million, **EA Engineering** was founded in 1973 by scientists from Johns Hopkins University. The company remains very scientifically oriented: 75% of its employees are scientists or engineers.

EA Engineering's primary business is consulting on toxic and hazardous waste disposal. Typically, the company studies a problem, suggests a solution, represents a client before the EPA or state or local authorities, and handles the actual remediation, or cleanup, of the mess. In effect, the company provides a turnkey service, enabling clients to avoid having to hire consultants and cleanup firms separately.

BUS Berzelius Environmental Services. In January 1990, a relatively new hazardous waste management company, **BUS Berzelius Environmental Services**, was listed on the Frankfurt Stock Exchange. The three-year-old company, a spinoff of the West German metals trading company **Metallgesellschaft**, has developed a new technology to process hazardous metals wastes. The company's plants in Germany, Spain, and Sweden already are recycling one-third of Western Europe's steel furnace dust.

In effect, the company is paid to cart away hazardous wastes; it then processes those wastes and resells the raw materials that it has refined back to industry. According to Helmut Maczek,

BUS's chief executive, "Customers pay us twice—to cart the waste away and then to buy it back."[32]

Revenues are expected to double in 1990 to $43 million and then to grow at a 70% annual rate over the next three years. Earnings are expected to triple in 1990 to $5.4 million and to nearly double again in 1991 to $10 million.

In 1980, Congress passed the Superfund program, intended as a short-term clean-up program for the worst hazardous waste sites in the country. By 1990, approximately 1,200 such sites had been identified for priority action and billions of dollars had been expended, but only about 45 sites were actually cleaned up.

According to **American International Group Inc.** (NYSE—AIG), the largest underwriter of commercial and industrial insurance in the United States, the reason for this dismal performance was that the Superfund legislation placed a higher priority on the establishment of liability than on remediation, necessitating the tracing of hundreds of users of hazardous waste dumps for the past 20 or more years. Indeed, at 422 sites, nearly 14,000 entities were notified that they could be liable for cleanup costs.

In **AIG's** opinion, this has meant "A bonanza for lawyers and consultants. And a tragedy for the environment [since at] some sites, as much as 60% of the money spent goes toward legal expenses . . . to assign liability instead of solving the cleanup problem. An avalanche of lawsuits has resulted, all aimed at getting someone else to pay."[33]

AIG's proposal for dealing with the problem is to create a National Environmental Trust Fund, fashioned after the National Highway Trust Fund, the resources of which would be used exclusively for cleaning up hazardous waste sites. It would be financed by adding a fee of 2% to commercial and industrial insurance premiums and an equivalent amount for self-insurers.

As **AIG** sees it, this would be "a new way to finance Superfund's mission without the need for new taxes, a new government agency and unproductive lawsuits." In promoting its proposal in newspaper and magazine advertisements, the company concluded with the rhetorical question: "Shouldn't we stop trying to fix the blame and start fixing the problem?"[34]

Maybe. But the risk here is that this smacks of being the kind of communal solution that has undermined the sense of personal responsibility—a major strength of the American politico-economic system. If we do not fix blame and hold the guilty responsible for their actions, what is the incentive to act responsibly in the first place? When all are held responsible for the actions of the few, all might as well act like the few and a short-term fix may turn into a long-term disaster.

AIG has suggested that this need not be the case. Its proposal is intended only to deal with old waste sites for which a system of retroactive liability had been established, so that it need not reduce the incentive to industry to deal responsibly with hazardous wastes in the future. Certainly, this is worth exploring, but precedents once established have a sticky way of becoming applicable in unintended situations and we would be somewhat wary over whether the distinction that **AIG** has proposed would be sustainable in practice.

WATER POLLUTION

Water pollution may occur in several different ways:

1.   Rainwater may seep into landfills, leaching toxic materials into the water supply. We commented on this problem earlier, in discussing the landfills solution to our solid wastes disposal problem.

2.   Similarly, chemical fertilizers and agricultural pesticides may also be leached by rainwater from farmlands, creating groundwater contamination. Aldicarb, for instance, a nerve poison which is the active ingredient in the insecticide *Temik*, was introduced by **Rhone-Poulenc Ag Company** in the United States in 1970. Nine years later, it was discovered in groundwater supplies in New York at 50 times the level considered safe by the EPA.

A year later, it was banned in New York's Suffolk County as well as in Wisconsin, where it was found in 19 wells. In 1983, wells in Florida, New Jersey, Massachusetts, California, and New York were found to be contaminated. Five years later, aldicarb was found in water supplies in 16 states; by 1989, the number was up to 22.

Nor is this problem limited to aldicarb or two or three other pesticides. According to Lawrie Mott of the Natural Resources Defense Council, 46 different pesticides have been found in water from agricultural runoff in 26 states.[35]

There are three ways to deal with this kind of problem. One, of course, is after the fact: to develop methods to clean groundwater after pollution has occurred. Several companies are doing just that.

But how much better would it be if we could avoid the problem to begin with by eliminating, or at least reducing, potential groundwater pollution from pesticides and fertilizers in the first place? This could be accomplished in two different ways.

The neo-Luddite approach would be to eschew the use of fertilizers and pesticides and return to agricultural methods that were in effect a century ago. This would work, but at what price! The availability and variety of fruits and vegetables would decline dramatically, the costs of foods would soar, and income of the agricultural sector would plummet—all in an effort to avoid the potential risk of groundwater contamination.

A much better approach, it seems, would be to seek to develop new pesticides and fertilizers that were less damaging to the environment. Such products have been developed, but the problem is that they are sometimes as effective against the crops they are designed to protect, as they are against the pests they are designed to combat. Thus a derivative goal then becomes the development of new strains of crops that would be resistant to those more environmentally benevolent herbicides.

Several companies have sought to do just that and with considerable success. **Calgene Inc.**, for instance, has developed a strain of cotton plants that is resistant to bromoxynil, a herbicide which is safer and degrades more quickly than others used on cotton. Thus, farmers can spray cotton crops grown from **Calgene's** seeds with less environmental risk.

Other companies, including **Monsanto Company** (NYSE—MTC), **American Cyanamid** and **DuPont** have sought to develop other crops that are resistant to more benevolent pesticides, but their lot has not been an easy one since the neo-Luddites have remained out in force. In March 1990, for instance, Senator Patrick Leahy introduced a bill prohibiting the use of federal funds for herbicide resistance research in order, as he put it, to "help farmers grow more with less pesticides, instead of helping chemical companies sell more herbicides."[36]

Still, some companies have succeeded in doing well for shareholders and aiding the environment at the same time, despite the opposition of the neo-Luddites. **DuPont**, for instance, has made a real contribution in this area: Its agricultural chemicals business has tripled over the last five years to $1.7 billion as the company developed a new generation of herbicides that leaves fewer residues than the old and, therefore, are less threatening to our groundwater.

3.   Industrial wastes may be dumped directly into rivers and streams. **General Electric Company** (NYSE—GE), for instance, is grappling with the problem of cleaning up the Hudson River toxic mess which it created by the dumping of polychorinated biphenyls (PCBs) in the river over a period of 30 years.

Between 1946 and 1977, **General Electric** dumped thousands of pounds of PCBs (which had been used since the 1930s as an insulator and lubricant in electrical components but which subsequently was implicated as a possible cause of cancer) into the Hudson River. In 1973, before the health hazards of PCBs were known for certain, the Fort Edward dam, located below **General Electric's** factories, was removed and PCB sediments, which had accumulated for years, flowed downstream. In 1976, **General Electric** paid a $3 million fine and, in 1977, stopped dumping PCBs into the river entirely.

It is now **General Electric's** responsiblility to clean up the mess, but there is a major disagreement between it and New York state as to how that should be accomplished. New York would like to dredge the river, subject to EPA approval, and bill **General Electric** $280 million to do it. The company, however, claims that dredging would stir up PCBs and worsen, not improve, the situation. Instead, it has proposed a process of bioremediation wherein bacteria in river sediments would feed on the PCBs and partially detoxify them. The **General Electric** proposal would be much less costly for the company.

4.   Air pollution can be converted into acid rain that can destroy our lakes. Virtually everyone agrees that this is a serious problem but there is considerable disagreement over just *how* serious it is and *what* should be done about it. Most environmental observers appear to agree, however, on the following facts:

a. Sulfur dioxide and nitrogen oxides, produced primarily by coal burning power plants, pollute the air and are the main cause of acid rain.

b. Acid rain, in turn, acidifies lakes, threatening aquatic life; it also damages forests.

c. Possible solutions to the problem include: legislating the cessation or reduction of coal as a fuel to generate electricity; mandating the use of scrubbers by electric utilities to reduce sulfur dioxide emissions; and liming acidified waters or the land draining into them.

What environmentalists disagree upon, however, are the following:

How serious is the problem? According to some, acid rain causes the premature death of up to 50,000 people annually; it has caused 6% of our lakes and streams to turn acidic and another 18% to be vulnerable, threatening marine life; it has destroyed forests; it has polluted the skies in 31 states; and it has damaged 35,000 historic stone buildings in the Northeast and tens of thousands of monuments and outdoor sculptures.

The facts, however, don't appear to bear out that most dismal appraisal. According to James R. Mahoney, director of the National Acid Precipitation Program (a 10-year $500 million study funded by Congress a decade ago): "Acid rain does cause damage, but the amount of damage is less than we once thought and it's much less than some of the characterizations we sometimes hear."[37] Among other things, Mahoney has pointed out that only 1,200 lakes have become fully acidified in the United States; that is only about 4% of all the lakes in the area where acidification might have been expected to occur.

Moreover, natural causes, such as decaying organic matter, often make lakes acidic, so that Florida, for instance, with little acid rain, has the highest proportion of acid lakes in the country. Furthermore, although acid rain has destroyed some lakes in the eastern United States, only a small percentage of them are too acidic to support marine life, and all are safe for swimming.

What should we do about it? The *Clean Air Act of 1990* would force electric utilities to spend about $4 billion to install scrubbers and/or purchase more expensive, cleaner coal. According to Mahoney, this will result in the revival of about 75 lakes over the next 50 years. By contrast, for an estimated $765,000 annually, he believes that we could lime the lakes and rivers and revive them all right away.

What do you think? When it comes to acid rain, does your cost-benefit analysis suggest that we'll really get our $4 billion worth out of the *Clean Air Act* or might not the liming of lakes be a much more economic and responsible approach?

5.   Inadvertent oil and chemicals spills can result in the pollution of our rivers, lakes, and oceans and the endangering of wildlife. Since the *Exxon Valdez* oil spill, this problem has moved to center stage. It has prompted hundreds of lawsuits against **Exxon Corp.** (NYSE—XON). It has galvanized Congress to introduce legislation mandating the retrofitting of existing tankers or at least the construction of new tankers with double hulls and double bottoms. And it has prompted stockholders to introduce resolutions at several companies to forestall such spills in the future.

In regard to double hulls and double bottoms, there are those who argue that this would *not*, necessarily, be a good solution to the problem of potential oil spills. *The Wall Street Journal*, for instance, has argued that double hulls not only would not have failed to prevent the *Exxon Valdez* oil spill but that they actually could increase the chances of major spills in the future and would drive up shipping rates.

So long as this difference of opinion exists, the passage of legislation mandating double hulls or double bottoms would seem inadvisable. However, that does not mean that an individual company, using its own best judgment, should not voluntarily build its future tankers with double hulls, if that is what it believes to be the most prudent course and if that is what its own stockholders desire.

That is exactly what **Conoco** (a wholly owned subsidiary of **DuPont**) has done. In the wake of the *Exxon Valdez* spill, **Conoco's** management determined to build all its future tankers with double hulls. It is voluntary action like that, rather than reaction to legislated mandates, which is the essence of corporate social responsibility.

Finally, we should mention a few of the companies that are in the business of providing water cleanup services. The **Chambers Works** subsidiary of **DuPont**, for one, runs the largest wastewater treatment operation in the country, serving 1,000 customers. **Groundwater Technology, Inc.** (OTC—GWTI), with annual revenues approximating $120 million, provides consulting and groundwater restoration services; its largest market is leaking underground gasoline tanks and its main customers are petroleum companies.

A third company, smaller still, but also deserving of comment is **Geraghty & Miller**, which provides engineering, consulting, and cleanup services to over 900 customers, including major oil and chemical companies and state and municipal governments. The company went public in early 1988; in 1989, its revenues approximated $54 million. According to Stephen Schweich, a security analyst at **Alex Brown & Sons, Geraghty & Miller** has "got the best reputation in the business."[38]

OZONE: TOO LITTLE OR TOO MUCH?

According to *The New York Times*,

> In 1988, New York's peak levels of ozone and carbon monoxide exceeded Federal health limits by more than 50 percent. New York exceeded Federal ozone health standards on 28 days that year. . . . [B]reathing elevated levels of ozone . . . can lead to a

host of health problems. . . . [O]zone can produce shortness of breath and, over time, permanent lung damage. Recent research indicates that ozone may be harmful at levels even lower than the current Federal standard.[39]

According to New York State's Department of Environmental Conservation, "Too much ozone in the air can make breathing difficult and painful. Shortness of breath, chest pain, throat and eye irritation, coughing and wheezing can occur."[40]

However, Gary Null has written that

If we continue to destroy our ozone layer as we have done over the past 30 to 40 years, there will be a gross increase in the number of skin cancers and other cancers, likely food shortages, ecological disasters, and a variety of other health injuries we have never had to deal with before because we never have been exposed to such great amounts of ultraviolet radiation.[41]

Similarly, *The New York Times* explained that

Chlorofluorocarbons . . . wreak havoc on the layer of ozone in the upper atmosphere which absorbs much of the ultraviolet radiation from sunlight. . . . [This could] lead to dramatic increases in skin cancer and eye cataracts. . . . According to the Environmental Protection Agency, the projected loss of ozone would lead to an extra 170 million cases of cancer by the year 2075 within the United States alone.[42]

Which position is correct? Do we produce too much ozone, endangering our lungs and our breathing? Or are we depleting our ozone, increasing the risk of cancer and ecological disaster?

Unfortunately, both positions appear to be correct.

At ground level, ozone is a major component of smog, created by the reaction of sunlight with the chemicals in automobile emissions, gasoline vapors, and industrial air pollution; as such, it is a threat to our breathing. At the stratospheric level, 10 to 30 miles above ground level, however, the ozone layer has a positive role, acting to filter out ultraviolet radiation; serious depletion of that ozone layer could increase the incidence of cancer substantially.

It would be wonderful if somehow we could shift excess ground level ozone to the stratosphere where it could do some good. But unfortunately that is impossible. So we really must examine the ozone question as two separate issues.

Depletion of the Ozone Layer

Turning first to the issue of stratospheric ozone, most observers seem to agree on the following facts:

1. Ozone is found in its greatest natural atmospheric concentration in the stratosphere where it performs an essential function of filtering out cancer-producing ultraviolet radiation.

2. Under normal conditions, the Earth's atmosphere would maintain ozone levels in the stratosphere at equilibrium, as a natural balance would develop between ozone formation and ozone destruction.

3. Manmade chlorofluorocarbons (CFCs) have had a large number of industrial uses, as solvents to clean electrical components, as refrigerants, as foaming agents in the production of polystyrene packaging, and as aerosol propellants. Once produced, however, CFCs are very stable and may remain airborne for 100 years. During that time, they may rise to the stratosphere, release highly reactive chlorine atoms, and break up the existing ozone. Scientists have estimated that just one chlorine atom can destroy 100,000 ozone molecules over time.

4. As a result, the amount of ozone in the stratosphere has declined by about 2% overall since 1969 and much more in some specific areas. In particular, a "hole" in the ozone layer appears to develop seasonally over Antarctica.

At this point, some differences of opinion do occur. Most observers argue that, in light of the forgoing, continued depletion of the ozone layer from the production of CFCs is extremely hazardous and that, as a consequence, we are justified in acting to terminate the use of CFCs as quickly as possible. Indeed, these observers note that even with a suspension in the production of CFCs, damage to the ozone layer will continue to worsen for many years to come, because of all the CFCs that have already been released into the atmosphere over the past 20 years.

There is a minority position, however, which was well-articulated by Michael Allaby, to the effect that this risk may not be nearly as serious as it has been made out to be, based on the following premises:

1. We cannot necessarily extrapolate the Antarctica experience to the rest of the Earth since climatic conditions at the South Pole, which permitted the development of the "hole" in the ozone, do not occur elsewhere (except possibly at the North Pole).

2. Even if there is a worldwide depletion of the stratospheric ozone layer, that wouldn't necessarily lead to greater ground level ultraviolet radiation since ozone may form at other levels and it is not the discrete ozone *layer* but the total ozone *column* through which light passes that matters. And, evidence suggests that the total ozone column is constant or increasing, compensating for any high altitude loss. Moreover, absorbers of ultraviolet radiation other than ozone, such as high altitude haze, have increased in recent years so that overall ultraviolet radiation reaching the ground actually has been decreasing, not increasing.[43]

In this situation, despite Allaby's arguments, prudence would seem to dictate that industry make an effort to eliminate, or at least reduce, the production of CFCs. In fact, corporate America has responded to the alarm, even going beyond what government has asked of it.

In 1987, 32 countries, including the United States, signed the Montreal Protocol, pledging to reduce CFC production by 50% by the year 2000. But many corporations did much more than that. **DuPont**, for instance, in 1988 announced that it would *totally* end production of CFCs by the year 2000—or even earlier, if possible. For **DuPont**, that meant walking away from a $750 million a year business in which it dominated the industry. By 1990, **DuPont** already had spent $170 million in the development of products to replace CFCs in cleaning, refrigeration and other uses and had committed to invest up to $1 billion in that effort.

Several other companies, including **Nissan Motor Co.** (OTC—NSANY), **Northern Telecom** and **Seiko Epson**, also announced their intentions to stop using CFCs. **General Electric** and **General Motors Corporation** (NYSE—GM) indicated that they were developing methods to prevent CFCs in air conditioners and refrigerators from escaping during maintenance. And **International Business Machines Corporation** (NYSE—IBM) said that it would stop using CFCs entirely by 1993—seven years before the Montreal Protocol called for just a 50% reduction. By 1990, it already had reduced its CFC emissions by 31%.

American Telephone & Telegraph Company (NYSE—T), one of the world's largest users of CFCs as solvents, announced that it would end all use by 1994 (which prompted the Council on Economic Priorities to nominate it in 1990 for a Corporate Conscience Award in Environmental Stewardship). In lieu of CFCs, the company began exploring the use of a natural solvent derived from orange peels.

Digital Equipment Corp. also devised a way to clean the most advanced type of circuit boards with a water solution that eliminates the need for CFCs. The company also said that it would provide directions on how to make and use the new solvent for free to other high technology manufacturers.

Ironically, while corporate America was stepping up its efforts to terminate the use of CFCs, the U.S. Government itself was holding back. An international meeting of about 50 countries in Geneva, preparing for a conference in London to strengthen the Montreal Protocol, proposed establishing a $100 million fund to which the United States would contribute about $15 to $20 million annually, the money to be used to assist third world nations in phasing out CFCs. Although the U.S. State Department, the EPA, and a U.S. industry association representing both CFC producers and consumers all urged the United States to participate, and although $15 to $20 million easily could be extracted from the $5 billion in excise taxes that will be imposed on the CFC industry over the next five years, the Administration initially opted not to participate, fearful of the precedent that might have set should similar requests be made in regard to global warming. (Ultimately, the United States did reverse its policy and agree to participate.)

In response, China and India, both of which had indicated their intentions to increase the use of CFCs said that they would not reduce or eliminate their use of these chemicals without substantial financial assistance. India added that it would urge developing nations that were signatories to the Montreal Protocol to withdraw if the fund were not established.

It is certainly something worth thinking about the next time someone suggests to you that the U.S. capitalist system is responsible for the Earth's environmental degradation. Here were **International Business Machines, American Telephone & Telegraph, Digital Equipment, DuPont**, and others acting responsibly to phase out CFCs, the U.S. Government dragging its heels and only participating reluctantly, and China and India willing to play a game of "chicken" with the Earth's ozone layer unless they were paid off by the very capitalist system they eschew. Surely it must give one pause.

Automobile Emissions and Smog

If depletion of the ozone layer is a danger in the stratosphere, here at ground level, the opposite is true: too much ozone, as a component of smog, not too little, is the real hazard. The major villain in the production of that smog is the automobile industry.

Although Americans constitute only 5% of the world's population, they drive more than one-third of the world's vehicles. In the United States, those vehicles produce half of all of the country's air pollution, including two-thirds of all carbon monoxide, one-third of all carbon dioxide (frequently held responsible for half of alleged global warming), more than 30% of all hydrocarbons, and more than 40% of all nitrogen oxides. Hydrocarbons and nitrogen oxides are primary factors in the creation of ground level ozone and, as such, are major components of urban smog; both also have been implicated in global warming, while nitrogen oxides also contribute to the creation of acid rain.

There are several different ways to deal with this problem. At one extreme is the neo-Luddite approach of mandating municipal, state, or federal controls on driving itself. In the 1970s, for instance, New York City considered a variety of controls, including: requiring that all truck deliveries be made at night, cruising by taxicabs be limited, and a reduction in the number of automobiles allowed to enter the city. Fortunately, reason prevailed and those measures, which would have amounted to throwing in the towel on the issue, were not adopted.

Three better proposals, all of which rely on technology and the free market to produce solutions to the problem, are:

1. the production of vehicles that don't burn polluting fuel at all (e.g., electric cars);

2. the development of cleaner emissions systems or devices in vehicles that would reduce or eliminate pollutants (e.g., catalytic converters); and

3. the creation of less polluting fuels (e.g., alternative fuels such as ethanol or reformulated gasolines).

Let's take a look at these three approaches.

1. At first, blush, converting to electric cars looks like an environmental free lunch. According to Daniel Berg, professor of science and technology at Renssalear Polytechnic Institute,

> Electrified vehicles would eliminate all the emissions from vehicles since the end use of electricity is 100 percent clean. . . . If only 5 percent of all urban fleets were electrified by the year 2000 . . . nitrogen oxide emissions in cities would be reduced by some 200,000 tons, hydrocarbons by one-quarter million tons and carbon monoxide by 2 million tons.[44]

As an aside, Professor Berg argues that this would also do wonders for our energy balance. As he points out,

If 5 percent of the urban miles traveled could be in electrified vehicles by the year 2000, four billion gallons of gasoline would be saved that year, our oil imports would decline by a quarter-million barrels per day, and the United States balance of trade would improve by $1.5 billion. The additional electricity required to power the vehicles would amount to . . . an additional 2 percent of our electricity production. Since this could be generated at night with capacity currently in reserve for the heavier daytime hours, the greater efficiency of plant operations would cause the average cost of electricity to decline."[45]

That certainly *looks* like a free lunch.

But is it? Electricity has to come from somewhere, too, and that somewhere seldom is from environmentally friendly solar or hydro plants. On the contrary, in the United States, more than 50% of all electricity comes from coal which also produces sulfur dioxide, nitrogen oxide, and carbon dioxide.

Tim Yau, in a detailed study for the Electric Power Research Institute, compared an electric car to a gas car, including "everything from the mine mouth to the rubber on the road." In that analysis, the electric car did come out well ahead, with much lower emissions of volatile organic compounds, nitrogen oxides, carbon monoxide, and carbon dioxide—although it did produce higher levels of sulfur dioxide.[46]

Steve E. Plotkin, of the Office of Technology Assessment, however, noted that the benefits of an electric car would depend to a great extent on where it was driven. In smoggy Los Angeles, the reduction in volatile organic compounds and nitrogen oxides would be a big plus but in a less smoggy area with a coal plant, there could be a net environmental loss because of the increase in sulfur dioxide.

Moreover, Plotkin pointed out that small changes in assumptions can alter results dramatically: Yau's gas pollution estimates, for example, were predicated on cars getting 40 miles per gallon; if that were increased to 60 miles, the difference between the two vehicles would narrow substantially. (While 40 miles per gallon is about the best that conventional cars can now get, increasing that by 50% can be no greater a technological feat than producing the electric car.)[47]

On balance, it still appears that electric cars would produce a net environmental gain, even if it wouldn't be quite the environmental free lunch it first appeared to be. Or are there still other costs?

As matters now stand, in small production runs of only a few thousands, electric cars would cost at least twice as much as comparably sized gasoline-powered automobiles. Maintenance would also cost at least twice as much since the cost of replacing batteries every two years would be double that of gasoline at $1 a gallon. Finally, the range for electric cars would only be about 120 miles, or less than half that of gas powered cars, and while refilling a gas tank only takes minutes, a full battery recharge would take at least six hours.

Meanwhile, **General Motors** is planning to introduce a mass market electric car, although just when is uncertain. In January 1990, the company displayed a prototype of its *Impact*, an aluminum skinned electric car that can accelerate from 0 to 60 miles per hour in 8 seconds and achieve a top speed above 100 miles per hour. The 2,200-pound car will be capable of being driven 120 miles at 55 miles per hour on one charge, but its 870 pounds of lead-acid batteries would have to be replaced every 20,000 miles at a cost of $1,500.

At present, it is too expensive to own and operate electric cars, despite their environmental benefits. However, as advances are made in the development of longer-lived batteries, and as environmental pressures increase demand to a level that could justify larger production runs than just a few thousand, the day of the electric car is likely to arrive. In fact, according to Paul B. MacCready, president of **AeroVironment Inc.**, the company that built the *Impact* prototype: "There's a 50–50 chance the internal combustion engine will go the way of the buggy whip by 2005."[48]

Meanwhile the **Southern California Edison Company** and the Los Angeles Department of Water and Power have announced a futuristic plan to build a road that transfers electric power from underground cables to surface vehicles without physical contact. Ultimately, this technology could make the range of electric cars almost infinite, even if it only were to be used on highways, since electric power on highways could not only run engines but could also recharge batteries to power vehicles between electrified segments. If that were to work, eventually parking spaces at curbs or in garages could also be electrified, enabling vehicles to be recharged overnight.

This plan is in its earliest stage with only a $2 million demonstration project over 1,200 feet of test road envisioned initially. To electrify all of the 12,000 miles of traffic lanes in the 1,700 freeway miles in the Los Angeles-San Diego region could cost $18 billion. Moreover, other major questions, including the effect of exposure to these magnetic fields on human health and the economics of billing drivers, still remain to be addressed.

Meanwhile, California's Air Resources Board has mandated that beginning in 1998, 2% of all new cars sold in that state must be electric and that, by 2003, that percentage must increase to at least 10% (or an estimated 200,000 cars). Jananne Sharpless, chairman of the Air Resources Board, admitted that "We recognize this is a very dramatic requirement we're imposing on automakers. It's going to take a lot of work, but we think it's in the realm of possibility."[49]

The automakers themselves, however, are not quite so sanguine (perhaps because it's always easier to mandate that someone else do something than that one do it oneself). Toni Harrington, manager of government and industry relations for **Honda Motor's** North American unit, perhaps expressed this best when he said, "We're concerned about the types of vehicles that we'll be able to offer our customers in California. They're not just pushing technology. . . . It's like mandating that you will cure cancer."[50]

2. Since the 1970s, even greater emphasis has been placed on the improvement of emission systems in conventional automobiles than on developing electric cars, cleaner gasoline, or alternative fuels—and with considerable success. Indeed, because of these improvements, over the past 20 years, hydrocarbon and carbon monoxide tailpipe exhaust emissions on new cars and trucks have been reduced 96%, while nitrogen oxides emissions have declined 76%.

It is sometimes argued that with so much progress already having been made in this area, the achievement of any further incremental improvement would be inordinately costly. But this is not necessarily so.

For example, in early 1990, **Camet Co.**, an affiliate of **W.R. Grace & Co.**, introduced a new kind of catalytic converter heated by electricity from a car's battery which promises to eliminate 50 to 90% of exhaust pollutants. This is expected to work because a car doesn't pollute the same amount for every mile it is driven: the greatest pollution occurs in the first few seconds after its engine is turned on and before the car has warmed up. Thus, by heating the catalytic converter, it can be made to kick in almost instantly, reducing the amount of pollution generated when it most matters.

As important as improving the emission standards of new cars is doing something about old cars on the road. Cars built before the introduction of the catalytic converter in 1975 produce 50 grams or more of carbon monoxide for every mile they are driven, compared to 20.7 for those with converters built after 1975 and as little as only 1.8 for those currently being built to California standards. The best thing to do would be to just get those old cars off the road.

Unocal Corporation (NYSE—UCL) is attempting to do just that. Unlike many of its oil company competitors that have been acting rapidly to reformulate their gasolines to reduce air pollution, **Unocal** believes that such changes are premature, pending legislative guidance. But it does want to do something because, as Richard J. Stegmeier, the company's chairman and chief executive, has said, "We're hearing from everybody—our customers, our shareholders and the communities in which we live—that corporations need to pay their dues, so to speak, for the operations that we engage in."[51]

Unocal chose to pay about $5 million in such dues, by offering to purchase 7,000 of the oldest and dirtiest cars in the Los Angeles area for $700 each, much more than their market value, and then recycling them. In addition to the $700, the company gave each car owner a one-month bus pass.

3.   The third approach to controlling pollution from automobile emissions involves the development of reformulated gasolines, which burn cleaner than conventional gasoline, or alterna-

tive fuels, such as natural gas, methanol, and ethanol. Among alternative fuels, the one which has received the most publicity is ethanol, a corn-distilled alcohol promoted by corn farmers and farm state legislators. Between 1978 and 1990, more than 800 million miles were traveled using ethanol blends, according to the Iowa Corn Promotion Board.

The nation's largest producer of ethanol is **Archer-Daniels-Midland Company** (NYSE—ADM), one of the largest food processors in the United States with annual revenues approximating $8 billion. In 1989, the company produced 700 million gallons of ethanol (about 70% of total U.S. capacity). Not surprisingly, **Archer-Daniels-Midland** has been a major beneficiary of federal tax subsidies for ethanol and import tariffs advocated by farm state congressmen. Many environmental groups also back ethanol, but the cost of using it as a gasoline additive could be substantial for drivers, amounting to anywhere from a few cents to as much as 25 cents per gallon.

Moreover, not everyone agrees that gasohol (gasoline mixed with ethanol) really would provide us with a net environmental benefit. Not surprisingly, there are tradeoffs here, too. In a study prepared by a California consulting firm for the oil industry, it was concluded that, although the use of ethanol would reduce carbon monoxide by 25%, it would also increase nitrogen oxide by 8 to 15% and hydrocarbons by 50%, which would result in a net increase of 6% overall in smog. According to Jerry Martin, a spokesman for the California Air Resources Board,

> The jury is still out. We do know that there seems to be a reduction in carbon monoxide but there seems to be some slight increase in nitrogen oxide. We have not determined as of yet which is the greater. We still are not certain whether there's a benefit or not.[52]

To Senator Phil Gramm of Texas (an oil state) the answer is obvious: as he sees it, subsidizing the production of ethanol or mandating its use in automobiles "is piracy aimed at benefiting one industry relative to another and its objective has nothing to do with clean air."[53] To Senator Thomas Daschle of South Dakota (a corn state), however, oil "industry opposition is generated solely by their desire to maintain their profitable monopoly on the gasoline market even at the expense of the health of the American public."[54]

According to Dick Wilson, director of the office of mobile resources at the EPA, natural gas, methanol, ethanol, and electricity eventually could reduce vehicle pollution by as much as 80%, whereas gains from reformulated gasoline may be limited to 30%. Nevertheless, over the near term, he believes that "the biggest bang for the buck will be from reformulated gasoline" and, as a consequence, he feels that "having the oil companies compete over who can produce the cleanest gasoline is great."[55]

And the oil companies at least have begun competing. In early 1990, **Atlantic Richfield Company** (NYSE—ARC) became the first of the major oil companies to introduce a reformulated gasoline, *EC-1*, for older cars in California; that gasoline reportedly reduced air pollution by 20% in cars using it. Then in September 1990, **Atlantic Richfield** introduced the second of its emission control gasolines, *EC-Premium*, which it claims reduces benzene emissions by 35%, aromatics by 17%, hydrocarbons by 21%, and carbon monoxide by 28%. According to **Atlantic Richfield**, the combined use of its *EC-1* and *EC-Premium* gasolines will enable its customers to eliminate eight million pounds of air pollutants monthly which otherwise would have been spewed into the atmosphere.

Along the way, between the time of the introduction of *EC-1* and *EC-Premium*, several other oil companies introduced their own reformulated gasolines. **Marathon Oil**, a unit of **USX Corporation** (NYSE—X), introduced a "clean" gasoline in Michigan, while **Conoco Inc.** and **Diamond Shamrock R&M** (NYSE—DRM) began selling reformulated gasolines for older cars in Colorado. The **Shell Oil Company**, a unit of **Royal Dutch/Shell Group**, announced the introduction of its own reformulated gasoline in 10 of the most polluted cities around the country: New York, Hartford, Chicago, Houston, Los Angeles, Philadelphia, Baltimore, Milwaukee, San Diego, and Washington, DC. And in November 1990, **Amoco Corporation** (NYSE—AN) announced that it had begun selling a cleaner gasoline in Washington, DC, Baltimore, Richmond, and Roanoke, Virginia, which was the first gasoline to meet the new standards for 1992 mandated by the *Clean Air Act* passed by Congress just one month earlier.

The Greenhouse Effect and Global Warming

Pick one:

1. By the indiscriminate burning of fossil fuels and the clearing of our tropical rain forests, we are creating so much excess carbon dioxide worldwide that the Earth's atmosphere is heating up at a rate that is unprecedented in human history. If this continues for another 60 years, the results will be cataclysmic: the Earth's temperature will increase by as much as 5 degrees Celsius, which would result in ocean levels rising by more that 2 feet, melting of the polar ice caps, global flooding, droughts, famines, epidemics, population migrations, and the collapse of civilization as we know it.

2. We are producing more carbon dioxide than ever before but this is good, not bad. The Earth's temperature will rise by about 2 degrees by the middle of the next century and this warming will make the world more habitable, not less. Combined with the additional carbon dioxide in the atmosphere, the rise in temperature will increase plant and crop growth, enabling us to produce more food for future generations.

3. The greenhouse effect is a myth: ignoring short-term random cyclical swings, the temperature of the Earth is not rising significantly at all.

4. Is the Earth getting warmer? We just don't know.

And the correct answer is. . .: 4. We just don't know.

What *do* we actually know? First, let's look at the case *for* global warming and the greenhouse effect.

1. The Earth's atmosphere does function like a greenhouse. Carbon dioxide and, to a lesser extent, methane, nitrogen oxides, and chlorofluorocarbons do trap heat in the atmosphere; if they didn't, the average temperature of the Earth would be 0 degrees Celsius rather than nearly 60 degrees.

2. Over the past 100 years, carbon dioxide concentration in the atmosphere increased from about 280 parts per million (ppm) to about 350 ppm. The primary factor underlying this increase has been our burning of fossil fuels since the advent of the Industrial

Revolution. Total greenhouse gases, including methane, nitrogen oxides, and chlorofluorocarbons (also generated by man), now stand at about 410 ppm.

3.   Over the past 160,000 years, based on laboratory analyses of glacial ice, it appears that global temperatures and the levels of carbon dioxide in the atmosphere have risen and fallen hand-in-hand. Thus it may seem logical to expect temperatures to continue to rise, if carbon dioxide and other greenhouse gases continue to increase as a percentage of the atmosphere.

4.   Temperature readings over the past 100 years suggest that the Earth has heated up by about 0.5 degrees Celsius during that time. The five warmest years of the last 110 all occurred in the 1980s.

5.   Computer models extrapolating from this data predict that global temperatures will rise between 1 and 5 degrees over the next 50 to 100 years, if we don't change our ways in regard to the burning of fossil fuels and the clearing of tropical rain forests. The lower range of estimates over a century might not be a problem, but the higher range over 50 years could cause cataclysmic floods and droughts.

But the holes in these arguments may be even bigger than the one in the ozone layer. Consider:

1.   When scientists analyzed the atmosphere, they found only half as much carbon dioxide as they expected based on estimates of how much had been produced over the last century by the burning of fossil fuels—and they don't know where the rest is. Indeed, when James Hansen of the National Academy of Science's policy committee (and a major supporter of the theory of global warming) was asked where the carbon dioxide is, he admitted: "We're not sure. There must be a carbon sink somewhere. Maybe it's the northern forest."[56] But if we don't know what happened to the carbon dioxide we produced in the past, how can we know what will happen to what we produce in the future?

2.   We also don't really know *why* there has been a close correlation between carbon dioxide levels and global temperature changes over the last 160,000 years. Certainly there is no evidence of a cause and effect relationship. And, in fact, there is even some evidence that it might have worked the other way

around, with changes in temperature, in some instances, having *preceded* rather than *followed* changes in carbon dioxide levels.

And what triggered those changes anyway? Evidently, some natural force other than man did it.

3.   Even the evidence that the Earth has warmed by 0.5 degrees over the last 100 years is open to question. Not only is that evidence based on surface readings that do not include huge regions of remote oceans, but those readings may also have been raised artificially by urban heat at land stations. Satellite measurements of the atmosphere between 1979 and 1988, however, showed wide swings in temperature readings, but no general warming trend.

4.   The computer models that scientists have used to predict global warming generally have not taken into account the manner in which changes in cloud formation affect global climate. Clouds behave paradoxically, both warming the Earth, by trapping heat, and cooling it, by reflecting sunlight back into space. No one knows how the greenhouse effect would affect the process of cloud formation but the net impact could be equilibrium or even a cooling, rather than warming. According to William Stevens, writing on the relationship of clouds to climate, "The computerized mathematical models on which climatologists largely rely in forecasting climatic change are so far out of touch with reality that they might have to be partly reconstructed, not merely adjusted."[57]

Given all of this uncertainty, what should we do in regard to the greenhouse effect and the risk of global warming? According to many environmental activists, we, nonetheless, should act immediately, decisively, and on a large scale to end the clearcutting of forests and to slash the emission of carbon dioxide and other greenhouse gases, even before all the evidence is in, lest it be too late to act by the time the scientific community can make a conclusive case. Klaus Topfer, West Germany's Minister for the Environment, has argued, for instance, that "Worldwide action against the climatic threat is urgently required, even if the complicated scientific interrelationships of climatic change have not all been fully understood. Gaps in knowledge must not be used as an excuse for worldwide inaction."[58]

But wouldn't what Topfer is advocating really amount to an abdication of humanity's responsibility to act rationally and logically based on scientific evidence, rather than emotionally on the basis of what *might* happen? And wouldn't such an approach be incredibly costly?

The answer to both questions is *yes*. According to Michael Boskin, chairman of the Council of Economic Advisors, cutting emissions of greenhouse gases in the United States by one-fifth by the year 2005, as some Western European nations have suggested, would cost "trillions of dollars—$100 billion to $200 billion a year would be in the ballpark . . . [and] it would mean a period of substantially higher unemployment and lower economic growth."[59] Indeed, a study by the Electric Power Research Institute put the cost of cutting carbon dioxide emissions by the year 2100 even higher—between $800 billion and $3.6 trillion.

Within this context, the Bush Administration has frequently been criticized for putting economic considerations ahead of environmental concerns. In response, the President has insisted that "To those who suggest that we're only trying to balance economic growth and environmental protection, I say they miss the point. We are calling for an entirely new way of thinking, to achieve both while compromising neither, by applying the power of the marketplace in the service of the environment."[60]

For corporate managements and socially responsible investors, the bottom line is this: At this time, concern over global warming and the greenhouse effect do not seem to justify draconian measures to slash carbon dioxide emissions substantially. President Bush's commitments to spend $1 billion for global climate research in 1991, to phase out chlorofluorocarbons, and to plant a billion trees would seem an adequate response, given what we know today. Companies and investors supporting these limited climatic goals are on the right track.

The Clean Air Act of 1990

In 1990, Congress passed its first clean air law in 13 years and the most comprehensive environmental legislation in history: the *Clean Air Act of 1990*. According to Senator George Mitchell of

Maine, it was "national in scope, comprehensive in coverage and historic in nature."[61] And in the words of Representative John Dingell of Michigan, "It is the most complex, comprehensive and far-reaching environmental law any Congress has ever considered. It is going to affect virtually every human activity."[62]

In one fell swoop, Congress mandated actions designed to reduce smog, acid rain, and toxic emissions and to encourage the production of cleaner burning fuels. Among other things, the law specifically required much tighter controls on automobile tailpipe emissions beginning with 1994 model cars; the sale only of cleaner burning reformulated gasolines in the country's smoggiest areas beginning in 1995; sharp reductions in power plant smokestack emissions by the year 2000; and a 90% reduction in the emission of 189 toxic chemicals over the next 10 years.

The good news is that this will virtually assure reduced smog, much better air quality, and fewer deaths from cancer, emphysema, and respiratory diseases. According to *The Wall Street Journal*, it has been estimated that air pollution now contributes to more than 50,000 deaths annually and costs Americans between $10 billion and $25 billion a year in health bills; implementation of this legislation should change all that.[63]

But the bad news is that these achievements will be very costly: estimates of the cost range upward from $25 billion annually by the time all of the law's provisions are phased in early next century—including the additional costs of reformulated gasolines, automobile emission control equipment on automobiles, smokestack scrubbers and/or low sulfur fuel for electric utilities, and so on. Some of these costs will be reflected in reduced corporate profits, tax payments, and dividends as well as lower employment in certain industries: an estimated 15,000 jobs in high sulfur coal mining could be lost by the year 2000, for instance, and another 25,000 in the steel industry by 2020 due to the closing of coke ovens.

Still, it may reasonably be assumed that most of these additional costs will be passed on to consumers in the form of higher prices. As one example, according to the EPA, the tougher controls on tailpipe emissions alone could add as much as $100 to the cost of a new car by 1994, and possibly as much as $500 by the year 2003. Another example: Consumers could end up paying anywhere from 3 to 10% more for electricity in the hardest hit states, such as Ohio.

But there will be positive economic tradeoffs, too. While some industries (e.g., automobile manufacturers, electric utilities, high sulfur coal mining, and oil refiners) may suffer, others (e.g., manufacturers of smokestack scrubbers, producers of alternative fuels, low sulfur coal mining, and natural gas producers) will clearly benefit. Specific beneficiaries might include **Fluor Corporation** (NYSE—FLR) (whose **A. T. Massey Coal Co.** subsidiary is the largest low sulfur coal producer in the eastern United States); **Ashland Coal Inc.** (NYSE—ACI), **Pittston Company** (NYSE—PCO), and **Westmoreland Coal Company** (OTC—WMOR) (three other low sulfur coal producers); **Corning Co.** and **Allied-Signal Inc.** (NYSE—ALD) (which manufacture catalytic converters and parts); **Pacific Gas & Electric Company** (NYSE—PCG) (which is opening natural gas stations in California and is providing some financing for **General Motors** pickup trucks which will run on natural gas); **Archer-Daniels-Midland Company** (NYSE—ADM) (the country's leading producer of ethanol); **Unocal Corporation** (NYSE—UCL) (which owns large reserves of natural gas); and such manufacturers of smokestack scrubbers as **General Electric Company** (NYSE—GE), **McDermott International Corporation** (NYSE—MDR) (through its **Babcock & Wilcox Co.** subsidiary), and **Air Products & Chemicals Inc.** (NYSE—APD) (through its **Pure Air** joint venture with **Mitsubishi Heavy Industries America Inc.**)

THE *VALDEZ PRINCIPLES*

Ceres was the Greek goddess of agriculture. CERES is also an acronym for the Coalition for Environmentally Responsible Economies, a spinoff from the Social Investment Forum, which formulated the *Valdez Principles*.

The *Exxon Valdez* oil spill occurred in March 1989, resulting in the dumping of 11 million gallons of oil into Prince William Sound, the death of thousands of birds and animals, and the pollution of miles of ocean, shores, and beaches. Six months later, CERES, representing a coalition of pension funds, environmental groups, churches, and socially responsible investors formulated the *Valdez Principles* to establish new goals for environmentally sound corporate behavior. Modeled after the *Sullivan Principles*, the *Valdez Principles* established standards for the evaluation of activities by corporations affecting the environment and outlined a code of corporate conduct for protecting the biosphere, using natural resources, recycling waste, disposing of hazardous wastes, and using energy efficiently.

Sponsors of the *Valdez Principles* initially included the controllers of New York City, New York state, and California; the National Audobon Society; the National Wildlife Foundation; the Interfaith Center on Corporate Responsibility; Co-op America; the Council on Economic Priorities; **Franklin Research and Development; Calvert Social Investment Fund; U.S. Trust Company**; and **Working Assets Money Fund**.

CERES' goals in formulating the *Valdez Principles* were admirable. They were intended to establish broad environmental standards to which all socially responsible corporate managements and investors might subscribe, to provide tools for investors to make their feelings better known, and to create an Environmental Auditing Standards Board to certify environmental audits, similar to financial audits, which eventually would be made available to stockholders and the public at large. In consequence, the *Valdez Principles* received considerable positive press.

But the *Principles* did have their shortcomings. For one thing, they were exceptionally vague and general, as even many of their supporters admitted. For another, none of the corporations that were asked to subscribe to the *Principles* had been involved in drafting them. To its credit, though, CERES did address both of these problems after the fact, by developing task forces including company representatives to further define each principle.

A third problem with the *Principles*, however, was that there seemed to be some confusion as to just how they were to be used. In an article in *The Forum*, the newsletter of the Social Investment Forum, Gordon Davidson, executive director of CERES, stated that "The Principles are not intended to threaten corporations with divestment."[64] But in an article in *Franklin's insight* introduced by Joan Bavaria, co-chair of CERES, the point was made that the *Principles*

> are structured to reward responsible corporate actions with significant investment dollars, and potentially to withdraw dollars from irresponsible firms. . . . Some strategies currently being utilized include . . . [d]ivestment. Several pension funds, including those of California, New Jersey, Philadelphia and Los Angeles, are considering asking their pension funds to only invest in *Valdez Principles* signatories. Could your pension fund do the same?[65]

(Joan Bavaria is president of **Franklin Research & Development** which publishes *Franklin's insight* and was one of the driving forces behind the creation of the *Valdez Principles*.)

In fact, several socially responsible *activist* investors filed resolutions in 1990 with 18 companies, requesting them to report within six months of their 1990 annual meetings on company programs and progress toward achieving each of the objectives outlined in the *Valdez Principles*. Of those 18, 11—**Aetna Life and Casualty Company** (NYSE—AET), **Amoco Corporation** (NYSE—AN), **Chevron Corporation** (NYSE—CHV), **Consolidated Papers, Eastman Kodak Company** (NYSE—EK), **Kimberly-Clark, Mobil Oil, Oryx Energy, Texaco Inc.** (NYSE—-TX), **Union Carbide Corporation** (NYSE—UK), and **Waste Management**—agreed to issue such reports before the resolution could even be brought to a vote so the resolution was withdrawn. The resolution was introduced and voted on at each of the other seven, however, although it did not receive more than 10% support at any of them; those seven companies were **American Express, Atlantic Richfield, Exxon, Federal Paper Board, Kerr-McGee Corporation** (NYSE—KMG), **Occidental Petroleum Corp.** (NYSE—OXY) and **Union Pacific**.

The following are the *Valdez Principles* to which corporations have been asked to subscribe:

1. *Protection of the biosphere.* We will minimize and strive to eliminate the release of any pollutant that may cause environmental damage to the air, water, or earth or its inhabitants.

We will safeguard habitats in rivers, lakes, wetlands, coastal zones, and oceans and will minimize contributing to the greenhouse effect, depletion of the ozone layer, acid rain, or smog.

2. *Sustainable use of natural resources.* We will make sustainable use of renewable natural resources, such as water, soils, and forests. We will conserve nonrenewable natural resources through efficient use and careful planning. We will protect wildlife habitat, open spaces, and wilderness, while preserving biodiversity.

3. Reduction and disposal of waste. We will minimize the creation of waste, especially hazardous waste, and wherever possible recycle materials. We will dispose of all wastes through safe and reponsible methods.

4. *Wise use of energy.* We will make every effort to use environmentally safe and sustainable energy sources to meet our needs. We will invest in improved energy efficiency and conservation in our operations. We will maximize the energy efficiency of products we produce or sell.

5. *Risk reduction.* We will minimize the environmental, health, and safety risks to our employees and the communities in which we operate by employing safe technologies and operating procedures and by being constantly prepared for emergencies.

6. *Marketing of safe products and services.* We will sell products or services that minimize adverse environmental impacts and that are safe as consumers commonly use them. We will inform consumers of the environmental impacts of our products or services.

7. *Damage compensation.* We will take responsibility for any harm we cause to the environment by making every effort to fully restore the environment and to compensate those persons who are adversely affected.

8. *Disclosure.* We will disclose to our employees and to the public incidents relating to our operations that cause environmental harm or pose health or safety hazards. We will disclose potential environmental, health or safety hazards posed by our operations, and we will not take any action against employees who report any condition that creates a danger to the environment or poses health and safety hazards.

9. *Environmental directors and managers.* At least one member of the Board of Directors will be a person qualified to represent environmental interests. We will commit management resources to implement these *Principles*, including the funding of an office of Vice President for Environmental Affairs or an

equivalent executive position, reporting directly to the CEO, to monitor and report upon our implementation efforts.

10. *Assessment and annual audit*. We will conduct and make public an annual self-evaluation of our progress in implementing these *Principles* and in complying with all applicable laws and regulations throughout our worldwide operations. We will work toward the timely creation of independent environmental audit procedures which we will complete annually and make available to the public.[66]

While in one sense, the environmental movement is an old one, harking back to Henry David Thoreau and John James Audobon, in another it is as fresh as tomorrow's headlines, addressing issues never dreamt of by Thoreau or Audobon. These include depletion of the ozone layer, the greenhouse effect, smog, the Valdez Principles and many of the others discussed in this chapter. Something similar might be said of racism and sexism: we may trace the roots of our concerns for these issues back to the pre-Civil War abolitionists and the women's suffrage movement or even earlier. But there are major current questions in these areas, too, which go well beyond anything that may have been countenanced by these movement's earliest leaders, including such matters as equal employment opportunity, affirmative action, and comparable worth. That's what the next chapter is all about.

8

Racism, Sexism, and Corporate Responsibility

THE RATIONALE BEHIND NON-DISCRIMINATORY BUSINESS PRACTICES

Socially responsible investors are virtually united in their opposition to racial, religious, and sexual discrimination in business, whether in employment practices, advertising, and marketing, or the selection of suppliers. But the rationale underlying that opposition varies greatly, depending on their political and philosophical orientations.

In the absence of legislation to the contrary, for instance, there are those who would *not* recognize any inherent moral imperative on the part of a *private* corporation, or even an individual for that matter, not to discriminate against persons on the basis of their race, religion, sex, or anything else—so long as that discrimination did not entail the initiation of the use of force or fraud against those persons. While they would recognize that it would be quite stupid to discriminate for such reasons, they would uphold the rights of individuals or private corporations, acting on their own behalf, to take such action.

Thus, they would contend that, just as an individual bigot has the right to avoid blacks, Jews, or gays in his personal life, so too does he have the right (in the absence of legislation prohibiting it) to refuse to hire them in his own company, to reject them as customers, or to avoid them as suppliers. Surely, to act that way would be dumb, but if it was his company and if he chose to run it foolishly, it would be his right to do so.

Moreover, the managers or directors of *public* corporations, even in the absence of legislation, would have no such right. This is not because public corporations are subject to any special moral imperatives to cater to selected ethnic or other minorities simply by virtue of their being public, but because of the ethical obligations of the managers of those corporations to their own stockholders. Remember that the directors or managers of public corporations are only the temporary custodians of the assets of those corporations (the hired hands of the shareholders, if you will). Those assets belong not to the managers but to their owners or stockholders and those managers are obligated to attempt to maximize profits for shareholders (within legal bounds). In attempting to do that, they are not at liberty to indulge their personal whims but must seek to hire the most competent people they can find and afford, irrespective of their race, religion, sex, national origin, color, age, sexual orientation, or, indeed, any other extraneous factor that would not bear on their ability to do the job.

Similarly, managers of public corporations should be "color-blind" and "sex-blind" in their marketing practices, in choosing suppliers or in making any other business decisions, since in those cases, too, the corporation itself (and, therefore, its owners or stockholders) might suffer if management arbitrarily limited its options for no good business reason. If a particular manager were prejudiced, say, against Jews, blacks, gays, or women, that might be his right and he need not associate with them in his private life; indeed, if he owned the company outright, perhaps he wouldn't even have a moral obligation to accept them as customers or consider them as suppliers (although he clearly would still have a legal obligation to do so, given the current state of the law). However, as the manager of a public corporation, he would have no right to act in a manner detrimental to the owners of the corporation simply because he felt like it. And, since limiting the choice of employees or customers or suppliers to a pool of white male heterosexuals certainly would provide the company with fewer options than if the pool in question also included women, gays, and ethnic minorities, the obligation to maximize profits for stockholders would translate into an imperative not to discriminate.

Liberals are equally opposed to discrimination in business, but they come to that position by a very different route. They do not argue that public corporations have no right to discriminate against blacks, women, or gays because to do so would not be in the interests of stockholders, but rather that public corporations are enjoined by an overriding ethical imperative not to do so. It is simply wrong to discriminate, they say, and so public corporations should not do it.

Many *conservatives* tend to agree with *liberals* on this one. They, too, predicate their opposition to discrimination in business not on the indirect consequences of managements' having to fulfill their responsibilities to stockholders, but rather on the inalienable rights of individuals to be treated equally. Where they differ from *liberals*, however, is in their understanding of the derivation of those inalienable rights. While *liberals* tend to see them as secular humanistic ethical abstractions, *conservatives* often believe that those rights are Godgiven.

THE CIVIL RIGHTS ACTS OF 1964 AND 1990

To some degree, however, the issue of whether or not a corporation has a social responsibility not to discriminate, at least in its employment practices, on the grounds of race, religion, national origin, color, or sex was made moot by the *Civil Rights Act of 1964*. Or at least it seemed to be. As interpreted subsequently by the *Equal Employment Opportunity Commission (EEOC)* and the courts, that act prohibited such discrimination outright, except as it resulted from "business necessity," and it provided for reinstatement and compensatory damages to victims in the event of its violation.

For some 24 years following passage of the law, the *EEOC* and the courts tended to interpret it more and more broadly, resulting in an expansion of the rights of aggrieved parties and a general acceptance that statistical imbalances in the racial configuration of a company's labor force might be presumed to be indicative of discrimination on a company's part, unless the company could prove otherwise. This was clearly at variance with the original intent of the law which was to prohibit individual cases of discrimination, not to balance workforces among the races and sexes, but it is what developed anyway.

(Indeed, in a memorandum to the U.S. Senate, inserted into the *Congressional Record* on April 8, 1964, Senators Clark and Chase, who were two of the act's main supporters, stated that

> There is no requirement in Title VII [of the *Civil Rights Act of 1964*] that an employer maintain a racial balance. On the contrary, any deliberate attempt to maintain a racial balance, whatever such balance may be, would involve a violation of Title VII because maintaining such a balance would require an employer to hire or refuse to hire on the basis of race. It must be emphasized that discrimination is prohibited as to any individual. . . .[1]

Similarly, the Department of Justice stated at the same time that

> it has been asserted that Title VII would impose a requirement for "racial balance." This is incorrect. There is no provision, either in Title VII or in any other part of this bill, that requires or authorizes any federal agency or federal court to require preferential treatment for any individual group for the purpose of achieving racial balance. . . . No employer is required to hire an individual because that individual is a Negro. No employer is required to maintain any ratio of Negroes to whites, Jews to gentiles, Italians to English, or women to men.[2]

Notwithstanding the clear intent of the law, however, the *EEOC* and the courts did interpret it over the years in such a way as to create statistical labor force balances by race and sex and, in some instances, de facto quotas. Then, in 1989, the Supreme Court, in effect, cried "Enough!" and handed down decisions in several cases which dramatically returned the state of the law to what had been intended in the first place. This meant that statistical imbalances in the workforce no longer would be sufficient to prove discrimination on the part of corporations; the burden of proving that such imbalances were the result of overt discrimination and not the consequence of normal "color-blind" or "sex-blind" business decisions in demographically unbalanced locales would revert to those plaintiffs alleging such discrimination.

But the game was not yet over. Congress responded by passing the *Civil Rights Act of 1990* in an attempt to put things back the way they were before the Supreme Court rendered its 1989 decisions. President Bush, however, vetoed the act and his veto was upheld by just one vote. So the proposed *Civil Rights Act of 1990* never did become law after all.

Had it become law, the *Civil Rights Act of 1990* would have shifted the burden of proof to employers to justify, in terms of "business necessity," any employment practices that have a "disparate impact" on different potential or actual employee groups. At the same time, it would have provided not only for reinstatement and compensatory damages for those found to have suffered from corporate discriminatory practices, but also for jury trials to determine punitive damages against those judged guilty of violating the law.

The net result of this, opponents of the proposed law claimed, would have been to force companies to adopt quota systems in their employment practices because they would not have been able to afford the enormous expenses necessary to document statistically "business necessity," nor afford the increased financial risk (in light of the jury trials and punitive damages provisions) of losing lawsuits wherein they were charged with willful discrimination. Thus, the law could have been a bonanza for lawyers but a disaster for corporate America. Whether or not it would have proved beneficial to those for whom it was proposed in the first place (i.e., women and racial and religious minorities) will never be known.

CORPORATE RESPONSIBILITY AND AFFIRMATIVE ACTION

Are quotas necessarily bad? Maybe the *Civil Rights Act of 1990* would have resulted in companies' incorporating quotas into their employment policies on hiring and advancement, but so what?

Might that not have been the best thing that could happen if, as a result, whole classes of people who previously had been excluded from sharing in the American dream—including blacks, Hispanics, Native Americans, the handicapped, gays, and women—would finally have gotten a chance to participate too?

Whether you think that would have been good or bad again will depend on your own political and philosophical orientation. But there are many who will look on quotas as horrific for the same reason that they were opposed to discrimination in the first place.

Affirmative action and quotas, after all, are a form of *reverse discrimination*, whether or not we choose to admit it. If a company intends to hire 10 employees or retain 10 suppliers and 2 of each group must be black, then the company will have to set a limit of 8 on the number of each group who could be white. And if the 10 best employees or suppliers candidates all turned out to be white, well, that would just be too bad—not only for the white candidates who would be excluded but also for the corporation's stockholders who would be deprived of their superior services. The company would just have to select two less well-qualified black employees or two less well-qualified black suppliers.

The net result would be that the corporation would not end up with the best possible employees or suppliers but with something less than that. If a corporate manager voluntarily hired workers or contracted with suppliers on this basis, he would be violating his responsibility to shareholders. If he did it because the law required it, then he couldn't be faulted on legal grounds, but the shareholders wouldn't be any better off.

Liberals would split down the middle on this. Traditional liberals who pride themselves on being "color-blind," on not discriminating under any circumstances, and on seeking *equality of opportunity* for all people, regardless of their sex, race, color, religion, national origin, or what-have-you would be as opposed to quotas today when blacks would benefit at the expense of whites and Asians, as they were when Christians benefited at the expense of Jews. For the fact remains that any time one group is given a gratuitous advantage, some other group is handicapped, and the true liberal recognizes that this is just plain wrong. And *conservatives* would agree with this.

As Stephen Barnett, professor of law at Berkeley, noted in regard to affirmative action in higher education: "If 'all' ethnic groups, including whites, are entitled to proportional representation, then no ethnic groups—including Asians—may be over-represented. A policy of guaranteeing parity for every ethnic group amounts to imposing a ceiling, or quota, on every other ethnic group."[3] Professor Barnett's observations are as applicable to the workplace as they are to the schoolroom.

Others who also call themselves *liberals*, however, have tended to focus on *equality of results* rather than *equality of opportunity* and are all for quotas and affirmative action. They start out by arguing that the experience of blacks in being brought to this country against their will and then being kept in slavery merits special recompense and that, if the white establishment, which was guilty of the importation and ownership of slaves, must now suffer a little as a result, that's only fair.

But somehow, lost in the shuffle of this argument, is the fact that the proposed beneficiaries of these quotas will be the fourth and fifth generation descendants of those black slaves who, it was argued, merited this special treatment in the first place—not the slaves themselves. In addition, those who would suffer, in most cases, would not even be the descendants of slaveowners but, rather, would be recent immigrants or first and second generation Americans who never were involved with slavery. Finally, even if there were any justification for special treatment for blacks because of the slavery experience, that would not justify any similar treatment for Hispanics, women, gays, or any other minority group.

WOMEN AND "COMPARABLE WORTH"

Most people today agree that corporations should not discriminate by paying whites more than blacks or Asians more than Hispanics or men more than women (or vice versa) for performing the *same* jobs. But the operative word here is *same*. A white truck driver should be paid as much as a black truck driver; an Asian carpenter should earn as much as a Hispanic carpenter; and a male administrative assistant should earn no more nor less

than a female administrative assistant. That is what equal employment opportunity laws, anti-discrimination measures and
even affirmative action are supposed to be all about. But there is
nothing to suggest that a truck driver, no matter what his color,
race, national origin, or sex, should be paid the same as a carpenter or an administrative assistant. That wouldn't seem to make
much sense.

In fact, we've made a lot of progress in accomplishing those
goals. For the most part, men and women, blacks and whites,
Asians and Hispanics, when they have the same skills, education,
and experience and are doing the same jobs at the same companies, *are* compensated equally. Yet, the fact remains that women,
overall, still earn only about 70% as much as men. Why is that?

There appear to be several reasons. For one thing, women
hold many more lower-level jobs than men. Many shorten their
educations or interrupt their careers to have children and raise
families and, therefore, don't attain the same educational levels
or have as much on-the-job seniority as men. Moreover, women
tend to gravitate to different fields than do men: Men become
construction workers, laborers, carpenters, and truck drivers
while women become nurses, teachers, secretaries, and typists.
And it is a fact that traditionally male-dominated fields such as
laborers, construction workers, carpenters, and truck drivers
earn more in our society than female-dominated fields such as
nurses, teachers, secretaries, or typists.

But why is that? Isn't it simply because the demand for truck
drivers and construction workers in our economy, relative to
supply, is greater than the demand for secretaries or typists? If
that is the case, why don't women typists or secretaries who want
to earn more money just become construction workers or carpenters instead?

Would that be because they are discriminated against in their
attempts to enter those traditionally male-oriented fields even
when they are qualified to do so? Or is it because, as a class, they
continue to prefer the *pink collar* occupations to the *blue collar*
ones?

If it is the former reason, that is one of the things which our
equal employment opportunity and affirmative action legislation
is designed to correct. That legislation should be enforced to the

fullest, ensuring that women are *not* precluded by discrimination from entering higher-paying traditionally male-dominated fields. But if it is the latter reason (whether because of innate differences between men and women or because of cultural and societal artificially induced differences or because of whatever other reason), then why should there be any responsibility on the part of companies to do anything about it?

Under those circumstances, after all, women simply would be making conscious choices, say, to trade off dollars for better working conditions. Might they not be saying, for instance, that, rather than being on the road and away from their families for days at a stretch as truck drivers, they would prefer to work for lower salaries as teachers so that they could spend more time with their children in the afternoons and during long summer, Easter, and Christmas vacations. Might many men not be saying just the opposite? Isn't that what free choice is all about?

Enter *comparable worth* theorists who argue that we need not concern ourselves with *why* truck drivers are paid more than teachers: maybe it's supply and demand and maybe it's discrimination but in either event it's true. Whatever the reason, it's still morally wrong—*if* a secretary's job is *worth* as much as a truck driver's. But that is a big *if*. If we don't accept the market's judgment as to the relative value of jobs, how should we determine what the word "worth" means and how should we calculate it?

Easy: Just get a bunch of self-proclaimed experts to evaluate jobs on the bases of their educational, skill, experience, effort, or responsibility requirements, as well as the working conditions that accompany them; rank them on those bases, one against another, and establish salary scales, accordingly. For jobs rated equally, pay employees the same, no matter what the market suggests wages should be.

Moreover, in doing this, don't lower any men's salaries to the levels of women's; just raise the women's. And if, strange as it sounds, some traditionally female jobs turn out to pay more than equally rated traditionally male jobs, well, just ignore it.

This is not a joke. It is the essence of the concept of *comparable worth* and, where it has been introduced, these are the kinds of problems that have developed.

In 1986, for instance, the State of Washington determined that there was a 20% gap between the average wages of its male and female employees and began a program to narrow the gap. As a result, compensation in many female-dominated fields was raised and the overall gap between the average wages of men and women was narrowed to only 5%. To finance this, no one had to take a pay cut but the state reduced across-the-board cost-of-living increases. As a consequence, in some male-dominated fields, wages fell 30% or more below levels for similar jobs in private industry and shortages developed as men left government work for the private sector.

In addition, other aberrations developed, with many clerk-typists, for instance, no longer vying for promotions to become bookkeepers, which had been a traditional route to advancement and increased compensation, because to do so would have entailed their taking pay cuts instead of earning more money. After four years went by and the program could be fairly evaluated, Mark R. Killingsworth, labor economist at Rutgers University, had this to say: "They made a mistake. It's like Prohibition. The solution is worse than the disease."[4]

In Ontario, Canada, the concept of *comparable worth* was pushed even further, having been mandated not only for the public sector, but for the private sector as well. The consequences were even worse. For example, at the **Toronto Sun Publishing Corp.**, a dozen female-dominated job categories ended up being better paid than comparably rated male-dominated groups, but the law didn't provide that men should get raises, only that women should. At the University of Toronto, some accountants discovered that they were about to earn less than the clerks they supervised.[5]

Adam Smith warned us about all this two centuries ago.

WOMEN'S RIGHTS AND FETAL PROTECTION

A particularly thorny problem has arisen for those socially responsible investors who are concerned about women's rights to equal employment and advancement opportunities but who, at the same time, recognize the importance of workplace safety and the protection of the unborn. If conditions in a particular workplace are threatening to the unborn children of women working there, say, because of the emission of radiation or chemical fumes, should employers have the right to bar fertile women from jobs in that area? Or would such action violate *Title VII* of the *Civil Rights Act of 1964* which prohibits discrimination in employment based on sex?

In 1980, five women agreed to be sterilized in order to retain their positions at an **American Cyanamid Company** (NYSE—ACY) plant, consistent with that company's fetal protection policy at the time. From time to time, other companies have had similar policies. But the issue is now coming to a head over the policy at **Johnson Controls Inc.** (NYSE—JCI) which bans fertile women from jobs in its battery plants that could expose them to low levels of lead.

The **Johnson Controls** policy was challenged by eight of the company's employees and the United Automobile Workers union both in the federal and California state courts and the arguments on both sides have been direct and to the point. For its part, **Johnson Controls** has maintained that an employer has a "legitimate interest in protecting the health of unborn children."[6] A company spokeswoman, Denise M. Zutz, stated that "You can't turn aside our concern for a child's health. That's at the center of our position. At the same time we have a legitimate position in protecting our shareholders' interests." According to the New York Times, Zutz explained that the company "sees the issue as both a humanitarian concern, protecting fetuses, and an economic one, avoiding both the costly protective measures that would reduce lead exposure and the risk of lawsuits if any babies are born damaged."[7]

On the other side, it is argued that women have the right to decide for themselves what risks to assume and whether or not to avoid pregnancy without necessarily being sterilized, and that the policy is a form of sex discrimination because it deprives women of job opportunities and does not equally concern itself with the known health risks to men of lead exposure.

A California lower court originally found in the company's favor, but that decision subsequently was overturned by a 3–0 vote of the California Court of Appeals which concluded that

Johnson Controls' policy was "blatant, overt gender-based discrimination [based on] unfounded, unscientific stereotypic notions about women." The court added that "We are in an era of choice. A woman is not required to become a Victorian brood mare."

Thus, for California, the question has been resolved, based on state law, but the rest of the country still must await the decision of the federal courts. A federal appeals court upheld **Johnson Controls'** policy by a 7–4 vote finding that the policy didn't violate *Title VII* but was justified under exceptions allowed in the statute. But a scathing dissent was filed arguing that if that position is correct, as many as 20 million jobs could be closed to women since many substances other than lead also pose fetal risks.

This decision has been appealed to the Supreme Court and it remains to be seen just how it will rule. Whatever the outcome, it is worth noting the irony here. On the one hand, socially conscious liberals traditionally have argued for a kind of paternalistic obligation on the parts of both business and government (e.g., to terminate the production of cigarettes or alcohol, whether or not consumers wanted to smoke or drink, because consumers presumably don't know what is best for themselves, or forbidding unsafe, unsanitary, or unduly onerous workplace conditions even if individuals are willing to contract voluntarily for such work under such conditions). On the other hand, conservatives frequently argued that individuals should have the right to make such decisions for themselves. In this instance, however, their roles appear to have been reversed: It is mostly those socially responsible investors of a conservative bent who have argued for the legitimacy of **Johnson Controls'** policy while more liberal investors have tended to see things the other way around.

WHAT SHOULD SOCIALLY RESPONSIBLE INVESTORS DO?

As a socially responsible investor, there are several things that you might consider doing to combat racism or sexism in this country and/or to encourage greater participation in the American dream by blacks, women, and other ethnic minorities. These might include one or more of the following:

Ideas for *Avoidance* Investors

1.   You might avoid the stocks of companies that have been found guilty of egregious job discrimination. In May 1990, for instance, although not admitting the charges against it, **General Dynamics Corp.** (NYSE—GD) agreed to pay over $500,000 in back pay and salary increases to women and minority workers as part of a settlement of job discrimination charges. The company's Space Systems division agreed to offer jobs to black engineers who allegedly were screened out of positions and to give over $260,000 in back pay to 21 black individuals. The company also raised salaries for over 100 women and minority men.

   General Motors (NYSE—GM), too, although not admitting any wrongdoing, agreed in January 1990 to compensate 10,000 current and former black employees who charged the company with having discriminated against them in hiring and advancement. That settlement could cost **General Motors** upward of $30 million.

2.   You might consider avoiding companies accused of attempting to exploit blacks or women by target-marketing undesirable products to them. **RJR Nabisco, Inc.** for instance, attempted to introduce a high tar and nicotine cigarette called *Uptown*, designed specifically to appeal to blacks; this created such an uproar that the cigarette was withdrawn. Then **RJR Nabisco** began test-marketing a new cigarette called *Dakota*, designed specifically to appeal to young, working-class women, and the adverse reaction was almost as strong.

   Indeed, many black militants, responding to the example of the Reverend Calvin O. Butts of the Abyssinian Baptist Church, took to painting over billboards in black communities that advertised tobacco and liquor products. But this kind of militancy is a two-edged sword: If black militants succeed in banning the advertising of products that they disapprove of, they will discourage companies from advertising to blacks entirely. And as John O'Toole, president of the American Association of Advertising Agencies, put it (in referring to Butts' actions of whitewashing billboards in Harlem): "He may call it civil disobedience in the spirit of Martin Luther King, but I call it bookburning in the spirit of Adolf Hitler."[8]

A better response to the problem of discouraging harmful products such as cigarettes, which are advertised extensively in black communities, however, was suggested by Benjamin Hooks, executive director of the National Association for the Advancement of Colored People. In a speech in May 1990, Hooks emphasized the fact that blacks can use all the advertising and public relations money that results from marketing products in their communities and still make their own decisions about the products being promoted.

3.   You might also consider avoiding the stocks of companies that are being boycotted by civil rights groups demanding that those companies promote more blacks and do more business with black-owned companies. If you do, be sure that you're really in agreement with the goals and evaluations of the boycotters.

Nike, Inc. (OTC—NIKE). Nike, Inc., for instance, is the largest athletic shoe manufacturer in the world; it also manufactures and markets dress and leisure footwear and other leisure and sports apparel. In recent years, its growth has been extraordinary: between fiscal 1987 (ended May 31) and fiscal 1990, revenues more than doubled to in excess of $2 billion while earnings per share increased more than sixfold from 93 cents to more than $6 (estimated).

The company has an exceptionally strong following among black youth and derives between 15 and 30% of its business from them. Some black families have sacrificed necessities in order to buy *Nike* sneakers at $50 to $125 a pair. Black inner city gangs have named themselves after the company and some black youths have sheared the name *"Nike"* into their hair. According to Dr. Carl Taylor, adjunct professor of criminal justice at Michigan State University and the author of the book *Dangerous Society*, which deals with urban youth culture: "[Many black young men] do not have dress shoes but have a dozen pair of Nikes at $100 a pop."[9] On occasions, teenagers have been killed over the shoes.

In August 1990, Operation PUSH, the civil rights organization founded by Jesse Jackson, attempted to launch a nationwide boycott against **Nike** in order to accomplish these objectives: to convince it to name a black to its board, to promote more blacks within the company, and to do more business with black-owned banks and advertising agencies. According to the Reverend Tyrone Crider, executive director of PUSH who directed the boycott, Nike practiced "a form of corporate apartheid"[10] and "all we're saying is that if Nike re-invests in the African-American community and does business with us, it makes good sense and contributes to the financial well-being of the black community."[11]

In response, Nike agreed to name a minority individual to its board, to increase the number of its non-white department heads by 10% within one year and to name a minority vice president within two years. But, the company still denied PUSH's allegations that it was not doing enough for the black community and it refused to commit itself to greater use of minority-owned banks, advertising agencies, and other service companies, and to accelerate its timetable for corporate promotions. Moreover, it implied that the PUSH boycott was a form of extortion, noting that it was begun only after **Reebok International, Ltd.** (NYSE—RBK), one of **Nike's** major competitiors, had purchased an advertisement in PUSH's magazine.

In its defense, Richard Donahue, **Nike's** president and chief operating officer, noted that, among other things, the company operates a special store in predominately black northeast Portland, Oregon, the profits of which were split with the community. In the same area, the company sponsored a program to teach carpentry skills to young blacks which enabled them to restore homes that had been abandoned or were being used as drug outlets. Finally, most of the company's $10 million annual charitable contributions went to minority programs.

No immediate bandwagon developed when the boycott was first announced. In fact, several black athletes denounced it. Michael Jordan, the basketball superstar who is also a spokesman for **Nike**, for instance, said that "It is unfair to single out Nike just because they are on top."[12]

Should you avoid the shares of **Nike** under these circumstances? Only you can answer that. You might decide that PUSH is right and that the stock should be avoided by socially responsible investors until the company agrees to invest more in the black community and promotes blacks within the company more rapidly. However, you might conclude that **Nike** actually has behaved very responsibly in regard to blacks so that not only should you not avoid the stock, but that, in fact, you should consider its purchase as a sign of your support for what the company has done. It's up to you.

Ideas for *Alternative* Investors

4.   This brings us to the flip side of *avoidance* investing. Just as some *avoidance* investors might choose to exclude **Nike** from their portfolios in support of PUSH's position, other *alternative* investors who disagree with PUSH and admire **Nike's** action in behalf of blacks might consider the stock an attractive investment.

There are, of course, many other companies that you might also consider as potential investments because of their positive actions on behalf of minorities or women. In seeking to find such companies, however, it is important that you cut through the rhetoric and determine who really is making progress. Lots of companies have highly publicized small programs that may help minorities or the disadvantaged or women to some slight degree, but which companies really make a major difference?

One which clearly does is **McDonald's Corp.** (NYSE— MCD). *Black Enterprise* magazine has cited **McDonald's** as one of the 50 best corporations for blacks to work for in America. According to Ben Wildavsky, the company "functions as a de facto job program by teaching the basics of how to work." It provides one out of 15 Americans with their first jobs; half of its store managers started with the company as low-paid hamburger flippers; 40% of its board of directors worked for the company at one time for hourly wages; and 17% of its managers are black.[13]

Another example is **Minnesota Mining and Manufacturing Co.** (NYSE—MMM) which has been commended by *Black Engineer* as having one of the best minority recruitment programs in the United States. The company recruits from 75 colleges and universities and makes a special point of encouraging minority participation in the sciences. Similarly, it sends many of its women scientists and technicians to schools to encourage girls to consider embarking on scientific careers as well.

Yet a third example is **Corning Inc.**, manufacturer of *Corning Ware, Pyrex*, and *Steuben* crystal. **Corning** has made one of the most all-encompassing efforts of any company in the nation in attempting to attract and retain blacks and women in its labor force. It recruits at black colleges such as Howard, Florida A&M, and North Carolina A&T. It grants raises and bonuses to its executives for recruiting, training, and promoting blacks and women. It assigns "coaches" to black and women recruits. And, perhaps most important, it makes a special effort to make its entire community one which blacks and women will want to live and work in. Thus, the company has recruited black barbers, hairdressers, and public school teachers, convinced a cable televison station to pipe in a black radio station and the Black Entertainment Network, and runs a day-care center for the three- to five-year old children of its employees.

Many other companies are also doing an outstanding job in providing opportunities for women, including a half-dozen cited by *Business Week* as "pacesetters." These include **Avon Products, Inc.** (NYSE—AVP), **CBS Incorporated** (NYSE—CBS), **Dayton Hudson Corp.** (NYSE—DH), **Gannett Company Inc.** (NYSE—GCI), **Kelly Services, Inc.** (OTC—KELYA) and **U.S. West Inc.** (NYSE—USW). In every one of these companies, at least 20% of top management posts are held by women, with at least one or two women reporting directly to the company's chief executive officer.

At **Avon**, which had two women on its board of directors, the company's initial effort to promote saleswomen from the field may be traced all the way back to 1977. At **Gannett**, 27% of the top jobs are held by women, including four women directors. And at **U.S. West**, women account for 21% of the top 1% of employees in terms of earnings.[14]

George Harvey, chief executive of **Pitney-Bowes Inc.** (NYSE—PBI) has encouraged the hiring of women and minorities at his company, arguing that: "It doesn't make sense to cut yourself off from half of the talented people in the world."[15] In implementation of that philosophy, he has mandated (since 1985) that at least 35% of all new hires must be women and at least 15% must be members of a minority. Managers' compensation is related to their success at achieving those goals. As a result, 17% of *Pitney-Bowes'* corporate officers were women in 1990 compared to virtually none a decade earlier.

In 1988, **Tenneco, Inc.** (NYSE—TGT) established eight women-only councils to advise James L. Ketelson, the company's chief executive officer, on the subject of helping women get ahead. On their recommendation, the company implemented bonus plans that penalized male managers who did not promote women and created benefit plans aimed specifically at women's needs. Within two years, the number of women in the company's upper management ranks had tripled from 10 to 30. Mary Lou Roaseau, treasurer of **Tenneco's Newport News Shipbuilding and Drydock** subsidiary, explained their progress: "What we've done is identify the barriers to women, and help Jim knock them down."[16]

Colgate-Palmolive Company (NYSE—CL) has done something similar: part of each of its executives' bonuses have been made contingent on their hiring or promoting additional women or minority members. As Reuben Mark, the company's chief executive, expressed it: "Putting money on the line puts teeth into management's value statements."[17]

5.   Another approach you might take might be to seek out those companies which provide blacks with opportunities to own important business franchises. Here, again, **McDonald's Corp.** deserves accolades. According to a survey by *Black Enterprise* in late 1989, **McDonald's** ranked first by a huge margin in the number of its franchised units that were owned by blacks: out of a total of 4,900 units, 418 or more than 8.5% were owned by blacks.

In second place, **Burger King Corp.**, a wholly owned subsidiary of **Grand Metropolitan PLC**, had 174 black-owned units, constituting 3.9% of its 4,491 units. In third place was **Popeye's Famous Fried Chicken and Biscuits Inc.** with 150 black-owned units or a whopping 21% out of a total of 714. Ranking fourth was

Kentucky Fried Chicken Corp., a wholly owned subsidiary of **Pepsico, Inc.** (NYSE—PEP) with 135 black-owned units or 3.8% out of 3,571. And in fifth place was **Subway Sandwiches and Salads** with 126 black-owned units or 3.7% out of 3,400.[18]

6. You might also invest in companies that actively seek relationships with minority-owned businesses. In the August 1990 issue of *Black Enterprise* magazine, for example, **Lockheed Corporation** (NYSE—LK) ran a full-page advertisement seeking minority suppliers: "Use this to get your foot in the door. If you're a small, minority-owned business with a product or service we need, and you can bid at a competitive price, call now. We're anxious to hear from you."[19]

Both **Monsanto Company** (NYSE—MTC) and **United Telecommunications, Inc.** (NYSE—UT) have also set up minority procurement programs, but with mixed results. At **Monsanto**, buyers have persisted in favoring established suppliers and the company has been forced to continue to try to educate them to broaden their horizons to encompass less traditional minority suppliers, too. At **United Telecommunications**, specific requirements were instituted such that a buyer must get at least one bid from a minority-owned or female-owned business—or explain in writing why he did not; as a result, orders with minority firms rose eightfold from $2 million in 1988 to an estimated $16 million in 1990.[20]

Even with the best of intentions, however, finding minority-owned companies to do business with often is much easier said than done, as even the California Public Employees Retirement System (Calpers) discovered in June 1990. With $58 billion, Calpers is the largest and possibly the most socially responsible of all the public pension plans in the country. It has taken the lead in areas of concern to socially responsible investors (ranging from stockholder rights to apartheid to environmental degradation). It tried to play a leading role in the hiring of black-owned money managers, too.

In 1989, Calpers hired a women-owned consulting firm and a black-owned consulting firm to solicit minority-owned and women-owned money management firms to manage a portion of its funds. But, fearful that a limited search specifically for women and minority managers would violate the laws regarding the use of racial criteria in hiring, Calpers opened its search to "emerging" managers, defined as those managing assets of between $20 million and $500 million. They did this with the belief that a good number of women- and minority-owned firms would still be included.

Their hunch was right. Eighty-five qualified firms, including four black-owned firms, were narrowed down to 29 finalists, including 2 women-owned firms, 4 Hispanic-owned firms, and 1 firm run by a disabled manager. But all the rest were owned by white males. Not one of the 4 black-owned firms made the cut to 29 finalists.

This effort alone might have been good enough for most socially responsible investors, but it wasn't for Calpers. As a result, Calpers reversed its decision and decided to interview all 85 firms, which included the 4 black-owned firms, rather than just the 29 finalists. Calpers determined that its search was flawed, rather than deciding that perhaps, just perhaps, for its purposes the 4 black-owned firms might not have been the best it could find.

After all was said and done, Calpers did hire 12 new managers, including 5 who were not among the original 29 finalists. They included 5 Hispanic-owned firms, 2 women-owned firms, 2 black-owned firms, 2 Asian-owned firms, and 1 owned by a manager with multiple sclerosis.

7. In addition, you might invest in companies such as **International Business Machines Corporation** (NYSE—IBM), **Anheuser-Busch Companies Inc.** (NYSE—BUD), **Honda Motor Co., Ltd.** (NYSE—HMC), **Ford Motor Company** (NYSE—F), **Delta Air Lines, Inc.** (NYSE—DAL), or **Toyota Motor Corp.** (OTC—TOYOY) which, by the examples they set in their own advertising programs, exert pressure on others to eliminate bias and prejudice in our society. In July 1990, for instance, all of these companies withdrew their plans for advertising during the telecast of the Professional Golfers' Association Championship which was scheduled to be held at the Shoal Creek Country Club in Birmingham, Alabama, when it became known that the club had an all-white membership and when its founder, Hall W.

Thompson, was quoted as saying that the club would not be pressured into accepting blacks because "We pick and choose who we want."[21]

The impact was immediate. Not only did the Shoal Creek Country Club agree to admit blacks to membership, but two other prestigious all-white golf clubs, Augusta National (the annual site of the Masters tournament) and Baltusrol Country Club (the proposed site of the 1993 United States Open) felt so threatened by what happened at Shoal Creek that they decided to admit blacks too. As Hord Hardin, chairman of Augusta National, put it: "When corporate America says it isn't going to be involved in television coverage, well, that wasn't the policy until two weeks ago."[22] It was a perfect example of the way in which the free market capitalist system, without government interference, brought about a major social good.

Or, as Arthur Ashe, the first black to win the U.S. Tennis Open, put it: "[Shoal Creek] shows you the enormous power just a few corporations have. Corporate America could almost overnight change these habits and practices if they wanted to. The most important force for change in this matrix is corporate advertising."[23]

Ideas for *Activist* Investors

8. In the 1990 proxy season, resolutions on racist or sexist issues were introduced at several corporations. Most ended up being withdrawn by sponsors before they could be brought to a vote, sometimes after private negotiations with corporate managements elicited commitments that were consistent with what the sponsors were seeking.

One which was brought to a vote, however, was at **Loews Corporation** (NYSE—LTR). Shareholders accused the company of having few black senior executives; its black managers were alleged to have cited obstacles to their own promotional success, including white executives discomfort with non-whites and whites' predilections to choose managers who have backgrounds similar to their own. Shareholders asked **Loews** to establish a policy of reporting to stockholders regarding its progress with equal employment opportunity and affirmative action programs, to inform shareholders (upon request) of the number of women and racial minority persons in upper management, and to develop a program to encourage racial minority and disadvantaged children to attend and graduate from college. The resolution was supported by 5.4% of votes cast.

You might want to keep abreast of resolutions such as this and make a point of voting your proxies in support of those with which you agree. An excellent source of information regarding proxy resolutions that have been filed by socially responsible investors is the Interfaith Center on Corporate Responsibility.

Discrimination in employment and advancement opportunities on the basis of race or sex is a major worry of socially responsible investors. But those are not their only concerns where workers are involved. In the next chapter, we'll discuss some others.

The Corporation's Responsibilities to its Employees

EMPLOYEES AS CORPORATE *STAKEHOLDERS*

As noted early in this book, there are many socially responsible investors who believe that corporations bear responsibilities not only to their stockholders, but also to a variety of other constituencies or *stakeholders*, as well (e.g., customers, suppliers, and the community at large). We discussed one of these *stakeholder* constituencies (customers) in Chapter 5 and alluded to another (all of mankind including unborn generations) in Chapter 7 when we talked about the environment.

But there is yet another major *stakeholder* group that should be considered: the constituency of employees or workers. This group did come up in Chapter 8 on racism and sexism, since a major concern of socially responsible investors involves combating those twin evils as they relate to employees or potential employees. But overall employee issues transcend matters of equal employment opportunity, affirmative action, or comparable worth, important as those matters might be. They also include such disparate issues as workplace safety, unionization, ESOPs, employee participation in management decisions, notices of plant closings, retraining, parental leave and child-care programs, pension and profit-sharing benefits, and the like. All of that certainly merits a chapter in its own right.

Many socially responsible investors look upon employees as the lifeblood of the corporation and deem them, as a class, to be even more important than the company's own customers or stockholders. To those of a Marxist bent who still subscribe to the discredited *labor theory of value*, the difference between a company's cost of goods and its selling price is accounted for solely by the *value added* by its workers; since it is only that value added which constitutes the company's profit, it is only the employees, they argue, who are entitled to it. Stockholders as owners of the corporation, or those who provided the capital for the company's formation in the first place, might be entitled to some return on their investment as the equivalent of rent of their capital, but they should not be entitled to the company's profits.

Those who take this position often argue further that, if it is the workers who should be entitled to all of a company's profits, then it is the workers, too, who must take precedence over the company's titular owners (or stockholders) or anyone else for that matter, as beneficiaries of the corporation's social responsibilities.

It is not our intention in this book to debate the merits of the *labor theory of value*. Enough has been written on that subject and the evidence of the marketplace is such that few continue to subscribe to it. In 1989–1990, the total collapse of communism throughout the Soviet Union and Eastern Europe was the most telling evidence of the wrongheadedness of this theory that totally ignored market realities.

But one does not have to subscribe to the *labor theory of value* to accept the premise that the corporation has at least *some* responsibilities to its own employees. One may come to that position on humanistic, religious, social, or ethical grounds, deriving simply from the relationship that exists between the corporation and its workers, or one may perceive those responsibilities as derivative from the corporation's obligations to its own stockholders.

At one extreme are those who admit that, yes, the corporation has responsibilities to its workers, but those responsibilities primarily entail the fulfillment of its contracts with them, its bargaining with them in good faith, its living up to its explicit and implicit promises, and its abiding by the labor laws. That means that the company must pay its employees what it has contracted to pay them; that it may not renege on its commitments regarding vacations, advancement opportunities, or fringe benefits; that it must negotiate in good faith with individual employees and their accredited unions; that it must pay legislatively established minimum wages; that it must provide workplaces that meet the safety requirements of federal and state law; that it may not discriminate in its employment practices to the extent that is prohibited by law; and so on.

But it does not mean that the corporation must pay any more than the minimum wage if it can find workers willing to work for that wage, no matter how low it is, how much its competitors are paying in similar situations, or what the value of the workers' labor might be, as determined in some non-market manner. It does not mean that the company must provide any safer or more pleasant working conditions than the minimum required by law (or voluntarily negotiated with individuals or unions). It does not mean that the company must make any special effort to benefit any particular disadvantaged group of employees or potential employees. And it does not mean that the company need do anything else in the way of wages, working conditions, or fringe benefits that was not negotiated for nor promised to employees nor mandated by law.

In addition, however, these investors would grant that if it were in the economic interests of stockholders that corporations do more than what was minimally required by law, then corporations would bear those additional responsibilities as well, as derivative of their responsibilities to stockholders themselves. This is the point we attempted to make in Chapter 8 concerning the argument against discrimination in employment practices, even in the absence of legislation on the subject. And, if stockholders directed managements of their corporations to do more than what was minimally required legislatively or economically, then fulfilling those instructions would become corporate responsibilities too, since managements are beholden to do what their companies' shareholders ask of them, even when that may not be in the shareholders' own economic best interests. This point was discussed in Chapter 1 in the section on ethical considerations.

Many liberals, and to a lesser extent some conservatives, however, frequently argue that the corporation's responsibilities to its employees go well beyond that, including the obligation to do more than the law or union contracts might require, whether or not that would be in the economic interests of stockholders and whether or not it was requested by them. In taking that position, they perhaps share Harold Williams' belief that

> As a society, we depend on private enterprise to serve as the instrument through which to accomplish a wide variety of goals—full employment, equal economic opportunity . . . and others. When viewed in light of these social implications, corporations must be seen as, to a degree, more than purely private institutions.[1]

But what employee responsibilites are ascribed to corporations? There are several. The degree to which you agree or disagree that these are legitimate company obligations will reflect your own philosophical and political leanings.

EQUAL EMPLOYMENT OPPORTUNITY, AFFIRMATIVE ACTION, AND COMPARABLE WORTH

These issues were discussed at some length in Chapter 8 and we will not go through them all again. Suffice it to say that, for most companies, the obligations to be fair and even-handed and not to discriminate on the basis of race, color, religion, national origin, or sex in hiring, advancement, and compensation practices has been mandated by the *Civil Rights Acts of 1964* and related laws. Even absent these laws, however, most investors would accept the substance of these claims as legitimate corporate responsibilities, either derivative of the corporation's obligations to its own stockholders or as devolving from higher ethical or religious principles.

So far as *equal employment opportunity* goes, we think that virtually everyone is for it—and should be. It is the ethically correct course. When we look at *affirmative action* issues, however, the moral imperatives are not nearly as clear-cut and opinions are much more divided, with reasonable arguments marshalled on both sides. And frankly, when we consider *comparable worth*, we are hard-pressed to see any merit to it at all and think that socially responsible investors would be well advised not to concern themselves with what we deem to be a bogus issue.

COMPENSATION: HOW MUCH IS FAIR?

Ben & Jerry's Homemade (OTC—BJICA) doesn't pay any employee more than five times what it pays its lowest paid worker, a fact which has been acclaimed by socially responsible investors as an example of the company's enlightened compensation policy. But this is an extreme example. What socially responsible investors are generally much more concerned about is whether a corporation pays its workers *decent* living wages, not the differentials in compensation between its highest and lowest paid employees.

As an example, when socially responsible *activist* investors filed resolutions in 1990 at **Dana Corporation** (NYSE—DCN) and **Parker-Hannifin Corporation** (NYSE—PH) requesting directors to develop a whole potpourri of global employment principles relating to wages, fringe benefits, overtime, unionization, safety, and the like, the very first principle that directors were asked to affirm was: "Equal pay for work of equal value, with consistent measures for determining the value of the job (allowing for regional differences), along with assurances that, based on local standards of living, fair and adequate wages will be accorded to ensure an existence worthy of human dignity."[2]

The first part of that statement (i.e., "Equal pay for work of equal value, with consistent measures for determining the value of the job") relates, of course, to the concept of *comparable worth*. We have had enough to say about that already and need not go into it again. But the second part (i.e., "assurances that, based on local standards of living, fair and adequate wages will be accorded to ensure an existence worthy of human dignity") does merit some comment.

There are at least three major difficulties with the idea of expecting socially responsible corporations to pay "fair and adequate wages . . . to ensure an existence worthy of human dignity"—if by that it is meant something more than the minimum required by law or competitive market conditions. Consider:

1. Who is to decide what "fair and adequate wages" are, what an "existence worthy of human dignity" is, or what is necessary to ensure such an existence? To the man with no job at all, $3 an hour might seem "fair and adequate," for it would represent the difference between life and death itself. To the individual working 16 hours a day, however, and sleeping in a cold-water flat, that minimum subsistence wage of $3 an hour might not seem "fair and adequate" at all, and his life may not be one of "human dignity." To him, "fair and adequate wages" might be $6, $8, or $10 an hour—or just enough to rent slightly better accommodations, to eat a little better, and to work a few hours less each day. But to the man already earning $6, $8, or $10 an hour, even that might not seem "fair and adequate," if it meant he still couldn't afford a telephone or a television set.

2. If a company pays higher wages than is required by law or the marketplace, will it put itself at such a competitive disadvantage that, as Milton Friedman has suggested, it would jeopardize its very existence? And if it did that, what would become of the employees who depended on it?

3. Finally, if a company paid some employees more than it had to, would it have to make up the difference by firing

others? Which would be the more ethical behavior: to pay each of two workers subsistence wages insufficient to enable either of them to live in "human dignity" but enough for both of them at least to stay alive; or to pay one twice as much as that, so that his "human dignity" was ensured, while refusing to employ the other at any wage at all and, thereby, allowing him to die?

These are not easy questions and we don't presume to have all the answers. But we do want to suggest that the knee-jerk response of looking on **Ben & Jerry's Homemade's** compensation policy as necessarily more admirable than, say, **McDonald's Corp.'s** (NYSE—MCD) payment of relatively low wages to unskilled youths, may not be fair. In the long run, perhaps it actually is **McDonald's** policy that would result in the greater good after all.

SHARING THE CORPORATE PIE

A way to avoid the problem of determining whether $5, $10, or even $100 an hour is a fair wage, however, might be to tie employees' compensation more directly to the level of corporate profits. Employee advocates might favor this as a way to enhance employees' self-esteem and provide them with a bigger share of the pie. Management and stockholders might also find that it resulted in greater effort on the part of employees and thus worked to their benefit.

Employees of **Worthington Industries** (OTC—WTHG), for instance, receive about 40% of their total compensation in the form of profit sharing which is distributed to them throughout the year. This has increased the sense of identification among employees, managers, and stockholders and it is why **Worthington** is Pete Peterson's favorite stock (Peterson runs the **Cardinal Fund**). According to Peterson, the company doesn't need time clocks or quality control because everyone is pulling together; they know that "the only way to get a fair piece of pie is to make the pie bigger."[3] Similarly, **Ford Motor Company** (NYSE—F), **Aluminum Com-**

pany of America (NYSE—AA), **E. I. du Pont de Nemours & Company** (NYSE—DD), and **Hewlett-Packard Company** (NYSE—HWP) are among the large group of companies that offer bonuses or incentive pay to most or all of their employees.

An even more dramatic way to get employees to identify with management and stockholders and to assure that they share in the fortunes of the companies for which they labor, however, may be through Employee Stock Ownership Plans (ESOPs). These are employee benefit plans, similar to profit-sharing plans, whereby companies fund the purchases of their own shares by a trust, the shares of which are then allocated to employees by some objective formula (such as salary).

The superficial advantage of an ESOP to the employee is obvious: He gains an asset at no cost to himself as an additional benefit of his employment. However, sometimes an ESOP is designed to replace some other employee benefit plan, such as a profit-sharing plan, and in that event, the employee might not be a net beneficiary after all. Moreover, the interests of employees are not always synchronous with those of stockholders. For instance, stockholders might be willing to defer immediate payoffs in exchange for long-term profits that could result from pouring more money into research and development and less into current salaries; employees, even when they secondarily are stockholders, seldom think like that.

The advantages of ESOPs to stockholders are also a mixed bag. On the one hand, ESOPs may be funded with corporate contributions that are tax-deductible to the company. Even more important, ESOPs may encourage employees to identify their interests more closely with those of management and stockholders, so that the profitability of the corporation becomes a priority to them too. On the other hand, sometimes corporate managements have used ESOPs to place stock in friendly hands, aligned with management, to forestall unfriendly takeover offers; in those instances, the creation of ESOPs might not be socially responsible at all—at least not from the point of view of stockholders.

The bottom line on ESOPs would appear to be as follows: when they are established to encourage greater employee identification with management and shareholders, or when they are intended to provide employees with additional benefits, their creation is clearly a socially responsible action. When the goal is the creation of tax benefits for the corporation, it is neither good nor bad. And when it is used to fend off unwanted corporate suitors, it is clearly socially irresponsible. Thus, there is no clear-cut answer as to whether or not the creation of ESOPs is socially responsible.

Interestingly, the market seems to have made the same kind of judgment regarding the value of ESOPs from an economic, rather than social, standpoint. In a study in the Spring 1990 issue of *Financial Management*, it was determined that shareholder wealth increased by 2 to 3% in the two days following the announcement of a new ESOP, when the ESOP was intended as an employee benefit plan, as part of a leveraged buy-out (LBO), or in exchange for wage concessions from employees, but when it was used as a takeover defense, stock prices declined by 3.3%. And a study by the National Center for Employee Ownership concluded that over a 10-year period, companies with ESOPs generated 40% greater sales and 46% more jobs than they would have without employee ownership.[4]

GENERAL WORKING CONDITIONS

Hiring practices, advancement opportunities, compensation, profit sharing, and stock ownership are not all that employees are concerned about. Equally or even more important to them are the conditions under which they must labor and the fringe benefits that their companies provide. Is the workplace safe? Are there risks from radiation, chemical fumes, toxic wastes, asbestos, indoor pollution, or dangerous machinery? Does the corporation provide attractive, subsidized dining facilities? Health and fitness centers? Day-care centers?

Perhaps most important of these issues to employees are the matters of safety and health. And little wonder: The National Safe Workplace Institute has estimated that occupational diseases cause the deaths of more than 70,000 U.S. workers annually and calls this issue the nation's "most neglected public health problem."[5] According to the Institute, 5 to 10% of the nation's 483,000 cancer deaths in 1987, 1 to 3% of the 964,000 cardiovascular disease deaths, and 2 to 4% of the 164,000 pulmonary disease deaths all resulted from previous occupational exposure to dangerous substances.

Estimates such as these are necessarily imprecise, but calculations of actual on-the-job accidents are much more reliable. In this safety area, at least two companies are especially noteworthy for having done an exemplary job. One, **DuPont**, has long been recognized as the leader in preventing worker accidents and work-related illnesses. In 1987, 1988, and 1989, **DuPont** had LWDI (Lost Work Day Incidence) rates of only 0.048, 0.038, and 0.050, respectively (i.e., 48 cases, 38 cases, and 50 cases per 100,000 employee workdays annually). This compared to 5,300 cases per 100,000 workdays for all manufacturers in 1987 and 5,700 cases in 1988. (As of this writing, data for 1989 were not available.) Moreover, 14 **DuPont** plants were on the National Safety Council's honor roll for having gone 10 million hours without a single lost workday; two of those plants went for more than 40 million hours without a lost workday.

Johnson & Johnson (NYSE—JNJ) is another exceptional company on this score. In 1987, 1988, and 1989, the company had LWDI rates of only 0.14, 0.12, and 0.14, respectively. By contrast, the LWDI rates for the pharmaceutical industry and the surgical appliances and supplies industry, of which **Johnson & Johnson** is a part, were 2.7 and 3.9, respectively, in 1987 and 2.4 and 3.8, respectively, in 1988. (Statistics for 1989 were not available as of this writing.)[6]

Moreover, **Johnson & Johnson** is not just concerned about its workers' on-the-job safety; it is equally concerned about their overall "wellness." To that end, it developed its voluntary *Live for Life* program, one of the most ambitious programs of its kind in corporate America, designed to encourage employees to stop smoking, improve their eating habits, get exercise, and generally improve their health.

With the assistance of a nurse, employees develop a personal health profile and learn what is best for them on an individual basis. The company also provides free use of a gymnasium where the average headquarters' employee works out twice a week. It also provides a selection of *healthy heart* foods in the employees' cafeteria. **Johnson & Johnson** has estimated that it costs approximately $200 per employee annually to provide all this, but it has also calculated that it has saved $378 per employee in the process by reducing absenteeism and health care expenses.

The success of **Johnson & Johnson's** program with its own employees prompted the company to develop a wellness program that it could market to other companies as well. As of mid-1990, its clients for these services included about 60 companies with more than 850,000 employees. Among the companies for which it designed fitness complexes were **International Business Machines Corporation** (NYSE—IBM), **Ford**, and **American Telephone and Telegraph Company** (NYSE—T). Other companies that have been leaders in the development of health, fitness, and wellness programs for their employees include **Tenneco Inc.** (NYSE—TGT), **Bristol-Myers Squibb Company** (NYSE—BMY), **United Technologies Corporation** (NYSE—UTX), **NCNB Corporation** (NYSE—NCB), and **Campbell Soup Company** (NYSE—CPB).

Of these companies, **International Business Machines** was also honored in 1990 with one of the Labor Department's first work-force quality awards. This award, *LIFT (Labor Investing for Tomorrow) America*, was given to **International Business Machines** in recognition of its "work/life" programs, whereby the company addressed family needs, including assisting employees with child care, spouse relocation, leaves of absence, schedule flexibility, seminars, and educational and career assistance. The company was also lauded for having pledged $25 million to increase the supply and quality of child-care and elder-care services in areas where its employees live and work.

In particular, the commitment to increase the availability of child care for its workers was noteworthy in being the largest financial commitment of that kind made by any company as of 1990. In its initial implementation of that commitment, **International Business Machines** announced that it would spend $3 million in 1991 to build five child care centers near its offices and plants to serve more than 500 children around the country. In addition, it indicated that it would spend another $500,000 in communities with large populations of company workers to improve existing centers and to recruit and train home-care providers.

Unquestionably, the issue of child care is of growing importance to workers, particularly women. With more and more mothers in the work force, some provision must be made for the day care of their pre-school age children. According to Child Care Inc., a non-profit organization in New York City which assists private and public groups in developing day-care programs, in 1987 there were 146,300 children under the age of five in New York alone who required day care but only 46,300 places for them in licensed day-care centers.[7]

Solutions to the problem range from public facilities to private day-care companies to accommodations provided by corporations themselves for their own employees. Of the three options, the third generally is the most convenient for working mothers but, of course, it is costly for companies to implement. Indeed, day-care centers are neither as easy nor as inexpensive to build and maintain as other workers' amenities such as cafeterias and fitness centers.

That, however, has not prevented a number of companies from stepping in to provide such facilities; in some cases they provide day care because they think it's the ethical thing to do, in other instances because they think it generates good public relations, and sometimes because they think that, in the long run, it will be in the company's own economic interest (e.g., by improving employee morale, reducing absenteeism, and so on). Whatever the reason (and sometimes it's all three), there is no denying that this is an employee benefit that is greatly appreciated by workers and socially responsible investors.

Outstanding among the larger companies that provide child-care centers for their employees' children (in addition to **International Business Machines**) are **Johnson & Johnson, Campbell Soup**, and **Stride Rite Corporation** (NYSE—SRR). Of these, **Stride Rite's** program may be the most ambitious and socially conscious of all: a leading marketer of high-quality children shoes, it provides day care not only for children but for the elderly as well, allowing the company's employees to work secure in the knowledge that not only their children but also their aging parents are being provided for while they are at work. And, the intergenerational contact between grandparents and grand-children appears to have paid off immeasurably in psychic divi-dends to all concerned as well.

JOB SECURITY, PLANT CLOSINGS, AND RETRAINING

But equal employment opportunity, affirmative action, compara-ble worth, compensation, profit sharing, ESOPs, job safety, well-ness, and child-care programs still don't tell the whole story. There is one other major area of concern to employees and to socially responsible investors on their behalf, and that is the issue of job security. Indeed, the issue of job security really predated the socially responsible investing movement as one of the earliest concerns of the American labor movement.

Today, responding to the competition and cultural influence of the Japanese, who provide virtually unconditional lifetime job guarantees to their workers, the United Auto Workers Union has been demanding similar treatment from the "Big Three" U.S. automobile manufacturers, **General Motors Corporation** (NYSE—GM), **Ford Motor Company** (NYSE—F) and **Chrysler Corp.** (NYSE—C). At the opening day of the UAW's convention in May 1990, Owen Bieber, the union's president, asserted that those companies should retain blue collar workers on their pay-rolls "unless [their] ability to survive is severely at risk as a result of conditions beyond their control."[8] This language is similar to the guarantees that the UAW negotiated with **Mazda Motors Corp.'s** U.S. plant as well as with joint ventures in this country between **Mitsubishi Motors Corp.** and **Chrysler** and between **Toyota Motor Corp.** (OTC—TOYOY) and **General Motors**.

This issue of job security extends to the rights of companies to close plants, if such closings would result in workers being unem-ployed. Many in the labor movement have argued that companies should not have unilateral rights to make such decisions, and some socially responsible investors have tended to agree with them.

In fact, the UAW sued **General Motors** for shutting down an assembly plant in 1988 which resulted in idling 1,700 **General Motors'** workers. The UAW contended that closing the plant violated a provision in its contract that forbids the plant closing but the arbitrator on the case agreed with **General Motors** that it had the right to lay off workers and close the plant in the face of a steep decline in sales of the *Pontiac* Fiero model which was being built at the plant.

Most labor experts had expected **General Motors** to prevail. As Dan Luria, a labor expert at the Industrial Technology Institute in Ann Arbor, Michigan, expressed it: "It's hard to see how one would enforce a plant closing ban in auto-assembly plants. What are you supposed to do if you're not selling the cars? Nobody is going to order a company to operate a plant to produce something that nobody is buying."[9]

Indeed, the solution to the problem of job security and plant closings is not to stand in the way of economic progress, not to attempt to restrain the "creative destruction" that is at the core of the free market capitalist system, and not to try to abrogate the economic laws of supply and demand by insisting that plants remain open and employees kept on the payroll, no matter what the economic cost. Rather, the answer is to work with employees and their union representatives, granting them ample notice of inevitable plant closings, attempting to alleviate their financial distress, and retraining them for alternative occupations.

General Motors did work with the United Auto Workers Union, however, in negotiating a precedent-setting contract at one of the plants of its A.C. Rochester division in August 1990, wherein it agreed to postpone the plant's closing for five years in order to allow workers time to reach retirement age. The five-year postponement was extraordinary in that no other contract at any of the "Big Three" automobile companies ever had provided for longer than a three-year postponement, which is probably why the contract was approved by a resounding 97% of workers who, only one day earlier, had threatened a crippling strike if the plant were closed and 600 workers laid off by 1992 as originally planned.

The agreement not only guaranteed the jobs of all 3,108 workers at the plant (including the 600 who had been scheduled for layoffs) but also stipulated that the company would spend another $21.3 million upgrading equipment and looking for other components that could be built there. The agreement was hailed by the union as "a model for the corporation" but it satisfied **General Motors** too: the company had been trying to pare down its aging workforce and had argued that retirement and normal attrition would allow it to do so with labor's cooperation. Since the average age of workers at the A.C. Rochester plant was 47 years and their average seniority was 24 years, this was an excellent place to start.[10]

Another company with a truly outstanding record in this area is **General Electric Company** (NYSE—GE) which set up programs to help more than 100,000 workers whom it was forced to lay off over a 10-year period. For starters, its outplacement centers are generally regarded as among the best in helping workers find new jobs. That's not all. Since the company provides a week's pay for each year of work when it is forced to lay off workers, many of its terminated employees have received severance checks in excess of $10,000; that has helped them to weather the financial shock of temporary unemployment and sometimes start a new small business of their own.

In addition, the company contributes between $750 and $1,500 to assist individual workers in moving to jobs at other **General Electric** plants, when they are available. It also allows workers to retain most of their benefits for a year after they are laid off. Moreover, workers are encouraged to apply for tuition reimbursement of up to $7,500 at any time over five years after losing their jobs.

At times the company has gone even further. When it was forced to close its Cicero, Illinois plant, it gave its workers there two and a half years advance notice of the closing. As William H. Bywater, president of the International Union of Electronic

Workers (**General Electric's** biggest union), has said, "We don't like closings [but, in retraining, **General Electric** is] one of the best."[11]

The responsibilities and obligations of corporations to their stock-holders, customers, employees, and, indeed, the world at large are all legitimate concerns of socially responsible investors. But there is one group and one issue that still stands out from all the rest. This group and this issue has captured the attention of investors throughout the world in a way no other group and no other issue has. We are referring, of course, to South Africa's blacks and the issue of apartheid; we will discuss this in the next chapter.

10

South African
Apartheid: The Distant
Challenge

THE BIGGEST ISSUE OF THEM ALL

The California Public Employees' Retirement System (Calpers) is the nation's largest public pension plan with approximately $58 billion in assets under management. Of that amount, it manages $17 billion itself in an index fund that seeks to replicate exactly the Standard & Poor's 500 Index—but with one unusual wrinkle: It completely excludes the stocks of any companies that invest in South Africa.

Calpers does not stand alone in its opposition to South African investment. By the end of 1989, 25 states, 19 counties, and 82 cities had also taken some economic action against companies doing business in South Africa; those actions often included divesting their public pension funds of any South African holdings. By mid-1988, 155 U.S. colleges and universities had also at least partially divested themselves of South African securities. In 1990, more than 100 U.S. companies and banks doing business in South Africa were subjected to stockholder resolutions urging them to cut not only their direct relationships but also their indirect ties to that country.

As a result of these pressures (as well as consumer boycotts and legislation), hundreds of American companies have disinvested from South Africa. Between 1982 and 1988, the total value of U.S. investment there plummeted from $2.3 billion to $1.3 billion and it is estimated that the total fell below $1 billion by the end of 1989. More and more investors have joined the ranks of those who conscientiously exclude the stocks of companies doing business in South Africa from their portfolios. In short, the issue of South African apartheid has galvanized socially responsible investors, especially institutional investors, as no other issue ever has.

But what is most extraordinary about this is that South African apartheid does not even deal directly with the interests of residents of the United States; in that way, it differs from all the other issues discussed so far in this book.

To be sure, questions concerning the rights of stockholders, customers, or employees don't only involve U.S. shareholders, consumers, or workers either but, in practice, that is what they generally are all about. Similarly, in discussing sexism or racism, we usually look at the effect of such policies on American women and American minorities. When dealing with tobacco or alcohol issues, although several multinational companies are involved, for the most part it still is the U.S. smoker or drinker, or the American affected by him, with whom we are concerned. Even in dealing with the environment, although some issues (e.g., the greenhouse effect or depletion of the ozone layer) are universal, most (e.g., solid waste disposal and the exhaustion of landfill space in the United States or air and water pollution in American urban centers and on American farms) are much more parochial.

The issue of South African apartheid is different, however, in that it is an issue primarily affecting people thousands of miles from our shores. In this instance, socially responsible investors in increasing numbers have been asking the managements of their mostly American companies to alter their actions in order to benefit or at least avoid injury to people located on the other side of the globe from themselves. Certainly, one might argue that there is a universal moral imperative for them to do so and that is probably true—the institution of apartheid is one of the unmitigated evils of our day. But, in a bottom line pragmatic sense, the goal of anti-apartheid socially responsible investors really has been to benefit people at a distant remove from themselves.

WHAT MADE IT HAPPEN?

How could such an extraordinary thing have occurred? After all, stockholders' rights became a major issue only because stockholders themselves forcefully advocated them. Workers' rights were championed by workers themselves and by their union representatives. Black rights were demanded by the black-led civil rights movement and women's rights by the women's liberation movement. How did the cause of South Africa's blacks, definitionally unrepresented in this country, come to be the biggest issue of them all?

It would be nice to believe that it came about simply because the horrors of apartheid were so overwhelming that no decent person could ignore them. There is at least some truth to that: the South African apartheid system is one of the most monstrous institutions of modern time. While whites represent barely 16% of the population of South Africa, they totally control the government and the society. Blacks, who constitute 75% of the population, are restricted to just 13% of the land; the rest is reserved for whites. Whites, and only whites, determine where blacks may live, where they may work, and where they may go to school. South African blacks may neither vote nor hold political office.

Blacks in South Africa earn only 26 cents for every dollar earned by whites. The South African Government spends five times as much on education and health care for its white citizens as it does for its black citizens. The mortality rate for white infants is 9 out of every 1,000; for blacks, it is 109. And the average life expectancy of a white South African, at 72 years, is 13 years longer than for his black counterpart.

Yet, this can't be the whole answer for we never saw anything even remotely comparable in the attitudes of socially responsible investors toward investing, say, in the Soviet Union, China, or the Arab states, despite records of human rights violations in

those nations which, in some cases, were comparable to those in
South Africa. A distinction is sometimes made to the effect that
South Africa is the only nation in which segregation is upheld by
law, but that really is a kind of sophistry. Whether or not upheld
by law, human rights abuses in other countries have been horrific
too.

Remember Soviet anti-Semitism and the refusal of the Soviet
Union to allow Jews to emigrate; the Tianamen Square massacre
in China; and the inherently anti-female nature of the Middle
Eastern Arab feudal societies. While it is true that voices have
been raised in reaction to those countries' policies, it has never
been on a scale even remotely comparable to the uproar over
South Africa. Colleges, universities, states, and cities sometimes
spoke out, but seldom did they seek to divest themselves of their
holdings of companies doing business in China, the Soviet Union,
or Saudi Arabia.

No, the answer is also a political one. The overwhelming
opposition to South African apartheid that has developed in this
country at least in part was a natural consequence of the American political system.

Ironically, it was the landslide re-election of Ronald Reagan
in 1984 that converted limited American opposition to South
African apartheid from one of many causes that stirred the American liberal community to the primary cause around which they
all might rally. In one fell swoop, the election served to demoral-
ize both the Democratic Party and American blacks.

Blacks not only felt ignored by the Republican Reagan Administration but also viewed its policy of "constructive engagement" toward South Africa as ineffective and insensitive. At the
same time, they felt betrayed by the Democratic Party for having
nominated Walter Mondale rather than Jesse Jackson as their
presidential candidate. This combination provided the Demo-
crats with a great political opportunity: by making a major issue
out of South African apartheid, they could recapture the hearts of
black Americans, mute their anger over the rejection of Jesse
Jackson, and adopt as their own at least one issue on which they
might score political points (the Republicans, after all, seemed to

have the basic issues of peace and prosperity all locked up). Perhaps this explains Senator Ted Kennedy's (Massachusetts) immediate visit to South Africa early in 1985.

Not that there was necessarily anything wrong with all that. While it is pretty obvious that there was a large measure of cynical self-serving on the part of those politicians who suddenly decided to jump on the anti-apartheid bandwagon, that does not change the fact that the cause itself is a worthwhile one. In the final analysis, it is results and consequences that count more than motivations: The best of intentions sometimes generate horrendous consequences and the most self-serving motivations sometimes produce considerable good. Thus, it is generally more important to consider what the results of a policy are likely to be than what motives may be underlying it.

This is as true for companies and investors as it is for politicians. If you grant, for instance, that apartheid is an evil institution which should be dismantled and you believe that certain actions by a company or investor are likely to contribute to its destruction, then you should support those actions, independent of the rationale behind them. Suppose, for instance, you are convinced that sanctions, withdrawal, and divestment work (i.e., that a company's withdrawal from South Africa or an investor's sale of stocks of companies doing business in South Africa are likely to contribute to the collapse of the South African apartheid system). Then you should support such withdrawal or divestment, no matter why those actions were undertaken in the first place.

Perhaps the company withdrew from South Africa out of fear of civil unrest in that country or because changes in the U.S. tax code made it unprofitable for it to continue to do business there. Perhaps it withdrew because it believed that remaining in South Africa would jeopardize its domestic contracts or because it feared adverse publicity—without caring a whit for the issue of apartheid itself. So what? You should support that company's policies because, in your opinion, they will lead to the results you desire.

However, suppose a company with the most enlightened business practices has the best of intentions in remaining in South Africa, believing that its presence there will be a force for good and it is determined to remain there despite the risks of civil unrest, the burden of double taxation, and the likelihood of adverse publicity and lost domestic contracts. You might admire and respect the company's management for its integrity and the strength of its convictions, but you really shouldn't own the stock since, in your opinion, the company is making a mistake and its actions are likely to lead to undesirable results.

Conversely, suppose you are convinced that by remaining in South Africa, enlightened American companies that subscribe to the *Sullivan Principles* (now the *Statement of Principles on South Africa*) can accomplish more good than if they were to withdraw. Under those circumstances, it is clear that you should support the decisions of those companies that remain, whether their motivations for so doing are economically self-serving or ethically based, just as you should oppose those who withdraw no matter what their motives might be. If your concern is to benefit South Africa's blacks and not just to pay lip service to some abstract principle, you would have no other choice.

We have gone into some length about this because we think it important that you, as a socially responsible investor, realize the need to make some very basic decisions before automatically subscribing to whatever anti-apartheid policy is currently the trend or deemed most *politically correct*. Perhaps those companies that have decided to withdraw from South Africa and cut all business ties with that country are, indeed, striking the biggest blow against the apartheid system because they are bringing the greatest pressure to bear on the South African economy—but only you can decide that. Perhaps those companies that have withdrawn from South Africa but continue to maintain trading, royalty, or service relationships there are accomplishing as much good without causing nearly as much suffering on the part of the black masses as a total severance of their business ties would cause—but that's for you to decide too. Or perhaps those companies that have remained in South Africa in order to set enlightened examples of inter-racial harmony are accomplishing the greatest good—but that too is for you to determine.

THE CASE FOR THE *SULLIVAN PRINCIPLES* (OR THE *STATEMENT OF PRINCIPLES ON SOUTH AFRICA*)

In 1977, The Reverend Leon Sullivan, a black minister and a director of **General Motors Corporation** (NYSE—GM), created the *Sullivan Code of Employment Practice* (generally referred to as the *Sullivan Principles*), the purpose of which was to eliminate apartheid at American companies operating in South Africa. American companies were asked for voluntary commitments to desegregate their South African workplaces, to pay equal wages to blacks and whites doing comparable work, to improve black training programs and advancement opportunities, and to enhance the quality of black workers' lives by spending more on community services.

Many American companies considered this to be the ideal approach to combatting apartheid. Far better, in fact, than a simple withdrawal from the country would be; by October 1985, 178 companies out of approximately 280 still doing business in South Africa had become signatories to the *Principles*. To be sure, even at the beginning, there were those who argued that it would be preferable if companies were to disinvest from South Africa entirely, since their very presence in the country could be interpreted as lending moral and economic support to the South African government; however, many companies still held firm to their beliefs that such withdrawals would make matters worse, not better, for South Africa's blacks.

Johnson & Johnson (NYSE—JNJ), for example, is one of the most respected companies in the United States and actually ranked first in *Fortune's* 1990 survey of companies most admired for their sense of community and environmental responsibility. Yet, **Johnson & Johnson** has steadfastly refused to withdraw from South Africa, preferring instead to subscribe to the *Sullivan Principles*, to finance housing for many of its mostly black 1,500 employees there, and to help build schools and hospitals in South African townships. Ralph Larsen, the company's chief executive officer, in defending his position, has said: "We'll stay as long as we can be a force for peaceful change."[1]

Similarly, at a 1985 meeting of leading American universities that rejected appeals to divest themselves entirely of their South African holdings, David McLaughlin, president of Dartmouth College, asserted: "We have an honest and strongly-held position that the corporate presence in South Africa is one of the positive forces for change."[2] And James Kinnear, chief executive officer of **Texaco Inc.** (NYSE—TX) which, with **Chevron Corporation** (NYSE—CHV), co-owns **Caltex Petroleum**, the last remaining U.S. oil company in South Africa, has stated that "Walking away is not the right way to fight apartheid."[3]

As one specific example of how the presence of a major U.S. company in South Africa can make a positive difference, consider **General Motors**. The company had been in South Africa since 1926 and, by the mid-1980s, it employed over 4,000 people, making it the largest U.S. employer in that nation. **General Motors** consistently received the highest rating for compliance with the *Sullivan Principles* which, after all, had been developed by one of its own directors.

In March 1986, Bob White, managing director of **General Motors** in Port Elizabeth, South Africa, announced that his company would provide legal and financial support to any of its black employees arrested for using a whites-only beach. This announcement almost surely contributed to the city council's subsequent decision to recommend desegregating the beaches.

Under continuing pressure from investors, however, **General Motors** announced later that year that it would withdraw from South Africa. Now the questions are: Were South Africa's blacks better off as a result of **General Motors'** withdrawal? Would the city council have recommended desegregation of the beaches if **General Motors** had never been there?

By 1984, however, coincidental with the Reagan landslide, the Reverend Leon Sullivan and much of the liberal anti-apartheid movement in this country had a change of heart, arguing that abiding by the *Sullivan Principles* might not be sufficient after all and that withdrawal from South Africa or disinvestment might be preferable. In October 1984, the Interfaith Center on Corporate Responsibility argued that: "We do not believe that being a responsible employer or active philanthropist in South

Africa offsets the many ways in which U.S. companies give the South Africa government support and sustenance."[4] In May 1985, the Reverend Sullivan stated that if apartheid were not abolished by 1987, he would urge that all U.S. companies withdraw from South Africa.

Ironically, a half-dozen surveys by American, British, German, and South African researchers indicated that most black South Africans actually opposed the total disinvestment of American corporations from their country. So did at least some of that nation's black leaders. Although Nelson Mandela and Archbishop Tutu have received considerable press for their unwavering support of sanctions and disinvestment, at least one other prominent black leader, chief Mangosuthu Buthelezi, head of the million-strong *Inkatha* movement and the Zulu nation, for one, has consistently opposed disinvestment (as well as sanctions) as not being in the practical best interests of South Africa's blacks.

With the Reverend Sullivan's withdrawal of support for the code he had created in 1977, the *Sullivan Principles* became known instead as the *Statement of Principles for South Africa.* As such, it has continued to have its subscribers but, gradually, its support has waned, as increased political and economic pressure has persuaded more and more U.S. corporations to disinvest entirely.

THE CASE FOR DISINVESTMENT

The argument for disinvestment is relatively simple: The withdrawal of U.S. corporations from South Africa will serve to ostracize the country morally and, even more important, it will undermine it economically. That, in turn, will force the government to dismantle the apartheid system in order to assure the nation's very survival. There are many who agree with this position including some who advocated it even before it became the politically correct posture to take.

Polaroid Corporation (NYSE—PRD). A major manufacturer of instant photographic cameras and films, **Polaroid Corporation**

also markets other optical, chemical, and electronic products. Its worldwide revenues are approaching $2 billion annually.

Polaroid was the first U.S. corporation to take a public position on the sale of its products in South Africa. As far back as 1971, it required its South African distributor, **Frank & Hirsch**, not to sell to that nation's government or to its military and to improve working conditions for its black employees. When it discovered in 1977, however, that its distributor was making secret sales to the government anyway, it withdrew from South Africa entirely.

Over the years, more and more companies have joined **Polaroid** in deciding to disinvest from South Africa, including such giants as **Exxon Corp.** (NYSE—XON), **General Motors Corporation, International Business Machines Corporation** (NYSE—IBM), **General Electric Company** (NYSE—GE), **Coca Cola Company** (NYSE—KO), **Chase Manhattan Corporation** (NYSE—CMB), and **Mobil Corp.** (NYSE—MOB). In some of those cases, no doubt, those decisions were prompted by moral re-evaluations and genuine changes of heart. In most instances, however, those belated decisions to disinvest probably were triggered at least in part by economic or political pressures.

Thus, Allen Murray, chairman of **Mobil Oil**, which long had argued that it believed it could do more good by remaining in South Africa and setting an example of enlightened management than by disinvesting, ultimately decided to throw in the towel as a direct result of the passage of the *Rangel Amendment*, which prohibited companies doing business in South Africa from deducting taxes paid to that nation. As Murray expressed it: "We had to weigh business considerations."[5]

These "business considerations" were of three forms. First, there was the effect of the aforementioned *Rangel Amendment*. In 1987, Representative Charles Rangel succeeded in getting Congress to pass legislation disallowing companies from claiming U.S. tax credits for taxes paid in South Africa. The impact was enormous. The U.S. Chamber of Commerce in South Africa estimated that this measure alone increased taxes for U.S. companies from 57.5 to 72% of their profits in South Africa.[6]

Second, there was growing concern over the economic and political stability of South Africa as a place in which to do business. The risks of riots, embargoes, and even civil war were increasing daily and rational businessmen, trained to calculate risk-reward tradeoffs in making business decisions, had to reconsider the attractiveness of continuing to do business in South Africa if the risks were increasing even as the potential after-tax payoffs were declining.

Finally, companies were being threatened with the potential loss of business in the United States if they persisted in remaining in South Africa. **International Business Machines**, for instance, was told by New York City that it might not receive any more city contracts if it continued to do business in South Africa; the business **International Business Machines** did in New York was much more important to it than the business it did in South Africa.

THE CASE FOR TOTAL WITHDRAWAL

Merely complying with the *Sullivan Principles* wasn't enough to satisfy many socially responsible investors who pressed strongly for disinvestment. And, superficially at least, they prevailed: by the middle of 1990, hundreds of American corporations, including some of the nation's largest, had disinvested from South Africa. Or did they?

If they did, why was it that *IBM* computers, *Ford* and *General Motor* vehicles, *Kellogg's* cereals, *Colgate* toothpaste, and *Coca-Cola* all remained in evidence throughout South Africa? The answer is that the companies manufacturing and marketing those products may have divested in a technical or legal sense by selling their South African assets and operations to other South African companies and investment groups but, in a practical sense, many really did not divest at all. In many cases, the American sellers continued to maintain licensing, distribution, servicing, franchising, or royalty arrangements with their successors. This allowed the sellers to take credit for virtuously withdrawing from South

Africa while at the same time continuing to benefit from sales made in that country.

From the point of view of South Africa's blacks, this may actually have been the worst of all possible scenarios since the groups that bought out the American companies generally had neither the power nor the inclination to concern themselves over the interests of their black employees to the degree that their American predecessors had. When **Ford Motor Company** (NYSE—F) left, for instance, the recreation center it had built for its black workers passed into white hands. **Ford Motor** was no longer in a position to assure its continued use by blacks but the company was obligated, under the terms of its disinvestment contract, to continue to provide vehicles plans, parts, and services to its successors. As a result, a safety net was provided to the South African white establishment—but not to the blacks whom disinvestment was intended to benefit.

These types of situations occurred again and again. The terms of disinvestment contracts frequently provided that the selling companies would not receive full purchase prices for their assets and operations immediately but only in installments over five years and then only if the sellers had continued to provide various goods and services.

One might interpret these results in either of two ways:

1. This proves that the disinvestment plan was a mistake to begin with. Instead of disinvesting, companies should have remained in South Africa and complied with the *Sullivan Principles*. In the long run, that would have been in everyone's best interest—not least of all the blacks themselves.

2. No, this only proves that the disinvestment plan didn't go far enough. Companies should have been pressured not only to sell their assets and operations, but also to withdraw completely from South Africa, terminating their royalty, servicing, franchising, or any other contracts as well. After all, at least some companies, such as **Eastman Kodak Company** (NYSE—EK), did do just that and it worked for them.

At this time, it would appear that most socially responsible investors are subscribing to the second interpretation. They are not prepared to give up on disinvestment, but they would like to see it work better than it has so far. To that end, they have been especially active in promulgating resolutions urging corporations not only to disinvest but to sever all other ties with South Africa as well.

ANTI-APARTHEID STOCKHOLDER RESOLUTIONS IN 1990

In the 1990 proxy season, resolutions dealing with apartheid in South Africa were introduced at more than 100 U.S. industrial corporations and banks. These resolutions fell into five broad categories.

1. *Adhere to the Sullivan Principles*. In a few cases in which companies continued to do business in South Africa but were not signatories to the *Statement of Principles on South Africa*, resolutions were filed urging those companies to sign on to the *Principles*. Three companies confronted by such resolutions, and the percentage of votes cast in favor of those resolutions at their annual meetings were:

CBI Industries Inc. (NYSE—CBH)	7.7%
Lubrizol Corporation (NYSE—LZ)	19.3%
Timken Company (NYSE—TKR)	10.7%

2. *Terminate Sales to the South African Government*. Several companies, whether they retained ownership interests in South Africa or merely functioned there through distribution agreements or other sales relationships, were urged not to sell goods to the South African military, police, or other government agencies, including, in some cases, the state-controlled Electricity Supply Commission (ESCOM) which provides 93% of South Africa's electricity. These companies, and the percentage of votes which were cast in favor of these resolutions at their annual meetings, were as follows:

Amdahl Corporation (ASE—AMH)   7.5%
American Cyanamid Company (NYSE—ACY)   8.1%
Caterpillar Inc. (NYSE—CAT)   9.8%
Chevron Corporation (NYSE—CHV)   11.8%
Foxboro Company (NYSE—FOX)   6.6%
General Motors Corporation (NYSE—GM)   16.6%
Ingersoll-Rand Company (NYSE—IR)   12.7%
Nalco Chemical Company (NYSE—NLC)   12.1%
Texaco, Inc. (NYSE—TX)   14.7%
United Technologies Corporation (NYSE—UTX)   10.1%

3. *Implement Withdrawal from South Africa.* Many companies were pushed even further: They were not asked simply to adhere to the *Sullivan Principles* nor even to agree not to sell goods or services to South African government agencies, but to disinvest from South Africa, shutting down or selling their assets and operations there to others. Resolutions to this effect were filed at the following companies and received the following percentages of votes cast at their 1990 annual meetings:

Avery International Corporation (NYSE—AVY)   12.6%
Baker Hughes, Inc. (NYSE—BHI)   11.8%
Borden Inc. (NYSE—BN)   12.9%
Caterpillar, Inc. (NYSE—CAT)   9.5%
Colgate-Polmolive Company (NYSE—CL)   14.3%
Deere & Company (NYSE—DE)   11.9%
Gillette Company (NYSE—GS)   11.5%
International Flavors & Fragrances Inc.
    (NYSE—IFF)   10.9%
International Paper Company (NYSE-IP)   13.5%
Pfizer, Inc. (NYSE—PFE)   14.3%
Phelps Dodge Corporation (NYSE—PD)   16.7%
Premark International Inc. (NYSE—PMI)   12.1%
Trinova Corporation (NYSE—TNV)   12.8%
Union Camp Corporation (NYSE—UCC)   14.2%
Union Carbide Corporation (NYSE—UK)   12.5%
United Technologies Corporation (NYSE—UTX)   9.2%
Upjohn Company (NYSE—UPJ)   12.0%
Warner-Lambert Company (NYSE—WLA)   17.0%

4. *Sever all ties to South Africa*. Turning the screw still tighter, socially responsible *activist* investors filed resolutions at several companies (some of which *had* and some of which had *not* already withdrawn from South Africa), asking them to terminate *all* business relationships with that country, including licensing, selling, servicing, franchising, and royalties.

For example, in introducing such a resolution at **International Business Machines**, more than 60 employees and 17 religious institutional investors argued that "We believe that IBM's computer sales to South Africa support apartheid." And according to Donna Katzin, director of the Interfaith Center on Corporate Responsibility's South Africa Programs,

> Although IBM announced in 1986 that it was departing from South Africa, it still holds the lion's share of the South African computer market. IBM sells hardware, software and services to the South African government as well as to companies, which supply the South African police and military, playing a key role in enforcement of apartheid.[7]

Among the companies confronted with such resolutions and the percentages of votes cast in favor of those resolutions were the following:

American Cyanamid Company (NYSE—ACY)	15.7%
American Express Company (NYSE—AXP)	13.5%
Boeing Company (NYSE—BA)	14.3%
Bristol-Myers Company (NYSE—BMY)	14.0%
CBI Industries Inc. (NYSE—CBH)	7.7%
Chevron Corporation (NYSE—CHV)	10.6%
Coca-Cola Company (NYSE—KO)	9.1%
Control Data Corporation (NYSE—CDA)	16.3%
Cummins Engine Company, Inc. (NYSE—CUM)	14.5%
Dow Chemical Company (NYSE—DOW)	12.8%
Emerson Electric Company (NYSE—EMR)	11.0%
Exxon Corporation (NYSE—XON)	9.7%
FMC Corporation (NYSE—FMC)	15.1%
General Motors Corporation (NYSE—GM)	16.3%
Goodyear Tire & Rubber Company (NYSE—GT)	16.4%

GTE Corporation (NYSE—GTE)	15.2%
Hewlett-Packard Company Inc. (NYSE—HWP)	9.5%
Ingersoll-Rand Company (NYSE—IR)	13.0%
International Business Machines Corporation (NYSE—IBM)	17.2%
Interpublic Group of Companies Inc. (NYSE—IPG)	10.8%
ITT Corporation (NYSE—ITT)	12.9%
Kimberly-Clark Corporation (NYSE—KMB)	12.2%
Lubrizol Corporation (NYSE—LZ)	16.2%
MCA Inc. (NYSE—MCA)	13.5%
Merck & Company, Inc. (NYSE—MRK)	14.2%
Monsanto Company (NYSE—MTC)	19.2%
NCR Corporation (NYSE—NCR)	13.5%
PepsiCo, Inc. (NYSE—PEP)	14.7%
Schering-Plough Corporation (NYSE—SGP)	13.8%
Schlumberger Limited (NYSE—SLB)	10.9%
Texaco, Inc. (NYSE—TX)	12.6%
Tokheim Corporation (NYSE—TOK)	15.2%
Unisys Corporation (NYSE—UIS)	19.6%
Westinghouse Electric Corporation (NYSE—WX)	14.6%
Wynn's International, Inc. (NYSE—WN)	2.6%
Xerox Corporation (NYSE—XRX)	17.3%

5. *End banking relationships with South Africa.* Several banks were criticized for maintaining correspondent banking relationships with South African banks and for having facilitated reschedulings of South African debt on terms considered favorable to the South African government. They were urged to terminate such relationships. Resolutions to that effect were introduced at the following banks and were supported by the following percentages of votes cast:

Bankers Trust New York Corporation (NYSE—BT)	13.7%
Chase Manhattan Corporation (NYSE—CMB)	14.8%
Chemical Banking Corporation (NYSE—CHL)	17.2%
Citicorp (NYSE—CCI)	20.3%

Manufacturers Hanover Corporation
(NYSE—MHC)   21.1%
J.P. Morgan & Company, Inc. (NYSE—JPM)   10.9%

WHAT SHOULD SOCIALLY RESPONSIBLE INVESTORS DO NOW?

If you are a socially conscious anti-apartheid investor, you must first determine which of the following three different courses of action makes the most sense to you:

1. *Invest in companies that are in South Africa but only if they adhere to the Sullivan Principles. Avoid those which are not signatories to the Principles.* This was the original approach of socially responsible investors to South African investment and it still has its adherents, although there are fewer today than there once were. The main arguments in favor of this approach are that American companies operating in South Africa and adhering to the *Sullivan Principles* accomplish more good than companies that just walk away from the problem since they seek to enforce nonsegregation in their workplaces and improve the quality of their workers' lives; that companies which disinvest instead hurt the blacks in South Africa more than the white establishment, since it is the black workers who then lose their jobs or are forced to work for South African firms that are less enlightened than their American predecessors; and that many blacks themselves have indicated that they would prefer that American companies adhering to the *Sullivan Principles* remain in their country.

Indeed, those who take this position note that when **Ford Motor Company** and **General Motors** left South Africa in 1986, 6,500 people lost their jobs. Most of them were black and most are still unemployed. **Ford's** recreation center, originally built for the use of blacks, was taken over by the police. With financial credits from the West cut off, the country has seen a net capital outflow of about $10 billion since sanctions were imposed; while this certainly put pressure on the white South African Government as intended, its toll in human terms on the blacks themselves cannot be ignored. Black unemployment has risen by an estimated 20,000 per year and funds for low-cost black housing largely have disappeared.

Furthermore, it is argued that even if sanctions and disinvestment made sense for a while as a way of bringing pressure to bear on the South African government, those policies have now served their purpose: Nelson Mandela, Walter Sisulu, and a host of other political prisoners have been released and a schedule has been established to repatriate 20,000 exiles and free all remaining political prisoners by April 1991. Thirty-six previously banned political organizations, including the African National Congress, have been legalized and political demonstrations are being tolerated. A four-year state of emergency, under which some 30,000 arrests were made, was lifted in all provinces. The *Separate Amenities Act*, which restricted public parks, swimming pools, and restrooms to whites only, was repealed. And negotiations have begun between black leaders and the South African Government.

It is these actions that prompted President Bush to state that "I think all Americans recognize that President de Klerk is courageously trying to change things. Our goal must be to support the process of change."[8] And it is under these circumstances that the time may have come to moderate stringent disinvestment demands as a way of rewarding F.W. de Klerk's government for the actions it has taken so far and encouraging it to continue in this direction.

According to Halton Cheadle, an attorney for COSATU, the largest South African union federation, only a bare majority of that union's members still favor sanctions while SACTU, the third largest union in the country, is clearly opposed to sanctions now. And according to Professor Pieter LeRoux, the Capetown University economist who helped to draft the African National Congress' latest economic policy statement: "Sanctions did their job, but the case against lifting them is now very weak."[9]

However, the fact remains that Nelson Mandela, the African National Congress and most South African black leaders continue to argue that sanctions and disinvestment should be maintained until much greater progress toward dismantling the apartheid establishment has been achieved. And they are quite correct in noting that the greatest strides toward South African freedom only occurred *after* sanctions and disinvestment were implemented, not *before*. Why stop now, before total victory is achieved, they ask.

You must decide. But if you do choose to adopt a *Sullivan Principles* approach, you might consider investing in one or more of the following major companies, all of which have significant ownership interests in South Africa but all of which also have received the highest rating for compliance with the *Principles*:

Abbott Laboratories (NYSE—ABT)
American Cyanamid Company (NYSE—ACY)
Borden Inc. (NYSE—BN)
Bristol-Myers Company (NYSE—BMY)
Colgate-Palmolive Company (NYSE—CL)
Gillette Company (NYSE—GS)
Johnson & Johnson (NYSE—JNJ)
Kellogg Company (NYSE—K)
Minnesota Mining & Manufacturing Company (NYSE—MMM)
Pfizer, Inc. (NYSE—PFE)
Schering-Plough Corporation (NYSE—SGP)
Warner-Lambert Company (NYSE—WLA)

2. *Avoid companies with ownership interests in South Africa, whether or not they are signatories to the Sullivan Principles. Instead, invest only in companies which have disinvested and withdrawn from South Africa.*

If, however, you believe that the best way to bring about an end to apartheid is for companies to withdraw from South Africa rather than remain there even as signatories to the *Sullivan Principles*, then the list of companies above is a *Sell List* for you, rather than a *Buy List*. No matter how well-intentioned a company or what it may have accomplished for blacks in South Africa, you won't want to own it if it still has assets and operations there. Instead, you'll want to select your investments from among those companies which have withdrawn from South Africa. The following is a list of some such companies that have disinvested from South Africa (although many retain licensing, distribution, or other sales relationships there):

Air Products & Chemicals Inc. (NYSE—APD)
Amdahl Corporation (NYSE—AMH)
American Brands Inc. (NYSE—AMB)
American Express Co. (NYSE—AXP)
American Home Products Corp. (NYSE—AHP)
Armco, Inc. (NYSE—AS)
Bausch & Lomb Inc. (NYSE—BOL)
Baxter International Inc. (NYSE—BAX)
Black & Decker Corporation (NYSE—BDK)
Boeing Company (NYSE—BA)
CPC International Inc. (NYSE—CPC)
Carter-Wallace Inc. (NYSE—CAR)
Coca Cola Company (NYSE—KO)
Control Data Corporation (NYSE—CDA)
Cummins Engine Company, Inc. (NYSE—CUM)
Dana Corporationm (NYSE—DCN)
Diebold Inc. (NYSE—DBD)
Dow Chemical Company (NYSE—DOW)
Eaton Corporation (NYSE—ETN)
Exxon Corporation (NYSE—XON)
FMC Corporation (NYSE—FMC)
Ford Motor Company (NYSE—F)
Foxboro Company (NYSE—FOX)
GTE Corporation (NYSE—GTE)
General Dynamics Corporation (NYSE—GD)
General Electric Company (NYSE—GE)
General Motors Corporation (NYSE—GM)
General Signal Corporation (NYSE—GSX)
Gerber Products Company (NYSE—GEB)
Goodyear Tire & Rubber Company (NYSE—GT)
Grace (W.R.) Company (NYSE—GRA)
Hewlett-Packard Company Inc. (NYSE—HWP)
Honeywell Inc. (NYSE—HON)
ITT Corporation (NYSE—ITT)
International Business Machines Corporation (NYSE—IBM)
International Minerals & Chemical Corp. (NYSE—IGL)
Maytag Company (NYSE—MYG)
McDonnell Douglas Corporation (NYSE—MD)

Measurex Corporation (NYSE—MX)
Merck & Company, Inc. (NYSE—MRK)
Motorola, Inc. (NYSE—MOT)
National Semiconductor Corporation (NYSE—NSM)
NCR Corporation (NYSE—NCR)
PepsiCo, Inc. (NYSE—PEP)
Proctor & Gamble Company (NYSE—PG)
Rohm & Haas Company (NYSE—ROH)
Sony Corporation (NYSE—SNE)
Square D Company (NYSE—SQD)
Storage Technology Company (NYSE—STK)
Tambrands, Inc. (NYSE—TMB)
Tektronix, Inc. (NYSE—TEK)
Tenneco, Inc. (NYSE—TGT)
Time-Warner, Inc. (NYSE—TL)
TRW, Inc. (NYSE—TRW)
USX Corporation (NYSE—X)
Unisys Corporation (NYSE—UIS)
Westinghouse Electric Corporation (NYSE—WX)
Xerox Corporation (NYSE—XRX)

3. *Only invest in companies that do no business in South Africa at all, i.e., those which not only have divested themselves of any ownership interests in that country but which also have no distribution, royalties, franchising, or other sales relationships there either.*

The list above includes 58 companies that have divested themselves of their assets and operations in South Africa but, for the most part, their products continue to be sold there through distributors and other marketing arrangements have been maintained. If you believe that the way to exert maximum pressure on the South African Government is not only to disinvest but to sever *all* business ties with that country, then you'll only want to invest in companies that maintain no such relationships. The companies on the following list meet that most stringent requirement: They not only have no ownership interests in South Africa, but they have no distribution, licensing, marketing, or other relationships there either.

Aetna Life & Casualty Company (NYSE—AET)
Alexander & Alexander Services, Inc. (NYSE—AAL)
Allied Products Corporation (NYSE—ADP)
AMAX Inc. (NYSE—AMX)
American International Group Inc. (NYSE—AIG)
American Telephone & Telegraph Company (NYSE—T)
AMR Corporation (NYSE—AMR)
Ashland Oil Inc. (NYSE—ASH)
Atlantic Richfield Company (NYSE—ARC)
Avon Products, Inc. (NYSE—AVP)
BankAmerica Corporation (NYSE—BAC)
Becton, Dickinson and Company (NYSE—BDX)
Bethlehem Steel Corporation (NYSE—BS)
Brunswick Corporation (NYSE—BC)
Champion International Corporation (NYSE—CHA)
Chrysler Corporation (NYSE—C)
CIGNA Corporation (NYSE—CI)
Citizen's & Southern Corp. (NYSE—CTZ)
Cooper Companies Inc. (NYSE—COO)
Corroon & Black Corporation (NYSE—CBL)
Crane Company (NYSE—CR)
Delta Air Lines, Inc. (NYSE—DAL)
Dravo Corporation (NYSE—DRV)
Eastman Kodak Company (NYSE—EK)
EG&G Inc. (NYSE—EGG)
Emerson Electric Company (NYSE—EMR)
Fluor Corporation (NYSE—FLR)
Foster Wheeler Corporation (NYSE—FWC)
Fuqua Industries Inc. (NYSE—FQA)
Hall (Frank B.) & Company (NYSE—FBH)
Harcourt Brace Jovanovich Inc. (NYSE—HBJ)
INCO Limited (NYSE—N)
Inland Steel Industries (NYSE—IAD)
Johnson Controls Inc. (NYSE—JCI)
LTV Corporation (NYSE—LTV)
Litton Industries Inc. (NYSE—LIT)
Lockheed Corporation (NYSE—LK)
Loews Corporation Inc. (NYSE—LTR)

Martin-Marietta Corporation (NYSE—ML)
McGraw-Hill, Inc. (NYSE—MHP)
Mellon Bank Corporation (NYSE—MEL)
Merrill Lynch & Company Inc. (NYSE—)
Northrop Corporation (NYSE—NOC)
Occidental Petroleum Corporation (NYSE—OXY)
Phillips Petroleum Company (NYSE—P)
Primerica Corporation (NYSE—PA)
Reebok International Ltd. (NYSE—RBK)
Rockwell International Corporation (NYSE—ROK)
Rorer Group, Inc. (NYSE—ROR)
Salomon, Inc. (NYSE—SB)
Security Pacific Corporation (NYSE—SPC)
Stanley Works (NYSE—SWK)
Stone & Webster, Inc. (NYSE—SW)
Sundstrand Corporation (NYSE—SNS)
Teledyne Inc. (NYSE—TDY)
Thomas & Betts Corporation (NYSE—TNB)
UAL Corporation (NYSE—UAL)
Wells Fargo & Company (NYSE—WFC)
West Point-Pepperell, Inc. (NYSE—WPM)
Weyerhaeuser Company (NYSE—WY)

The fact that secure, white, American investors can identify with and champion the rights of downtrodden black South Africans on the other side of the world is a testament to the universality of human life. But there are those who carry the concept of the sacredness of life yet one step further, applying it not only to all of humanity but to the entire animal kingdom. We shall take a look at the position of these animal rights activists in the next chapter.

11

Animal Rights

A DIFFERENCE IN KIND

The issue of animal rights differs from all the others we have discussed so far (e.g., apartheid, racism, sexism, tobacco, shareholder rights) in one obvious and important respect. In every other case, the ethical responsibilities of corporate managements and investors were to other human beings—whether they are stockholders, customers, or employees; South African blacks, American ethnic minorities, or women; potential victims of environmental degradation, side-stream smoke, or drunk driving accidents. Here, however, the concern is for species *other* than our own: animals.

At the extreme, some animal rights advocates argue that species other than ours are deserving of all the moral and ethical considerations to which humans are entitled. Thus, they contend that humans have no more right, for instance, to eat lamb, beef, or chicken or to wear fur coats or leather shoes than they have to eat human flesh or to wear clothing made from human skin. Similarly, they assert that there is no more justification to our confining animals in zoos or circuses than there was to our confining black slaves to Southern plantations before the Civil War.

As Peter Singer, the philosopher and author of *Animal Liberation*, has expressed it:

237

> The tyranny of human over non-human animals . . . has caused and today is still causing an amount of pain and suffering that can only be compared with that which resulted from the centuries of tyranny by white humans over black humans. The struggle against this tyranny is a struggle as important as any of the moral and social issues that have been fought over in recent years.[1]

Similarly, the Animal Rights Front (ARF), an activist group of animal rights advocates, has justified its position as follows:

> Because nonhuman animals have the capacity for both pain and pleasure, we believe they also have the right to fulfill their basic needs for food, comfort, space and movement, and to express their preference for either solitude or society.
>
> ARF members also believe that no one species is superior to another, and that any advantage human animals may have over nonhuman animals does not justify our tyranny of them. Simply put, ARF believes that nonhuman animals have the right to their own lives. Ultimately, ARF's goal is animal liberation, the freeing of all nonhuman animals from human institutions and structures of oppression and forced domestication.[2]

Other animal rights advocates, however, take a much more moderate position. They believe that human beings are unique and that they have the right to use animals for their own benefit, whether as beasts of burden, seeing eye dogs, sources of food or clothing, pets, the subjects of scientific experiments, or what have you, but they still contend that special efforts must be made to treat animals with consideration in those instances. In other words, this contingent argues that animals may be raised for food or clothing, but that they should be bred and slaughtered in a manner which results in minimal pain and suffering. While they accept the legitimacy of experiments being conducted on animals if absolutely essential to advance our medical knowledge and potentially save human lives, they insist that such experiments be conducted as humanely as possible. They object to the performing of gratuitous experiments that would be likely to add little to our knowledge and the benefits of which might be obtained in other ways—especially if such experiments would be likely to result in pain, suffering, mutilation, or death of the animal subjects.

Of course, among those who consider themselves to be animal rights advocates, not everyone clusters at one end of the spectrum or the other. Thus, while there are those who are absolute vegetarians, not only refusing to eat beef, pork, lamb, chicken, or fish, but also refusing to eat eggs or milk, there are others who draw the line differently, perhaps declining to eat the flesh of mammals but eating poultry or fish, or drinking milk and eating eggs while eschewing flesh of any kind. Similarly, many who refuse to eat meat have no qualms about wearing clothes derived from animals. Others might not wear fur but see no harm in wearing leather shoes or belts or woolen skirts and suits.

Some animal rights advocates focus on endangered species and even think it acceptable to sacrifice industrial progress in order to maintain viable habitats for threatened species as diverse as snails, whales, and owls. Some attempt to raise selected remnants of threatened species in captivity before returning them to the wild in order to improve the chances of those species' survival; others object to any interference by man with the natural course of nature. Some are exercised by the threat to dolphins from tuna fishing, but don't seem concerned over the much more direct threat to the tuna themselves. Often there is considerable concern for whales, seals, calves, and other "cute" mammals but much less for rodents or insects.

The issue of animal experimentation is another area of conflict among animal rights advocates. Some are opposed to any experiments on animals at all, just as they would be opposed to such experiments being performed on non-consenting humans. They see such experiments on animals as comparable to the Nazi medical experiments that were conducted on human beings during World War II. Others oppose experiments on animals for what they consider to be fatuous purposes, such as the development of beauty products, but don't object to experiments for the purpose of researching or developing new drugs or medical treatments. Others don't object to any experiments per se, but do object to any that would be likely to cause pain and suffering.

Socially responsible investors fall into each of these categories.

VEGETARIANS: THE ULTIMATE ANIMAL RIGHTS ADVOCATES

If you are totally opposed to the use of animals for human purposes, including as a source of food, and you are a socially responsible *avoidance* investor, there really is not much in which you *can* invest. Obviously you couldn't invest in any meat packing companies, poultry farms, or fisheries—but that would only be the beginning. Virtually every major food processing company you could think of also markets at least some food products that incorporate some form of fish, meat, or poultry, whether in spaghetti sauces, microwavable frozen dinners, or even pet foods. Obviously you couldn't invest in most shoe companies either, nor most clothing companies that use leather, fur, or feathers in their manufacturing processes. Eliminate the grocery chains and the retail stores too, since they market those goods.

But don't stop there. You'll have to eliminate most financial service companies, including banks and insurance companies as well, since they're involved in financing or insuring these operations, too.

Most animal rights advocates who are also socially responsible investors, however, aren't that extreme. Rather, they tend to focus their attention in the following more limited areas:

1. The protection of endangered (and sometimes not so endangered) species.
2. The improvement of farming and slaughtering methods to mitigate animal pain and suffering.
3. An end to unnecessary sport hunting, fishing or trapping (i.e., for purposes other than the production of food).
4. A ban on raising or trapping animals for the manufacture of fur coats.

5. The total elimination of animal experimentation or the assurance that such experiments will only be conducted for essential medical and scientific purposes and/or in a manner that will cause no suffering of any kind to the animal subjects involved.

Let's take a look at these areas.

THE PROTECTION OF ENDANGERED (AND OTHER) SPECIES

Animal rights advocates have frequently joined forces with environmentalists in the cause of endangered or threatened species, such as spotted owls, red squirrels, whales, squawfish, seals, and dolphins. In the Pacific Northwest, for example, they succeeded in having the spotted owl designated an endangered species, making it illegal to destroy the old growth forests which are the owls' natural habitat (despite vehement opposition from the timber industry which claimed that anywhere from 10,000 to 102,000 jobs could be lost as a result). Similarly, plans for a mountaintop astronomical observatory in Arizona were threatened over concern for the red squirrels that make their home there.

American conservationists at the International Whaling Commission's annual meeting in the Netherlands in 1990 succeeded in turning back a request by Iceland to take 200 whales in the mid-Atlantic; a five-year moratorium on commercial whaling was thus maintained. In South Africa, environmentalists succeeded in blocking a government plan to allow the killing of 30,500 fur seals annually. And, as we have already noted, socially responsible investors were part of the broad coalition of consumers, environmentalists, and animal rights advocates who succeeded in convincing **H.J. Heinz** (NYSE—HNZ) and its principal competitors to change their tuna fishing practices in order to eliminate the risk of killing dolphins.

Issues such as these are, of course, high on the agendas of many animal rights advocates. But bear in mind that here, as everywhere else in life, tradeoffs are required, too. As Steven Goldstein, a spokesman for Secretary of the Interior Manuel Lujan, has said: "There are people who make it their life's work protecting endangered species and their motives are laudable and sincere. But there are others who occasionally use the Endangered Species Act to stop economic progress or development because they oppose a particular project."[3]

So even if you are a staunch animal rights advocate, before jumping on the bandwagon for every allegedly endangered species, you ought to consider what price might have to be paid in lost jobs or production. And if, as a socially responsible investor, your concerns also extend to the economically underprivileged among us, you might find that in some cases the price required is just too high.

FACTORY FARMING, HUNTING, AND FISHING

As noted, some animal rights advocates are vegetarians and, as such, are opposed to the raising of animals as a food source under any and all circumstances. But most animal rights advocates don't take that extreme a position. Rather, they accept the ethical legitimacy of small family farms while steadfastly opposing the kind of factory farms that raise pigs that never see the light of day, chickens that are debeaked with hot knives to prevent them from pecking one another to death under the most stressful conditions, or calves that are chained in narrow stalls in which they cannot even turn around and are intentionally fed iron-deficient diets.

Animal rights advocates opposed to factory farming do not just object to raising farm animals under such conditions, however. They are generally equally opposed to hunting, fishing, and trapping wild animals as a food source, too. They are particularly opposed when such actions are not even undertaken to obtain food but are engaged in simply for sport or fun. As a result, the socially responsible investors among them are specifically opposed to the purchase of stocks in those sports equipment companies that manufacture hunting rifles, fishing equipment, or animal traps.

THE ANTI-FUR MOVEMENT

The anti-fur movement may be looked on as just a subset of the anti-hunting, fishing, trapping, and factory farming movements, but it still probably merits comment in its own right. Between 1971 and 1986, fur sales in the United States climbed constantly to a record high of nearly $2 billion. During the subsequent five years, however, at least in part as a result of the actions of the anti-fur animal rights movement, fur sales basically flattened out. At about $1.9 billion in the year ended February 1990, they were no higher than they had been five years earlier.

In early 1990, **Fur Vault, Inc.** (ASE—FRV), the nation's second-largest fur retailer with a national chain of 11 stores and 10 *Bloomingdale's* salons, announced that it was getting out of the fur business and changed its name to **Banyan Corp**. (ASE—BYC). While management denied that this represented capitulation to the anti-fur movement, Robert H. Miller, president and chief executive officer of the company, did admit that "In my view, fur as a fashion statement does not have the same allure that it had years ago."[4] That, of course, was precisely what the anti-fur movement had been attempting to accomplish.

In a way, though, **Banyan Corp.'s** decision to get out of the fur business may not have been that much of a victory for animal rights advocates. In withdrawing from the fur business, the company opted instead to market leather outerwear, a product that should logically be as anathematic to animal rights advocates as are fur coats.

DRUGS, COSMETICS, AND ANIMAL EXPERIMENTATION

Probably the major issues exercising animal rights advocates are those involving animal testing and experimentation. In the opinion of many, if not most, animal rights advocates, the testing of products on animals and animal experimentation for medical purposes is not only cruel, but unnecessary.

The test which is usually cited in support of this contention is the Draize Eye Irritancy Test which was developed by Dr. John Draize in 1944 as the standard test for products that might cause irritation or damage if they got into the human eye. The test entails placing concentrated doses of the products to be tested (*e.g.*, shampoo, detergent, or mascara) into the eyes of rabbits which have been immobilized but not anesthetized; the rabbits cannot wipe away the substances and their tear ducts cannot wash them out. These tests have been performed on thousands of rabbits (which have been considered the best proxies for human beings for these purposes), resulting in their blindness, rupture of their eyeballs, bleeding, and ulceration.

Despite that, the value of the test to humans remains questionable: Dr. Murray Cohen, assistant professor of Clinical Psychiatry at Mount Sinai Medical Center in New York, for example, has been quoted as saying, "I consider the Draize test archaic, cruel, irrational and dangerous, and the rationale for its use has nothing to do with human welfare."[5]

In 1980, the Coalition to Stop Draize Rabbit Blinding Tests launched a major campaign in the press and in demonstrations at several corporations' headquarters, with considerable success: as a result, **Revlon** agreed to make a $750,000 grant to Rockefeller University to search for alternative tests.

It was quickly followed by **Avon Products, Inc.** (NYSE—AVP) which also supported the search for alternatives.

Eventually, several companies agreed to stop testing on animals. In addition to **Avon** and **Revlon**, they included **Faberge, AMWAY**, and **Mary Kay Cosmetics**.

There remains a large number of companies, however, that persist in testing their products on animals including the following corporate giants which socially responsible animal rights advocates might, therefore, want to avoid:

Alberto-Culver Company (NYSE—ACV)
American Cyanamid Company (NYSE—ACY)
Bristol-Myers Company (NYSE—BMY)
Carter-Wallace Inc. (NYSE—CAR)

Clorox Company (NYSE—CLX)
Colgate-Palmolive Company (NYSE—CL)
Dow Chemical Company (NYSE—DOW)
Gillette Company (NYSE—GS)
Helene Curtis Industries, Inc. (NYSE—HC)
Johnson & Johnson Company (NYSE—JNJ)
Johnson Products Company, Inc. (ASE—JPC)
Kimberly-Clark Company (NYSE—KMB)
Eli Lilly and Company (NYSE—LLY)
Neutrogena Corporation (OTC—NGNA)
Pfizer, Inc. (NYSE—PFE)
Proctor & Gamble Company (NYSE—PG)
Schering-Plough Corporation (NYSE—SGP)
Scott Paper Company (NYSE—SPP)
Squibb Corporation (NYSE—SQB)
Syntex Corporation (NYSE—SYN)
Upjohn Company (NYSE—UPJ)
Warner-Lambert Company (NYSE—WLA)

One institutional investor that decided (in November 1990) to divest itself of the holdings of companies that use animals for testing cosmetics and household products was the Connecticut Humane Society. At that time, the Society indicated that, within a year, it intended to divest itself of some $2.5 million worth of stock in 10 companies that experimented on animals, including **Upjohn** and **Johnson & Johnson**.

Nevertheless, the most radical of animal rights advocates have argued that the Humane Society's policy did not go far enough since it will still invest in companies that use animals for medical research if the research is conducted humanely and cannot be accomplished in some alternative fashion. Which brings us to the argument on the other side (there is always another side).

While animal rights advocates have argued that the use of animals for medical experimentation is not only cruel but unnecessary, there are those who, while also concerned for animal welfare, feel that the need to put the interests of humanity first necessitates the use of at least some animals in medical research. Dr. Louis W. Sullivan, Secretary of Health and Human Services, for instance, has argued that "Animal research has saved millions of human lives." While readily admitting that "Virtually every-one agrees that unnecessary animal research or the cruel use of animals is wrong," he still has contended that medical experimen-tation on animals "is an integral part of mankind's striving for the betterment of humanity."[6]

Similarly, Dr. William E. Jacott, a trustee of the American Medical Association, has said that "There is a growing number of animal activists whose sole goal is to halt all biomedical research using animals. To these groups, the importance of the research to human medicine doesn't matter."[7] And Dr. Torsten Wieles, a Nobel Laureate for brain research, has gone even further, argu-ing that "Modern biomedical research would come to a halt if researchers no longer had animals available."[8]

Whether or not you are opposed to animal experimentation for the sake of medical research, let's assume that you *are* op-posed to it for the purpose of testing cosmetics or other house-hold products. In that event, there are, as we have seen, several stocks in which you would not choose to invest (see the list preceeding). But suppose that you are an *alternative*, rather than an *avoidance* investor, and that you wish to make a *positive* investment statement in support of your animal rights convic-tions. Is there any stock in which you might consider investing? The answer is yes.

Body Shop International is a fast-growing natural cosmetics franchiser based in Great Britain which was founded in 1976. By 1990, the company had 320 stores in 37 countries, including 22 in the United States. It only markets natural cosmetics that have not been tested on animals (e.g., those derived from honey, beeswax, or almond oil). In addition, the company is very environmentally conscious, using recycled paper wherever possible, offering cus-tomers the opportunity to refill their original **Body Shop** contain-ers in order to avoid unnecessary new packaging, and only pro-viding products that are biodegradable.

And what if you are an *activist* investor? Never fear. There are many opportunities for you to make your feelings known too.

In 1990, People for the Ethical Treatment of Animals (PETA) filed resolutions at four companies urging them to reduce testing on animals. The percentage of votes cast which those resolutions received at the four companies were: **Bristol-Myers** (9.7%), **Gillette** (6.9%), **Johnson & Johnson** (5.3%), and **Schering-Plough** (8.9%). In addition, 10.3% of stockholders voted to ask **International Business Machines** to report on its use of animals in research and testing. And, at **U.S. Surgical**, 10% of stockholders asked the company to report on its use of dogs in medical testing.

By now we have discussed most of the major issues of concern to socially responsible investors (ranging from tobacco to apartheid to animal rights) but there are still a few issues left which we really shouldn't omit. So in the next chapter we'll take a quick look at three such issues that we believe are of more than a mere passing interest to socially responsible investors: armaments and defense; charitable contributions; and Northern Ireland and the MacBride Principles.

12

Charity, Defense, and the *MacBride Principles*

DIFFERENT STROKES FOR DIFFERENT FOLKS

In the first 11 chapters of this book, we discussed the major issues of concern to socially responsible investors, including the rights of stockholders, employees, and customers; tobacco, alcohol, and gambling; racism and sexism; and environmentalism, apartheid, and animal rights. But there are probably as many more issues that we have not even touched on, including the marketing of infant formula, the sale of Salvadorean coffee beans, AIDS research, discrimination on the basis of sexual orientation, abortion, alternative energy sources, and so on. In this final chapter of Part Two of this book, we will briefly address just three of those other issues with which socially responsible investors appear to be most concerned: corporate philanthropy; armaments and defense; and Northern Ireland and the *MacBride Principles*.

THE CASE FOR AND AGAINST CORPORATE PHILANTHROPY

Perhaps the most difficult of all corporate social responsibility issues to resolve is that regarding the legitimacy or illegitimacy of corporate contributions to charities or cultural or educational

249

institutions. On the one hand, some socially responsible investors argue that the *only* real evidence of a management's sense of corporate responsibility is what it does over and above its day-to-day business, not how it manages the business itself. Their reasoning is that it is *expected* for a company to produce quality products, to treat its employees and customers fairly, to refuse to support totalitarian regimes through its business activities, and to refrain from polluting the environment; if it didn't do those things, it would be acting immorally, not amorally. So, the sign that a company is socially responsible can only come from the *extra* things it does (e.g., what it gives in charitable contributions to the community or society, irrespective of how it runs its business).

On the other hand, other investors, who consider themselves to be just as socially responsible, argue that the giving of charitable contributions is *not* a legitimate function of corporations since, in the absence of some economic or moral imperative to make such charitable contributions, such giving would constitute a waste of corporate assets and a violation of those corporations' responsibilities to their own stockholders. Ironically, socially responsible investors who take this position begin by accepting the premises of those who defend the legitimacy of corporate charity—but they draw very different conclusions from those premises.

Yes, they agree, corporations do have inherent obligations not to pollute, not to discriminate, not to produce dangerous or shoddy merchandise, not to perform experiments on animals, or not to support the apartheid regime of South Africa, because to do those things would be wrong. But that, they contend, is what social reponsibility is all about.

Beyond that, whence, they ask, is the corporation's obligation derived to use its stockholders' money for anything that does not improve their profits and does not alleviate a wrong for which the corporation itself is responsible? They agree that there is a moral imperative not to initiate the use of force or fraud on another, and from that moral imperative might be derived such disparate obligations as the need to end cigarette production, animal testing, discriminatory employment practices, or environmental degradation. A corporate recycling program, for example, might be justified (even if it is costly to the company), if it is intended to alleviate the pollution generated by the company's own goods, packaging, or production process. Equal employment opportunity, affirmative action, or comparable worth programs might be justified as correctives for past illegal corporate discrimination. The development of cosmetics that do not require any animal testing might not be cost-effective, but could still be justifiable as socially responsible policies, if the alternative would be to do wrong by performing painful experiments on animals. But in all these cases, the socially responsible actions asked of corporations are intended to correct their own shortcomings.

But what has that got to do with charitable contributions? Why should **Philip Morris Companies, Inc.** (NYSE—MO) support the Whitney Museum or **Dayton-Hudson Corporation** (NYSE—DH) contribute to Planned Parenthood? Is there any comparable moral imperative to sacrifice the interests of shareholders to the interests of others (e.g., the sick, the poor, art lovers, or the community at large) by donating corporate profits to charities absent the kinds of considerations that prompted the other socially responsible activities of corporations and investors discussed in this book?

Indeed, **Occidental Petroleum Corporation** (NYSE—OXY) was sued by stockholders (including the California Public Employees' Retirement System) because it planned to spend an estimated $95 million to build and operate the Armand Hammer Museum of Art and Cultural Center to house Hammer's $250 to $400 million art collection. Stockholders claimed that that would constitute a clear waste of corporate assets for which they would get little in exchange. **Occidental's** directors, however, argued that the museum would provide enormous goodwill for the company. Interestingly, neither side argued that the public would or would not benefit from the building of the museum (that was a non-issue), but only whether the expenditure would or would not benefit stockholders.

Sometimes, of course, corporate charitable contributions really have primary (or at least ancillary) purposes that are in the giving corporations' own best interests, such as the generation of positive publicity, better worker morale, or improved relations with consumers or the community. When that is the case, there is no question of the legitimacy of corporate charity. If it is good business for **Philip Morris**, say, to sponsor the Whitney Museum, no rational investor, socially responsible or otherwise, would disapprove. In such a situation the socially responsible consequences of the action would only be a by-product effect, not the motivating cause—and that would be just fine.

An issue would only arise when a company contributed to charities for purposes *not* in its own best economic interest and *not* because of its ethical obligations not to do harm or to correct the harm it may have done, but rather because it thought that that was the right thing to do. It is up to you to decide if that is the kind of company you wish to invest in or not.

It would appear that you have three choices:

1. You may invest in companies that give large amounts to charities, over and above what they reasonably think might be in their own best economic interests, simply because they think that that is the morally right thing to do. You might say that their emphasis is on "doing good, even if the consequence is that they don't do so well."

2. You may invest in companies that give little or nothing to charities, perhaps considering charitable giving to be a waste of shareholders' assets and preferring to leave it to stockholders themselves to donate their money as they see fit. You might say that their emphasis is simply on "doing well and letting their stockholders themselves handle the question of doing good individually if they so desire."

3. Or, you may invest in companies that give reasonable amounts to charities, in a manner which generates favorable publicity and goodwill for the companies or their products or otherwise also inures to their own benefit. You might say that their emphasis is on "doing well by doing good."

It is in this third area that we believe corporate charitable contributions make the most sense. There are many examples of the success of such strategies, both from a business and a social point of view.

Federal National Mortgage Association (NYSE—FNM), for example, concentrates its charitable efforts in areas related to housing and homelessness because that's what it knows best—and where it gets the best payoff in national publicity. **Aetna Life and Casualty Company** (NYSE—AET) emphasizes services to youth, civil justice reform, and urban neighborhood revitalization; according to Sanford Cloud, Jr., vice president of corporate public involvement at **Aetna**, "When society is healthy and prosperous, our own company's chances of success are enhanced. We can sell products to receptive markets and find people to fill jobs."[1] Similarly, the managements of industrial and technology companies, such as **International Business Machines Corporation** (NYSE—IBM) and **Westinghouse Electric Corporation** (NYSE—WX) often focus their charitable efforts on educational grants supporting engineering scholarhips, not necessarily for the public relations benefits that it could generate, but certainly cognizant of their companies' potential needs for skilled engineers in the future.

One sort of corporate charitable giving that has clearly had a positive impact on society (it is estimated to generate $100 million annually for various charities) is "cause-related marketing." The first, and certainly the best known, example of this was **American Express Company's** (NYSE—AXP) classic campaign to raise money to restore the Statue of Liberty in 1983. The campaign raised $1.7 million, but also resulted in a 28% increase in **American Express'** credit card use in the last quarter of that year. Similarly, **Coca Cola Company** (NYSE—KO) raised $5 million in its *Hands Across America* campaign against hunger and gained great publicity for itself in the process. **Ralston Purina Company's** (NYSE—RAL) *Pets for People* program to help senior citizens adopt healthy dogs and cats helped the elderly and reinforced the company's image while expanding its market.

Even if you believe that companies should contribute generously to charities, the question remains: To whom should they give? You might answer that it doesn't matter to you, that any museum, college, medical facility, research laboratory, orphanage, or homeless center would be good enough for you and that, just as you wouldn't expect to second-guess managements on their day-to-day business decisions, you wouldn't want to second-guess them on the question of which charities they ought to contribute to either. Sounds easy and enlightened. But is it?

Dayton-Hudson Corporation (NYSE—DH). One of the largest retailers in the United States, **Dayton-Hudson** operates hundreds of department stores, discount stores and other retail outlets under the *Dayton's, Hudson's, Marshall Field's, Mervyn's* and *Target* names. In the 1980s, the company's sales rose at an average annual compound rate of 17%, its earnings climbed at a rate of 12% annually, and its dividends (which were increased every year) grew at a rate of 11% annually.

At first blush, **Dayton-Hudson** may seem to be just the kind of corporation in which you'd want to invest, if contributing generously to charities is one of your criteria for measuring a company's sense of social responsibility. After all, it was **Dayton-Hudson** in 1946 which became the first American corporation to announce a policy of contributing 5% of its pre-tax earnings to charity—and that was nearly 30 years before the Greater Minneapolis Chamber of Commerce formed the nation's first 5% club to encourage corporations to donate that much to charity. And, in recognition of **Dayton-Hudson's** consistently outstanding record of corporate giving, The Council on Economic Priorities' named the company the 1989 winner of a Corporate Conscience Award for Charitable Giving.

So far, so good. However, one of the charities that **Dayton-Hudson** had been contributing so generously to was Planned Parenthood which, among other things, advocates women's rights to abortion. Under pressure from the Christian Action Council, an anti-abortion group, **Dayton-Hudson** agreed to withdraw its support of Planned Parenthood. But then the pendulum swung the other way as hundreds of **Dayton-Hudson's** customers who supported abortion rights cut up their credit cards in protest demanding that **Dayton-Hudson** reverse its decision. Elizabeth

Holtzman, a trustee for the New York City Employees Retirement System, which owns more than 400,000 shares of **Dayton-Hudson** stock, joined the ranks of those urging the company to reverse its decision, declaring that "By antagonizing consumers, they're threatening the value of our investment."[2] The company capitulated, agreeing to resume its $18,000 grant to Planned Parenthood, albeit only after being assured that the money would not be used to advocate abortion.

There are several issues involved here, only the least of which is whether you are pro-choice or pro-life. More important, should the company have the right to use your money to support a pro-choice (or pro-life) organization? If not, should their stockholders make that decision? How? Should companies capitulate to economic pressures in situations such as this, if they believe it to be in their stockholders' best economic interest that they do so? Or are there other values that should transcend their stockholders' economic interests in cases such as these? Or should they avoid *any* potentially controversial issues—which would mean avoiding a lot of worthwhile, but controversial charities?

This is not an easy matter. Suppose the charity wasn't Planned Parenthood but a civil rights group and the issue wasn't advocacy of abortion rights but advocacy of affirmative action. Would that matter? Honorable men may differ on a variety of issues. Should the company decide for them, with their money? If so, how?

American Telephone and Telegraph Company (NYSE—T) found itself in a situation similar to the one which confronted **Dayton-Hudson**. It also was a supporter of Planned Parenthood and was targeted by the Christian Action Council. The company withdrew its support and then was picketed by several dozen pro-choice protesters. Unlike **Dayton-Hudson**, however, **American Telephone** did not renew its support of Planned Parenthood despite opposition by individual and institutional investors. (Trustees of the New York City Employees' Retirement System, which owned three million shares of **American Telephone** stock, for instance, wrote to the company to express the fact that they were "deeply disturbed" by the company's action.)[3]

Through it all, the company held firm. Robert E. Allen,

chairman and chief executive officer, explained the company's position as follows: "Much to our regret, Planned Parenthood has raised the level of their political advocacy with respect to abortion. . . . Our contribution to a specific segment of Planned Parenthood has become tainted and tarnished with a number of our constituencies because their actions were interpreted as being in favor of a pro-abortion stance. That is not an issue on which this corporation ought to come down either one way or another."[4]

What all of this means is that if you truly do see yourself as a socially responsible investor and you believe that generous charitable contributions by corporations are desirable, you still shouldn't just settle for investing in the stocks of those companies that contribute a lot and let it go at that. It really is incumbent upon you to try to determine *what* it is that they are contributing to, so that you can be sure that the charities being supported are ones that you want to support too.

On average, corporate giving as a percent of pre-tax profits has been declining since 1985, when it peaked at almost 2%. Since then, it has declined annually to 1.6% in 1988, the last year for which data were available.

Within that context, we might call attention to the activities of some unusually charitable companies:

Cummins Engine Company, Inc. (NYSE—CUM) won the Council on Economic Priorities 1990 Corporate Conscience Award for Charitable Giving. The company budgets 5% of its average domestic pre-tax profits for charity. Recipients have included groups that assist poor and dispossessed people. In Columbus, Indiana, where the company is based, **Cummins** helped to found a day-care center for the elderly and a homeless shelter.

Tasty Baking Company (ASE-TBC), another 1990 nominee of the Council on Economic Priorities for its Corporate Conscience Award for Charitable Giving, contributes at least 5% of its pre-tax income to charity, in cash alone. In addition, the company makes considerable donations of its baked goods to food banks, churches, and youth groups in Philadelphia.

Anheuser-Busch Companies, Inc. (NYSE—BUD) contributes more than 2% of its pre-tax income annually to charities, focusing its efforts in the areas it knows the most about. It is a major supporter of *Students Against Drunk Driving (SADD)* and *Mothers Against Drunk Driving (MADD)*. **Ben & Jerry's Homemade, Inc.** (OTC-BJICA), received the Council on Economic Priorities 1988 Corporate Conscience Award for Charitable Giving and contributes 7.5% of its pre-tax income to charity.

Other companies that historically have contributed generously to charities include **American Express Company** (NYSE—AXP), **Colgate-Palmolive Company** (NYSE—CL), **Adolph Coors Company** (OTC-ACCOB), **Digital Equipment Corporation** (NYSE—DEC), **H. B. Fuller Company** (OTC-FULL), **General Mills, Inc.** (NYSE—GIS), **International Business Machines Corporation** (NYSE—IBM), **McCormick & Company, Inc.** (OTC-MCCRK), **McDonnell Douglas Corporation** (NYSE—MD), **Noxell Corporation** (OTC-NOXL), **J. C. Penney Company, Inc.** (NYSE—JCP), **Polaroid Corporation** (NYSE—PRD), **Proctor & Gamble Company** (NYSE—PG), **Sara Lee Corporation** (NYSE—SLE), and **Xerox Corporation** (NYSE—XRX).

DEFENSE AND ARMAMENTS

A substantial number of socially responsible investors object to investing in companies that contribute to our defense effort, either through the manufacture and sale of armaments or through the sale of any goods at all (even food and clothing) to the U.S. Department of Defense. Indeed, there are those who even refuse to purchase general obligations of the U.S. Government because much of the money borrowed by the Government through the sale of bills, notes, and bonds is used to support our military effort; these investors frequently invest instead in the debt instruments of the **Federal National Mortgage Association,** the **Federal Home Loan Bank**, or the **Student Loan Marketing Association** so that they may be assured that the money that they are lending to the U.S. Government will only be used to support education or housing, not defense.

Some of those who originally took this position were avowed Marxists, who honestly believed that in the post-World War II

Cold War period, the West was mostly in the wrong and the Communist bloc mostly in the right. They thought that the peoples' republics of the Communist bloc were truly peace-loving while the Western capitalistic nations were the real warmongers. Given those misconceptions, they saw the United States as a major threat to world peace and, consistent with that view, they objected to supporting our military establishment.

Others adopted only a slightly less unrealistic attitude: They didn't think we were any more dangerous than the Russians or the Chinese but they didn't think we were any less threatening either. Totally ignoring the realities of the post-war world, their attitude might be summed up in the phrase: "A plague on both your houses."

Then there were the true pacifists, who believed that if you took guns away from people, they wouldn't fight any more. Placing the cart solidly before the horse, they argued that guns kill people, not that *people* with guns kill people.

In the face of the collapse of the Communist bloc and the desperate plea of its people for freedom, capitalism, and democracy, these charades were impossible to sustain and all the old reasons given for opposing military support went by the boards. After all, it was tough to argue any longer that the United States, not the Communists, were the threat to world peace when even the Gorbachevs and Yeltsins as much as admitted the opposite. It was even hard to argue for any kind of moral equivalence between the two.

But then the argument was turned on its head. The same people who had maintained that we ought not support our military establishment because we were the bad guys, suddenly argued that we shouldn't support it because the Communist threat was no longer there (i.e., that we *had* been the good guys after all but that now that the bad guys had given up, we no longer needed so strong a military capability).

Maybe this time they were right.

But what about Saddam Hussein? Or Muammar Khadafi? Or whoever might come after them?

In a way, we think it somewhat ingenuous to suppose that maintenance of a strong military establishment by the United

States is not desirable but, if that is how you feel, either because you think it is not necessary for our security or world peace, or even if you think it is necessary but just not as essential as housing or education (or cancer research or welfare), then, by all means, you have a right to that opinion. If you do feel that way, there are a number of companies you ought to avoid.

For starters, you probably should avoid investing in the stocks of the country's largest defense contractors. In 1989, these were the 25 with the largest dollar contracts with the United States Department of Defense:

1. McDonnell Douglas Corporation (NYSE—MD)
2. General Dynamics Corporation (NYSE—GD)
3. General Electric Company (NYSE—GE)
4. Raytheon Company (NYSE—RTN)
5. General Motors Corporation (NYSE—GM)
6. Lockheed Corporation (NYSE—LK)
7. United Technologies Corporation (NYSE—UTX)
8. Martin Marietta Corporation (NYSE—ML)
9. Boeing Company (NYSE—BA)
10. Grumman Corporation (NYSE—GQ)
11. GTE Corporation (NYSE—GTE)
12. Rockwell International Corporation (NYSE-ROK)
13. Westinghouse Electric Corporation (NSE-WX)
14. Honeywell Inc. (NYSE—HON)
15. Litton Industries Inc. (NYSE—LIT)
16. International Business Machines Corporation (NYSE—IBM)
17. TRW, Inc. (NYSE—TRW)
18. Unisys Corporation (NYSE—UIS)
19. ITT Corporation (NYSE—ITT)
20. Texas Instruments, Inc. (NYSE—TXN)
21. Tenneco, Inc. (NYSE—TGT)

22. Textron, Inc. (NYSE—TXT)

23. Allied-Signal Inc. (NYSE—ALD)

24. Avondale Industries, Inc. (OTC-AVDL)

25. FMC Corporation (NYSE—FMC)

If you're an *avoidance* investor, these are some of the companies you'll want to avoid. But there may be others too, depending on where *you* choose to draw the line for yourself. You might want to avoid the 50 largest defense contractors or the top 100 or any company doing, say, more than $10 million or $100 million worth of military business. Or maybe you'll just want to avoid companies that do any military business at all.

You might also make the test one of the *significance* of military business to the company involved, eliminating any that derive more than, say 5% or 10% of sales or profits from the military. Or you might want your standards to be some combination of the two, say companies that derive more than 5% of their revenues or profits from defense business *and/or* have $10 million worth or more of such business.

You'll also want to decide just what you mean by "defense business." Do you mean just distinctively military goods such as guns, tanks, planes, or ammunition, marketed by companies such as **Boeing, Lockheed**, or **McDonnell Douglas?** Or would you also include companies like **Philip Morris** which did rank among the top 100 defense contractors among publicly owned corporations in 1989, although what it sold to the military was the same kind of products (cigarettes and foodstuffs) that are standard civilian fare? Only you can draw those lines in the way that makes the most sense for you.

Suppose, however, that you see yourself as an *alternative* investor, rather than an *avoidance* investor? Are there any particular companies in which you might invest?

One such company might be **Ben & Jerry's Homemade, Inc.** (OTCF-BJICA), which we discussed earlier in this book. This company, one of the most socially responsible of any in the nation by conventional standards, started the *1% for Peace* program. This organization lobbies for 1% of the U.S. defense budget to be diverted to the funding of social programs.

What if you are an *activist* investor? Here there is a good deal you can do to make your feelings known. In 1990, for example, resolutions were introduced at three companies that are largely dependent on military business, urging them to report the following items to shareholders: the capacity of employees to transfer their skills to civilian production; the company's policies for diversification away from military and toward commercial business; and corporate plans for identifying new commercial markets and products. Shareholder votes cast in favor of these "conversion" resolutions amounted to 2.5% at **United Technologies Corporation** (NYSE—UTX), 6.0% at **Motorola, Inc.** (NYSE—MOT), and 8.1% at **Textron, Inc.** (NYSE—TXT).

Resolutions were also filed at **General Motors** and **Honeywell**, urging those companies' managements to report to shareholders regarding their efforts in developing space weapons. Those resolutions received more than 5% of the votes cast at both companies. More than 7% of stockholders also voted to urge **EG&G Inc.** (NYSE—EGG) to establish a special committee to evaluate that company's nuclear weapons operations. And a shareholder proposal asking **General Electric Company** (NYSE—GE), which manufactures neutron "triggers" for weapons (as well as nuclear fuels for commercial power plants), received a little more than 6% of votes cast at that company's 1990 annual meeting.

The main thrust of many of those resolutions was that companies shouldn't just get out of the defense business by laying off workers and shutting down plants. Rather, they should convert those plants and retrain those workers to produce civilian goods and services that would enhance the quality of life. Or as Valerie Heinonen, director of ICCR Programs Against Militarism at the Interfaith Center on Corporate Responsibility, said, "While corporate managers and scientists play the high-tech war games of the Star Wars program, they waste money that could be spent for housing, job training and education. Religious investors agree with more than 7,000 scientists nationwide who have called Star Wars misguided and destabilizing."[5]

Many defense companies, however, including **Boeing**, **McDonnell Douglas**, **Lockheed**, **Grumman**, **General Dynamics**, and **Northrop**, have tried to convert to non-defense businesses in the past, but with little success. **Boeing**, for instance, failed in its attempt to build subway cars. **Grumman** couldn't make it in minivans, buses, or solar power systems. And **McDonnell Douglas** lost money in the computer services business.

Nor has this just been a matter of random bad luck: There is a basic difference between succeeding at government defense work and succeeding in civilian commercial businesses. In the former situation, huge bureaucracies have been developed over time to market to just one customer, the U.S. Defense Department, while in the latter, companies must develop the flexibility to market to many prospective customers at once. According to Murray Weidenbaum, director of the Center for the Study of American Business at Washington University, the reason that it is so difficult for defense companies to convert to civilian business is that those companies are

> very good at what they are set up to do: design and produce state-of-the-art weapons and related civilian aircraft . . . but are woefully ignorant of the basics of commercial business: products, production methods, advertising and distribution, financial arrangements, funding of research and development and dealing with demanding customers.[6]

To be sure, many of these companies would *like* to expand somewhat into civilian business (if only to cushion the cyclical swings in their defense businesses), but for the most part, they don't see total conversion as economically feasible. Thus, **Boeing,** for instance, hopes eventually to apply its satellite-killing laser technology to the design of medical lasers to destroy cancer cells while the **Hughes Aircraft** subsidiary of **General Motors,** hopes to reduce its defense-to-commercial ratio from the current 80–20 to 60–40 by the mid-1990s. But in both cases, that would still mean that the majority of **Hughes'** and **Boeing's** businesses would still be defense related.

Many defense company executives are even more outspoken in their skepticism regarding the ultimate possibility of their total conversion from military to civilian business. John O'Brien, chairman of **Grumman**, for one, has said: "It's a waste of money, a concept that won't work. Employees can be retrained to produce cars or buses or trucks, but where's the market for these product?"[7] Thomas L. Phillips, chairman of **Raytheon**, has said "You can't just start with a bunch of people who have done nothing but compete in the military market for 30 years and sprinkle holy water on them."[8] And Kent Kresa, chief executive of **Northrop**, has taken the same position arguing that "We are principally a defense contractor and we are in the business to stay."[9]

NORTHERN IRELAND AND THE *MACBRIDE PRINCIPLES*

Neither as well known as the *Sullivan Principles* (on South Africa) nor the *Valdez Principles* (on the environment), the *MacBride Principles* nonetheless are at least as important to those socially responsible investors who are concerned with finding a peaceful solution to the conflict between Protestants and Catholics in Northern Ireland. In the opinion of many, years of employment discrimination against the Catholic minority by the Protestant majority was one of the major underlying causes of the conflict. It was that conviction on the parts of Sean MacBride (the Catholic founder of Amnesty International and winner of the Nobel Peace Prize), John Robb (a Northern Ireland Protestant surgeon), Inez McCormack (a Protestant former director of the Fair Employment Agency), and Father Brian Brady (a Catholic civil rights activist) that prompted them to issue the following statement (which has come to be known as the *MacBride Principles*) in 1984:

> In light of decreasing employment opportunities in Northern Ireland and on a global scale and in order to guarantee equal access to regional employment, we propose the following equal opportunity/affirmative action principles:
>
> **1.** Increasing the representation of individuals from underrepresented religious groups in the work force including managerial, supervisory, administrative, clerical and technical jobs.
> **2.** Adequate security for the protection of minority employees both at the workplace and while traveling to and from work.

3. The banning of provocative religious or political emblems from the workplace.
4. All job openings should be publicly advertised and special recruitment efforts should be made to attract applicants from underrepresented religious groups.
5. Layoff, recall and termination procedures should not, in practice, favor particular religious groupings.
6. The abolition of job reservations, apprenticeship restrictions, and differential employment criteria, which discriminate on the basis of religion or ethnic origin.
7. The development of training programs that will prepare substantial numbers of current minority employees for skilled jobs, including the expansion of existing programs and the creation of new programs to train, upgrade and improve the skills of minority employees.
8. The establishment of procedures to assess, identify and actively recruit minority employees with potential for further advancement.
9. The appointment of a senior management staff member to oversee the company's affirmative action efforts and the setting up of timetables to carry out affirmative action principles.[10]

Between 1984 and 1990, 12 states and 25 cities in the United States passed legislation linking their investments and/or their purchases of goods to a company's equal employment record in Northern Ireland. Similar legislation was pending in 13 other states by the end of that period.

In 1990, resolutions were introduced at several corporations urging them to subscribe to these principles. Some of those companies and the percentage of votes cast at each that those resolutions received were:

Baker Hughes, Inc. (NYSE—BHI)	9.9%
Dun & Bradstreet Corporation (NYSE—DNB)	12.5%
Exxon Corporation (NYSE—XON)	5.7%
International Business Machines Corporation (NYSE—IBM)	11.7%
Marsh & McClennan Corporation (NYSE—MMC)	8.8%
McDonnell Douglas Corporation (NYSE—MD)	6.3%
Minnesota Mining & Manufacturing Company (NYSE—MMM)	4.4%

Mobil Corporation (NYSE—MOB)	10.6%
NCR Corporation (NYSE—NCR)	7.9%
Unisys Corporation (NYSE—UIS)	14.0%
Xerox Corporation (NYSE—XRX)	11.5%

———————

Thus ends Part Two where we have discussed a variety of specific issues of concern to socially responsible investors. In Part Three we will deal with the practical question of how you might actually go about implementing your own socially responsible investing program, either by investing in socially responsible mutual funds, retaining an independent socially responsible investment advisor, or doing it all on your own.

INVESTMENTS

13

Socially Responsible Mutual Funds and Investment Advisers

THE CASE FOR MUTUAL FUNDS

There are several means by which socially responsible investors might seek to put their principles into practice: (1) they might do their own financial and social research and invest on their own, perhaps with the assistance of a good broker who also shares their social values; (2) they might delegate the responsibility to an investment adviser with experience and expertise in socially responsible investing; or (3) they might purchase the shares of one or another of the socially responsible mutual funds. Of these three approaches, the third is probably the easiest, most economical, and most commonly utilized by individual investors for several reasons:

1. Investing in mutual funds enables investors to benefit from the economies of scale that result from the pooling of their assets with those of other like-minded investors (e.g., lower commissions on volume transactions, the spreading of research costs among many investors, etc.).

269

2. It is a way to get professional management, not just on the financial side but also on the social responsibility side. That is, the resources available to a fund's manager to screen and evaluate companies and securities on both scores are much greater than those typically available to individual investors.

3. Investing in most mutual funds generally also provides the advantages of diversification, which tends to reduce risk relative to the investor's potential return. Most individual investors are not in a position to purchase enough different securities on their own to achieve such diversification. (Note, however, that not all funds are *diversified*. Some are *specialized* to the point of investing in just one area, and while some of them may also be attractive to investors whose interests are coincident, it is tautological that they cannot provide the benefits of comparable diversification.)

4. Finally, mutual funds usually also provide investors with greater liquidity than they could achieve through the purchase of individual securities.

However, there are also disadvantages to investing in mutual funds. For one thing, an investor in a fund generally wouldn't get the individualization or personalization of his portfolio that he might achieve by managing his assets himself or by having them managed for him in an individual account by an independent professional investment adviser. Such an investor, for example, might be opposed to the proliferation of nuclear energy and weapons systems but might not, necessarily, favor disinvestment from South Africa. If he were to purchase shares in the **Calvert Social Investment Fund** he would, indeed, avoid investments in companies with significant nuclear or military capabilities but he'd also be precluded from all South African investments, even though that didn't matter to him, because that fund simply doesn't invest in companies doing business in South Africa either.

Or an investor might be anti-tobacco and anti-alcohol, but not necessarily anti-gambling. Too bad. Most funds which avoid tobacco and distilling companies don't invest in gambling casinos either, so if he wanted to use mutual funds to avoid the one (or two), he'd just have to avoid all three. Suppose there were specific other issues such as abortion, the importation of coffee beans from El Salvador, corporate charitable contributions, or the marketing of infant formula that really were important to him; it might be just a matter of luck whether or not the particular socially responsible fund in which he chose to invest cared about those specific issues too.

If you are considering the purchase of shares of a socially responsible mutual fund, however, the first thing you ought do is answer the following questions to your own satisfaction:

What Are Your Financial Investment Objectives?

Different funds have different investment objectives, ranging from very conservative preservation of capital to aggressive growth. It really does not make sense for you to invest in one whose goals are significantly different from your own, no matter how well it is managed. That would be like retaining a wonderful interior decorator who specialized in French Provincial furnishings to redecorate your home, when your own taste ran to ultramodern. He might do a fine professional job, but it just wouldn't work for you.

Therefore, the first thing you should think about is what your own goals are. Are you most concerned with preserving the capital you already have and generating an income from it with minimal risk? Or would you prefer to defer current income and accept a reasonable amount of risk in seeking long-term capital appreciation? Are you willing to accept an even higher level of risk in order to have a shot at even bigger returns? Or do you want something in between—perhaps a combination of current income and some capital appreciation potential?

In considering this question you should take into account your overall financial position, your obligations, your age, and your psychological make-up. Are you relatively young, single, perhaps, or married without children, and with no or few immediate pressing financial obligations? In that case, it might make sense for you to incur a relatively high level of risk in order to seek above average returns. After all, if you lose, you'll still have a lifetime in which to recover and no one would have to suffer as an immediate consequence.

Or are you in your middle years, with family responsibilities, paying off a mortgage, perhaps, or providing for your children's college educations, but with adequate personal insurance, a savings safety net, a secure job and several years of productive employment still ahead of you? If so, you might not want to *shoot the moon* in a high-risk investment venture, but you probably could afford to forgo current income for the chance of seeing your assets grow before your ultimate retirement.

Or are you already at or near retirement age with most or all of your productive earnings years behind you? In that event, you probably would want to ensure that the assets you've worked a lifetime to accumulate aren't lost in the stock market and that they are invested to generate the highest current return possible for you at minimal risk, because that's what you're going to need to live on. You might not be able to afford the risk of much equity ownership and might be better advised to concentrate on investments that emphasize the preservation of capital and the generation of current income.

Of course, in all of these instances, it is equally, if not even more, important to know just who *you* are and what *you're* comfortable with. Even if you're young and can afford it financially, it wouldn't make sense for you to invest in a particularly risky fashion if that would cause you many sleepless nights. However, if you really are a risk-taker by nature, you might want to incur somewhat greater risk with your money, even in your later years, than the standard retirement manuals and guidebooks recommend, since it is *your* life and that's what will make *you* happy.

Which Fund or Funds Are Designed to Help You Achieve Your Particular Goals?

Once you've decided what *your* goals are, you still have to find the right fund to help you achieve them. Fortunately, there are both more and less risky mutual funds (and that includes socially responsible mutual funds) structured to achieve each of these objectives and there is a good chance that you can find one that is suitable for you. In general, these funds might be classified as follows:

1. *Income Funds* include bond funds and money market funds whose primary concerns are current income and preservation of capital. Examples of such socially responsible funds would be **Working Assets Money Fund**, the nation's largest socially responsible money market fund which limits its investments to only the highest quality short-term money market instruments; **Calvert Social Investment Fund's** *Money Market Portfolio* which also invests only in short-term high-grade money market instruments; and **Calvert's** *Bond Portfolio* which invests in a variety of fixed-income securities of varying durations.

2. *Capital Appreciation* or *Growth Funds* generally invest in common stocks and other equity equivalents. Several socially responsible mutual funds fall into this category including **Calvert Social Investment Fund's** *Equity Portfolio*, **Calvert-Ariel Growth Fund**, **Dreyfus Third Century Fund**, **New Alternatives Fund**, and **Parnassus Fund**. All of these funds adhere to some socially responsible criteria and all of them hold capital appreciation or growth as their primary objectives.

3. *Balanced Funds* have goals that are a combination of capital appreciation and income and generally seek to achieve those dual objectives through a combination of investments in cash equivalents, fixed-income securities, and equities. If you are interested in such a combination of growth potential and current income, you might consider a fund such as **Calvert's** *Managed Growth Portfolio* which invests in cash equivalents, fixed-income securities, and equities, although in no fixed predetermined proportion. Or you might consider **Pax World Fund** whose primary objective is income and conservation of principal but whose secondary objective is long-term growth of capital. **Pax World Fund** attempts to maintain a balance of investments with about 70% in equities and 30% in fixed-income securities.

What Is the Fund's Particular Style of Management?

It is not enough, however, just to know whether a fund is of the income, balanced, or growth type, for there are important differences among funds even within those categories. In the growth category, for instance, **Calvert-Ariel Growth Fund** is especially aggressive, investing primarily in smaller, relatively unknown companies with annual sales of only $100 to $200 million. **New Alternatives Fund** is relatively aggressive too, but in a different fashion. Although it commits at least 75% of its assets to companies listed on the New York or American stock exchange, it also concentrates at least 25% of its investments in companies in the solar or alternative energy industries.

Indeed, a major difference among funds is that while most, such as **Dreyfus Third Century Fund** or **Pax World Fund**, are *diversified*, some, such as **New Alternatives Fund**, are *concentrated*, and others, such as **Freedom Enviromental Fund**, are *specialized*.

At one end of the spectrum are the *index funds*, which are diversified to the point of seeking to replicate the popular market averages as closely as possible. In a real sense, of course, indexing is inconsistent with socially responsible investing (or any other kind of *active* investing, for that matter) since indexing entails buying everything (or proxies for everything) and socially responsible investing (or any other form of active investing) entails being selective in avoiding certain issues or purchasing others. But within limits, even index funds can accommodate the needs of some socially responsible investors. Calpers, after all, has been able to structure an index fund that excludes all companies doing business in South Africa and does not seem to have suffered from its actions.

Most socially responsible funds are not index funds, of course, but they are *diversified*, which means that they invest in a large number of different industries. True, most exclude one or more economic sectors, say defense contractors or tobacco companies or companies with ownership interests in South Africa, but they do invest in enough different areas that they can still manage to achieve the benefits of diversification for their shareholders.

Some funds including socially responsible ones are *concentrated*, which means that while they are generally *diversified*, they do emphasize certain sectors. **New Alternatives Fund**, for instance, concentrates at least 25% of its assets in the solar and alternative energy area. Even this seldom prevents investors from realizing most of the benefits of portfolio diversification.

At the opposite extreme from the *index* funds, however, are the *specialized* funds which make little, if any, attempt at diversification. These funds make a conscious effort to concentrate their assets in just one area, say pollution control companies or high technology stocks, and they are willing to trade off the benefits of diversification for the chance of realizing the bigger potential score that may come from exclusive concentration in just one sector. In effect, they have put all their eggs in one basket because they believe it is the best basket to carry eggs in and they watch that basket very closely.

In 1989 and 1990, with the explosive worldwide development of interest in environmentalism, a number of specialized environmental funds were launched. Most of those really weren't socially responsible funds in that they did not establish social criteria for the selection of portfolio investments; rather, they were structured to capitalize on investments in companies that might benefit from legal or economic changes produced by the environmental movement, whether or not those particular companies were or were not socially responsible in their own right. Nevertheless, some of these funds may also be of serendipitous interest to some socially responsible investors.

Less aggressive than **Calvert-Ariel Growth Fund** but still a growth fund in its own right is **Calvert Social Investment Fund's** *Equity Portfolio* which is described as "neither speculative nor conservative in its investment policies."[1] Where **Calvert-Ariel** looks for relatively unknown companies, **Calvert's** *Equity Portfolio* tends to own the stocks of major listed big capitalization companies. As of year-end 1989, its 10 largest holdings were all listed on the New York Stock Exchange. **Dreyfus Third Century Fund** also tends to purchase larger, big capitalization (albeit not necessarily listed) companies.

You should also find out how a particular fund actually goes about making its investments in order to be sure that you are personally comfortable with its methodology. Is it very fundamentalist in its approach, such as **Parnassus Fund** which prides itself on following a *contrarian* strategy in the footsteps of Benjamin Graham and utilizing a whole array of very rigid mathematical screens and filters? Or is it more freeform in its approach like **Pax World Fund** with fewer rigid guidelines?

Is stock selection all in the hands of one man, such as Jerome Dodson at **Parnassus Fund**? Or is there more of a committee system? Is the entire investment decision-making process delegated to a sub-adviser, as **Dreyfus Corporation**, investment adviser to the **Dreyfus Third Century Fund** now does with **Tiffany Capital Advisors, Inc.** or as **Calvert Asset Management Company, Inc.**, investment adviser to the **Calvert Social Responsibility Fund** does with **U.S. Trust Company of Boston**? And what is the actual background and experience of those responsible for the fund's management? **Dreyfus Corporation** and **U.S. Trust Company of Boston** have been around for decades and have managed billions of dollars for investors; other advisers, however, have much shorter histories and more limited records.

How Has the Fund Actually Performed Over Time?

This is a bottom-line question: When all is said and done, has the fund in which you are considering investing outperformed or underperformed comparable funds over time? In answering this question, however, it is not enough just to see how much the fund in question appreciated or depreciated in its latest quarter or the latest year and how that compared to the Standard & Poor's 500 Index or the Dow Jones Industrial Average. Rather, it is really essential to examine performance over as long a period as possible in order to determine how the fund actually has performed over a full market cycle and under differing conditions.

It is also important to remember that there are two, not one, dimensions to performance measurement. *Reward*, on which investors usually focus, is important but it is only half the equation; *risk* is the other, and equally important, half.

Measuring *reward* is easy—just add dividend or interest income to realized and unrealized appreciation and depreciation and you've got total return, that's it. But measuring *risk* is much tougher, raising all sorts of practical and abstract problems. Generally, however, variability in rates of return has been regarded as a reasonable proxy for *risk*; and this is something you ought to look at, too.

All that this really means, of course, is that a fund whose returns are volatile is riskier than one that does not fluctuate widely, even if their overall average returns are comparable. Ignoring dividend and interest income, if *Fund A*, for example, appreciates 40% one year and declines 10% the next it will have grown by 26% over the two-year period, generating a compound rate of return of just about 13% annually. If *Fund B* appreciates 14% one year and 10% the next it will also have grown by about 26% over the two-year period, producing about the same 13% average annual compound rate of return. But clearly *Fund A* was the riskier holding and, all other things being equal, most investors would prefer to own *Fund B*, the much less risky investment vehicle which provided just as good an overall return.

Finally, in comparing the performance of different mutual funds, it is important that you not fall into the trap of comparing apples to oranges. Certainly it makes no sense to compare the income, appreciation, total return, or variability of rate of return of a bond fund with that of an equity fund—they have different goals and styles and invest in different types of securities so that major differences in results are to be expected. However, it certainly is legitimate for you to compare the yield over time of one money market fund with that of another, or the total return of one bond fund with that of another, or the variability and total return of one aggressive growth fund with that of another. We urge you to do that.

What Are the Fund's Social Criteria and How Do They Square with Your Own?

Finally, you must decide which social issues are important to you and which are not, and then find a fund whose values accord closely with your own. Remember that just as there are huge differences in values among socially responsible investors, there are also large differences in the social criteria adhered to by different socially responsible funds. So it's important that you find one that's right for you.

If, for example, one of your major concerns is to avoid South African investments, most socially responsible mutual funds will meet your requirement—but **Pax World Fund** wouldn't because it hasn't adopted any standards in that area. If you are opposed to smoking, drinking, or gambling, you might consider investing in **Parnassus Fund** or **Pax World Fund**, but an investment in **Dreyfus Third Century Fund**, any of the **Calvert** funds or **Working Assets Money Fund** wouldn't make sense for you because they don't have those restrictions. The **Calvert** funds won't buy companies in the nuclear or weapons businesses, but **Dreyfus Third Century Fund** will.

Still, if you are considering going the mutual fund route, there are several socially responsible funds you should look at. They include:

> **Calvert Social Investment Fund** (including the *Money Market, Managed Growth, Equity* and *Bond Portfolios*)
>
> **Calvert-Ariel Growth Fund**
>
> **Dreyfus Third Century Fund, Inc.**
>
> **New Alternatives Fund, Inc.**
>
> **Parnassus Fund**
>
> **Pax World Fund Incorporated**
>
> **Working Assets Money Fund**

The following brief descriptions of these funds may assist you in making these decisions.

CALVERT SOCIAL INVESTMENT FUND

1700 Pennsylvania Avenue, N.W.
Washington, DC 20006
Telephone: (800) 368-2748 or
    (301) 951-4820

Calvert Social Investment Fund was founded in 1982. By 1990, it had over $270 million in assets, making it the largest of all socially responsible fund groups by a wide margin. The Fund's principal underwriter is **Calvert Securities Corporation**.

This is the only socially responsible mutual fund offering a choice of four different investment portfolios: (1) the *Money Market Portfolio*, (2) the *Managed Growth Portfolio*, (3) the *Equity Portfolio*, and (4) the *Bond Portfolio*. All of the portfolios are managed by **Calvert Asset Management Company, Inc.**, the investment adviser to the fund, in a manner consistent with **Calvert's** belief that long-term rewards to investors will come from those organizations whose products, services, and methods enhance the human condition and the traditional American values of individual initiative, equality of opportunity, and cooperative effort.

To that end, **Calvert** seeks to invest in companies that meet the following criteria:

1. They deliver safe products and services in ways that sustain our natural environment.
2. They are managed with participation throughout the organizations in defining and achieving objectives.
3. They negotiate fairly with workers, providing environments supportive of their wellness.
4. They do not discriminate on the bases of race, sex, religion, age, ethnic origin, or sexual orientation; they do not consistently violate regulations of the Equal Employment Opportunity Commission; and they provide opportunities for women, disadvantaged minorities, and others for whom equal opportunities often have been denied.
5. They foster awareness of commitments to human goals, such as creativity, productivity, self-respect, and responsibility within the organization and the world and they continually create contexts within which those goals may be realized.
6. They do not produce nuclear energy or manufacture equipment to produce nuclear energy.
7. They do not do business with South Africa (including franchising or licensing agreements) or other repressive regimes. (**Calvert** prides itself on having been the first fund to have taken a position on divestment from South

Africa and to have offered a South Africa-free investment to mutual fund shareholders.)

8. They do not manufacture weapons systems.

9. They do not manufacture alcoholic beverages.

10. They do not manufacture tobacco products.

11. They do not operate gambling casinos.

Calvert Asset Management Company selects individual investments for the *Money Market Portfolio,* **U.S. Trust Company of
Boston** is a sub-adviser to **Calvert Social Investment Fund** and
selects the specific investments for the *Managed Growth, Bond*
and *Equity Portfolios*. It also applies the social screens for all the
Calvert portfolios.

U.S. Trust pioneered the concept and practice of social investing and has managed socially screened portfolios since 1974. In
1990, it had over $1.2 billion in assets under management, includ-
ing over $400 million in socially responsible accounts. It also
provides technical assistance to advocacy groups such as the
Tobacco Divestment Project and the African National Congress.

All potential investments are first screened for financial
soundness and then evaluated according to the fund's social criteria. To the greatest possible extent, investments are made in
companies which, in managements' opinion, exhibit unusual positive accomplishments with respect to one or more of the criteria
but companies must also meet the fund's minimum standards for
all the criteria. With respect to government securities, the Fund
attempts to invest primarily in debt obligations issued or guaranteed by agencies or instrumentalities of the Federal Government
whose purposes further or are compatible with the fund's social
criteria, such as obligations of the **Student Loan Marketing Association**, rather than general obligations of the Federal Government, such as Treasury securities.

Calvert doesn't only attempt to manage the assets in the funds
entrusted to it in a socially responsible manner; it also seeks to
promote positive social goods within its own organization and in
the community and world around it. Thus, the company has made
a point of converting to the use of recycled paper and eliminated

the use of plastic wrappings in mailing prospectuses. **Calvert** was also cited by *Good Housekeeping* as one of the best companies employing working mothers.

Sales charges on the *Managed Growth, Equity* and *Bond Portfolios* are a maximum of 4.5%; there is no sales charge on the *Money Market Portfolio*. Management fees may range from a maximum of 0.7% of the *Managed Growth* and *Equity Portfolios* to 0.65% of the *Bond Portfolio* and 0.5% of the *Money Market Portfolio*. The minimum initial investment in any of the portfolios is $1,000 (except in the case of certain retirement plans where it may be less); subsequent investments of $250 or more may be made at any time.

Managed Growth Portfolio

Calvert's flagship fund, the *Managed Growth Portfolio*, was founded on October 21, 1982. By year-end 1989, it had nearly 25,000 shareholders and assets under management exceeding $220 million.

The objective of the *Managed Growth Portfolio* is to achieve a total return above the rate of inflation through an actively managed, diversified portfolio of common and preferred stocks, bonds, and money market instruments that offer income and capital growth opportunity and satisfy the social criteria established by the **Calvert Fund.**

From its inception through December 31, 1989, the *Managed Growth Portfolio's* average annual total return was 14.13%. After deducting sales charges, the return was 13.40%.

Annual returns in each of the five years 1984 to 1989 were 18.72% in 1989, 10.73% in 1988, 4.97% in 1987, 18.11% in 1986, and 26.85% in 1985.

As of year-end 1989, the fund's total assets approximated $222 million and its yield was 3.1%. Fixed-income securities accounted for more than half of the portfolio with the bulk of those investments in issues of the **Federal National Mortgage Association,** the **Federal Home Loan Bank Board,** and the **Student Home Loan Marketing Association.** The remaining 43% was in common stocks valued at nearly $95 million.

As of December 29, 1989, the 10 largest equity holdings in the *Managed Growth Portfolio* were:

Shares	Company	$(000)	%
105,000	Albertson's Inc. (NYSE—ABS)	5,828	2.62
45,000	Bell Atlantic Corporation (NYSE—BEL)	5,006	2.25
100,000	Illinois Tool Works, Inc. (NYSE—ITW)	4,488	2.02
100,000	Consolidated Papers, Inc. (OTC—CPER)	4,400	1.98
15,000	Washington Post Company (ASE—WPO.B)	4,223	1.90
75,000	R.H. Donnelly & Sons Company (NYSE—DNY)	3,844	1.73
75,000	Student Loan Marketing Association (NYSE—SLM)	3,600	1.62
48,000	American Information Technologies (NYSE—AIT)	3,264	1.47
75,000	Clorox Company (NYSE—CLX)	3,150	1.42
50,000	Quaker Oats Company (NYSE—OAT)	2,888	1.30

Equity Portfolio

The *Equity Portfolio* was introduced on August 30, 1987. By year-end 1989, it had 1,645 shareholders and assets of nearly $12 million.

The *Equity Portfolio* seeks growth of capital through investment in equities perceived to offer opportunities for potential capital appreciation and which satisfy **Calvert's** investment and social criteria. It normally invests at least 80% of its net assets in equity securities including common stocks, convertible securities, and preferred stocks.

In 1988, the *Equity Portfolio's* first full year of operation, it achieved a total return of 14.76%. In 1989, its total return was 27.45%.

As of December 29, 1989, the 10 largest equity positions in the *Equity Portfolio* were:

Shares	Company	$(000)	%
9,000	American Information Technologies (NYSE—AIT)	612	5.13
5,000	Bell Atlantic Corporation (NYSE—BEL)	556	4.66
7,000	Quaker Oats Company (NYSE—OAT)	404	3.39
7,000	Albertson's Inc. (NYSE—ABS)	399	3.26
7,500	Student Loan Marketing Association (NYSE—SLM)	360	3.02
7,000	R.R. Donnelly & Sons Company (NYSE—DNY)	359	3.01
7,500	Illinois Tool Works, Inc. (NYSE—ITW)	337	2.83
5,000	W.W. Grainger Inc. (NYSE—GWW)	323	2.71
10,000	Sysco Corporation (NYSE—SYY)	316	2.65
7,500	Clorox Company (NYSE—CLX)	315	2.64

Bond Portfolio

The *Bond Portfolio* was also introduced on August 30, 1987. By year-end 1989, it had 1,447 shareholders and assets of over $15 million.

The *Bond Portfolio* seeks to provide as high a level of current income as is consistent with prudent investment risk and preservation of capital through investment in bonds and other straight debt securities, selected pursuant to the fund's investment and social criteria. Under normal conditions, the *Bond Portfolio* invests at least 80% of its assets in publicly traded straight debt securities that have a rating within the four highest grades as determined by Moody's Investors Service, Inc. or Standard &

Poor's Corporation, obligations issued or guaranteed by the U.S. Government or its agencies or instrumentalities, or cash and cash equivalents.

In 1988, the *Bond Portfolio* generated a total return of 8.07%. In 1989, it returned 13.56%.

As of September 29, 1989, the 10 largest holdings of the *Bond Portfolio* were all issues of the **Federal National Mortgage Association,** the **Federal Home Loan Bank,** or the **Student Loan Marketing Association.** Together, these issues accounted for more than half of the *Bond Portfolio's* total net assets.

Money Market Portfolio

The *Money Market Portfolio* seeks to provide the highest level of current income, consistent with liquidity, safety, and stability, through investment in money market instruments, including securities issued and guaranteed by agencies of the U.S. Government and repurchase agreements with banks and brokers secured by such instruments, selected in accordance with the fund's investment and social criteria. The *Money Market Portfolio* is designed for short-term cash management and for investors who require stability of principal.

CALVERT-ARIEL GROWTH FUND

1700 Pennsylvania Avenue, N.W.
Washington DC 20006
Telephone: (800) 368-2748 or
  (301) 951-4820

Calvert-Ariel Growth Fund commenced operations on September 29, 1986. At year-end 1989, it had more than 20,000 shareholders and net assets of nearly $180 million. Like **Calvert Social Investment Fund, Calvert-Ariel Growth Fund** is managed by

Calvert Asset Management Company, Inc. and is distributed by **Calvert Securities Corporation.**

The fund's investment adviser is **Ariel Capital Management, Inc.**, a privately held minority-owned, full-service money management firm. **Ariel** provides investment advice to the fund and is responsible for the selection of its investments.

Calvert-Ariel Growth Fund seeks to provide long-term capital appreciation by investing primarily in common stocks, although it may also invest in other securities including preferred stocks. In seeking capital appreciation, the fund attempts to discover relatively unknown and undervalued companies that have demonstrated potential for growth. It seeks issuers who have experience in providing quality products or services and avoids those in cyclical or recently deregulated industries.

In particular, **Calvert-Ariel Growth Fund** seeks issues trading at price-earnings ratios of 10 or less, with low prices relative to their estimated earnings, book value, and assets. Emphasis is placed on companies with annual sales of $100 to $200 million, demonstrated annual earnings per share growth of 12% to 18%, and the potential to generate annual returns on equity of 15%.

In terms of its social criteria, the fund will not invest in issuers engaged in business in South Africa (defined as those with five or more employees or agents in that country, those with subsidiaries, affiliates, or franchises there, or those with loans to South African companies or the South African Government). In addition, the fund does not invest in companies engaged in the manufacture of weapons systems, the production of nuclear energy, or the manufacture of equipment to produce nuclear energy.

The maximum sales charge on the **Calvert-Ariel Growth Fund** is 4.5% and the management fee is 0.65% annually. The minimum initial investment is $2,000 (or less for certain retirement plans); subsequent investments may be made with as little as $250.

Annual total returns in the three fiscal years (ended November 30) 1987 to 1989 were: 25.11% in 1989, 39.93% in 1988, and 11.40% in 1987.

The 10 largest equity positions in **Calvert-Ariel Growth Fund's** portfolio as of December 29, 1989 were:

Shares	Company	$(000)	%
211,800	Clorox Company (NYSE—CLX)	8,896	4.95
274,150	Fleming Companies Inc. (NYSE—FLM)	8,259	4.59
306,600	Russell Corporation (NYSE—RML)	8,010	4.45
452,200	United Stationers Inc. (OTC—USTR)	7,235	4.02
262,700	Morrison, Inc. (OTC—MORR)	7,027	3.91
351,060	Herman Miller (OTC—MLHR)	6,933	3.86
241,600	Ecolab Inc. (NYSE—ECL)	6,886	3.83
374,400	Interface, Inc. (OTC-IFSIA)	6,646	3.70
301,800	Handleman Company (NYSE—HDL)	6,338	3.52
202,000	Angelica Corporation (NYSE—AGL)	6,136	3.41

DREYFUS THIRD CENTURY FUND, INC.

666 Old Country Road
Garden City, NY 11530
Telephone: (800) 645-6561, (718) 895-1206, or
(516) 794-5200

Originally launched in 1972, the **Dreyfus Third Century Fund** was the second explicitly socially responsible fund in the country (preceded only by the **Pax World Fund** which had been launched just two years earlier). By year-end 1989, the fund's total net assets exceeded $180 million and it had nearly 15,000 shareholders.

At its inception, the **Dreyfus Third Century Fund** was structured to invest two-thirds of its assets in companies demonstrating social commitments in four areas:

1. Protection and improvement of the environment and the proper use of natural resources.

2. Occupational health and safety.

3. Consumer protection and product purity.

4. Equal employment opportunity.

The fund's secondary focus was to invest in companies whose activities enhanced the quality of life in the United States in the aforementioned areas and which made meaningful contributions or advancements in the fields of health, transportation, housing, and education. The remaining third of the fund's portfolio assets were to be invested in such companies.

In 1985, the fund also determined not to invest in any companies that had direct operations in South Africa.

For a variety of reasons, these methodologies did not work out as effectively as the fund's management had hoped, at least not in the late 1980s, as companies that management was considering investing in grew increasingly reluctant to divulge the detailed information that the fund relied upon for its screening decisions. Also, changes in federal requirements regarding the disclosure of EEOC data and limitations on the availability of primary OSHA data exacerbated the problem. As a consequence, the fund found that its universe of potential investments was severely circumscribed and that some alterations in its operating policies, even if not in its underlying socially responsible investment philosophies, were in order.

With that in mind, in March 1990, the fund's directors proposed several changes in the fund's operations, including:

1. Thenceforth, companies were to be identified and evaluated individually, not by industry.

2. Third-party research would be employed for the first time to supplement **Dreyfus'** own research. Previously only direct **Dreyfus** research had been utilized.

3. The distinction between the "two-thirds" and the "one-third" companies would be eliminated. All companies would be reviewed and evaluated in the same manner while companies making active contributions would continue to be sought out aggressively.

4. The South African exclusion would be expanded to include any company with more than a 10% direct interest in another company operating in South Africa.

5. Tiffany Capital Advisors, Inc., a minority-owned investment manager, would be designated as a sub-adviser to the fund.

All of these changes were approved by shareholders at the fund's annual meeting on August 27, 1990. But some things weren't changed. The minimum initial investment in the fund remained at $2,500 (or less for certain retirement plans) and additional investments may still be made with as little as $100. The fund remained "no-load," which means that there is no sales charge. The annual management fee remained at 0.75%. The fund's investment manager continued to be the **Dreyfus Corporation,** which has been in the mutual fund business for nearly 40 years and which manages or administers almost $50 billion in assets for more than 1.6 million investors. The distributor is still **Dreyfus Service Corporation**, a wholly owned subsidiary of **Dreyfus Corporation**.

One can never rely with certainty on past performance in projecting probable future investment results. That is especially true when methodologies change as strikingly as they are changing at **Dreyfus Third Century Fund**. But for what it may be worth, the Fund's performance record for the five years 1985 to 1989 was: 17.34% in 1989, 23.24% in 1988, 2.60% in 1987, 4.55% in 1986, and 29.75% in 1985.

As of May 31, 1990, the 10 largest equity positions in the fund's portfolio were:

Shares	Company	$(000)	%
250,000	Astra A Free	22,898	11.70
150,000	Fed. Nat. Mortgage Association (NYSE—FNM)	5,963	3.05
200,000	Tandem Computers, Inc. (NYSE—TDM)	5,600	2.86
150,000	General Motors, Class E (NYSE—GME)	5,363	2.74

Shares	Company	$(000)	%
70,000	Dayton-Hudson Corporation (NYSE—DH)	5,294	2.71
125,000	Costco Wholesale Corporation (OTC—COST)	5,109	2.61
75,000	Sigma-Aldrich Corporation (OTC—SIAL)	4,950	2.53
100,000	Intel Corporation (OTC-INTC)	4,825	2.47
75,000	Reuters Holdings A.D.S. (OTC—RTRSY)	4,584	2.34
100,000	Pacific Telesis Group (NYSE—PAC)	4,575	2.34

NEW ALTERNATIVES FUND, INC.

295 Northern Boulevard
Great Neck, NY 11021
Telephone: (516) 466-0808

New Alternatives Fund began operations on September 3, 1982. As of year-end 1989, it had 1,400 shareholders and assets of nearly $11 million. The fund's investment manager and principal distributor is **Accrued Equities, Inc.**

The fund's primary objective is long-term growth which it seeks to achieve by investing in the solar and alternative energy industries. As it uses those terms, solar and alternative energy refer to energy sources other than petroleum or nuclear power. In implementation of that goal, the Fund concentrates at least 25% of its assets in the stocks of such companies. **New Alternatives Fund** also emphasizes companies listed on the New York or American stock exchanges and invests no more than 25% of its assets in companies that aren't listed.

Management of the fund considers itself to be "affirmatively socially responsible" and notes that "alternative energy, resource recovery, conservation—our environmentally oriented investments—are a positive form of social investment."[2] Since alternative energy technologies are intended to replace the burning of carbon-based fuels and the emissions therefrom, it believes that this, in turn, will contribute toward the reduction of both acid rain and the greenhouse effect.

In addition, the fund tries to find new areas of investment in pollution control, recycling, and clean water. It excludes investments relating to atomic energy, considering them to be unsafe and expensive because of the potential for accidents, unresolved radioactive waste disposal problems, excessive costs, and community opposition to such programs. It will not invest in companies that do business in South Africa. And, for its cash deposits, it utilizes socially conscious banks, such as Chicago's **South Shore Bank** which has long been noted for its interest in rebuilding housing for the less affluent.

The fund's maximum sales charge is 5.66% and its annual management fee is 1% (scaling down on assets above $10 million). The minimum initial investment is $2,650 (or less for qualified retirement plans) and subsequent investments may be made with at least $500.

In the five years 1985 to 1989, the fund's average annual total return, after deducting sales charges, was 16.76%. Annual total returns during that period were: 26.04% in 1989, 23.96% in 1988, 3.16% in 1987, 22.47% in 1986, and 24.03% in 1985.

As of January 31, 1990, the 10 largest equity positions of **New Alternatives Fund** were:

Shares	Company	$(000)	%
16,500	Diversified Energies, Inc. (NYSE—DEI)	561	4.78
13,000	Burlington Resources Inc. (NYSE—BR)	543	4.63
14,000	Zurn Industries, Inc. (NYSE—ZRN)	522	4.45
11,500	NICOR Inc. (NYSE—GAS)	476	4.06
35,000	AMETEK Inc. (NYSE—AME)	442	3.77
10,000	Corning Glass Works (NYSE—GLW)	425	3.62

Shares	Company	$(000)	%
14,500	Ogden Corporation (NYSE—OG)	422	3.60
11,000	Equitable Resources Inc. (NYSE—EQT)	415	3.54
20,000	Archer-Daniels-Midland Company (NYSE—ADM)	400	3.41
16,000	Wellman, Inc. (NYSE—WLM)	396	3.38

PARNASSUS FUND

244 California Street
San Francisco, CA 94111
Telephones: (800) 999-3505 or
  (415) 362-3505

Parnassus Fund was founded on December 27, 1984 by Jerome L. Dodson, a graduate of the University of California at Berkeley and the Harvard Business School. A member of the diplomatic corps in Vietnam in the late 1960s, Dodson subsequently entered the world of finance, eventually becoming president and chief executive officer of **Continental Savings and Loan Association** in California. In 1982, he founded and became the first president of **Working Assets Money Fund**, a socially responsible money market fund, and continues to serve as a trustee of that fund.

As of year-end 1989, **Parnassus Fund** had over 3,700 shareholders and its assets approximated $23 million. The fund's investment adviser and distributor is **Parnassus Financial Management**.

Parnassus Fund is a "low-load" fund with a maximum sales charge of 3.5%. The annual management fee is 1% on assets up to $10 million and scales down on amounts above that. The minimum initial investment is $2,000 ($1,000 for certain employee benefit or tax-qualified retirement plans) and additional investments may be made with as little as $100.

Parnassus Fund's primary investment objective is to achieve long-term growth of capital; current income is a secondary objective. Management of the fund attempts to do this by investing primarily in equity securities, defined as common stocks, convertible preferred stocks, convertible debentures, or warrants. The fund emphasizes the securities of large companies, defined as those that are (1) traded on the New York Stock Exchange, (2) traded on the American Stock Exchange or the NASD's National Market System and have been in business for more than 10 years and pay a dividend, and/or (3) are listed as a *Fortune 500* company. Up to 30% of the fund's assets may be invested in smaller companies that do not meet those criteria but, in general, the fund attempts not to invest in companies with annual sales below $50 million.

The fund's adviser has three basic criteria in selecting securities for the fund's portfolio:

1. *The Contrarian Principle.* The fund seeks stocks that are out of favor with the investment community and, therefore, may be undervalued. This entails searching for stocks selling at depressed prices compared to the market as a whole and their own price histories. Specifically, stocks are sought whose market prices are no more than 125% of their book values (except for smaller or high-growth companies that may sell for up to 175% of book value. Prices should also have declined to 65% or less of the highest prices at which these stocks sold over the previous five years. Price-earnings ratios should be below that of the Standard & Poor's 500 Index and the stocks' own averages of the previous 10 years. And price-sales ratios should be low relative to the market as a whole. These are intended as guidelines, not absolute limits, and a stock might be purchased even if it did not meet all of them. However, it would not be bought if it did not meet any.

2. *Financial considerations.* Companies must be financially sound and have good prospects for the future. These facts would be determined through an analysis of the company's balance sheet, a comparison of the company's current sales to its sales five years ago, an appraisal of the outlook for future earnings, an evaluation of net cash flow, and an examination of the company's earnings and dividend history for the past decade.

3. *"Renaissance factors."* Next we come to those qualitative factors which would be indicative of a company's sense of social responsibility or, as management of the **Parnassus Fund** has put it, which are reflective of "enlightened and progressive management."[3] These "renaissance factors" are:

a. the quality of a company's products and services;

b. the degree to which a company is marketing oriented and stays close to its customers;

c. the sensitivity of a company to the community in which it operates;

d. a company's treatment of its employees; and

e. a company's ability to innovate and respond well to change.

The fund usually seeks positive reasons for investing in a company, including a good environmental protection policy, an effective equal employment opportunity policy, a record of civic commitment, and a history of ethical business dealings. In addition, however, the fund will automatically exclude certain companies from its portfolio. Companies automatically screened out include:

a. Manufacturers of tobacco products.

b. Manufacturers of alcoholic beverages.

c. Companies involved with gambling.

d. Companies with operations in South Africa. (Prior to 1987, **Parnassus Fund** invested in companies that did business in South Africa if they met certain standards including adherence to the *Sullivan Principles*. Those standards included treating black and white employees equally and making social contributions to the black communities in which they operated. In 1987, however, despite some mixed emotions on the subject, the fund changed its policy to exclude all companies doing business in South Africa, in order to conform to what by then had become the accepted practice of the socially responsible investment community.)

e. Weapons contractors. (The fund does not automatically exclude all companies doing business with the Defense Department, if the products or services provided to the military are the same as those provided to civilians (e.g., toothpaste or computers.) It only chooses not to invest in companies specializing in weapons contracting that it considers an inherently unstable business which has bad effects on the economy and society.

f. Companies that generate electricity from nuclear power.

In the five years 1985 to 1989, **Parnassus Fund** achieved the following performance results: 2.84% in 1989, 42.44% in 1988, 8.01% in 1987, 2.41% in 1986, and 18.60% in 1985.

As of September 30, 1989, the 10 largest equity positions in **Parnassus Fund's** portfolio were:

Shares	Company	$(000)	%
135,000	ASK Computer Systems, Inc. (OTC—ASKI)	1,283	5.64
55,000	Tandem Computers, Inc. (NYSE—TDM)	1,265	5.56
180,000	Altos Computer Systems (OTC—ALTO)	1,215	5.34
12,500	Digital Equipment Corporation (NYSE—DEC)	1,141	5.02
19,000	Cummins Engine Company, Inc. (NYSE—CUM)	1,093	4.80
90,000	3Com Corporation (OTC—COMS)	1,091	4.80
55,000	FirstFed Michigan Corporation (OTC—FFOM)	1,073	4.72
70,000	Zenith Electronics Corporation (NYSE—ZE)	1,015	4.46
35,000	Southwest Airlines, Inc. (NYSE—LUV)	936	4.12
100,000	Advanced Micro Devices, Inc. (NYSE—AMD)	888	3.90

PAX WORLD FUND INCORPORATED

224 State Street
Portsmouth, NH 03801
Telephones: (800) 343-0529 or
  (603) 431-8022

Originally organized in 1970, **Pax World Fund** was offered to the public as the nation's first socially responsible mutual fund on August 10, 1971. By the end of 1989, it had more than 11,000 shareholders and a market value in excess of $93 million.

    Pax World Fund was founded by Anthony S. Brown, Luther E. Tyson, J. Elliott Corbett, and Paul V. Brown, Jr., all of whom remain actively involved in the fund's management: Anthony Brown is vice president, treasurer, director, and portfolio manager of the fund and an officer and director of the fund's adviser, **Pax World Management Corp.**; he is also employed as a registered representative with **Fahnstock & Co.**, members of the New York Stock Exchange. Both Tyson and Corbett are Methodist clergymen and ethicists; Tyson is president and a director of the fund while Corbett is vice president and a director and president of *Pax World Foundation*. Tyson, Corbett, and Paul Brown are also officers and directors of **Pax World Management Corp.**

    The fund pays **Pax World Management Corp.** an annual investment management fee of 0.75% of the first $25 million of the fund's net assets and 0.5% of assets over that. The fund is *no-load* which means that there is no sales charge. Minimum initial investment is only $250 and additional investments may be made with as little as $50.

    Pax World Fund is a *balanced* fund whose primary objectives are income and conservation of principal and whose secondary objective is long-term growth of capital. In seeking to achieve those goals, the fund invests about 70% of its assets in common and preferred stocks and 30% in bonds and debentures.

    It is not coincidental that the fund was launched during the Vietnam War. As Brown explains it: "We were outraged that the country was wasting boys' lives in a war that no one wanted. We decided that we could make a political statement by investing ethically."[4]

To that end, the fund was established with a mandate to limit its investments to companies that were not engaged in manufacturing defense or weapons-related products. It excluded any companies appearing on the Department of Defense's "100 Largest Defense Contractors' List" as well as any other companies deriving 5% or more of their sales from Department of Defense contracts.

Instead, the fund attempts to invest in what it refers to as "firms producing life-supportive goods and services,"[5] including companies in such industries as health care, education, pollution control, food, retail, housing, renewable energy, and leisure time. From time to time, it has invested in the securites of the **Federal National Mortgage Association** which makes mortgage loans to low and moderate income families; in bonds of the **World Bank**, a significant amount of whose profit goes to the **International Development Association** for long-term low-interest loans to poorer countries; and **Student Loan Marketing Association** bonds which provide low-interest loans to students.

In addition, **Pax World Fund** does not invest in companies in the tobacco, alcoholic beverages, or gambling industries. And in a positive way, it seeks out companies with fair employment and pollution control policies and practices, and some international development.

In the five years 1985 to 1989, **Pax World Fund** realized the following total returns: 24.81% in 1989, 11.70% in 1988, 2.49% in 1987, 8.45% in 1986, and 25.79% in 1985.

As of December 31, 1989, **Pax World Fund's** 10 largest equity positions were:

Shares	Company	$(000)	%
170,000	Brooklyn Union Gas Company (NYSE—BU)	5,461	5.87
240,000	Bay State Gas Company (NYSE—BGC)	5,460	5.87
68,000	Proctor & Gamble Company (NYSE—PG)	4,786	5.14
60,000	Merck & Company, Inc. (NYSE—MRK)	4,650	5.00

Shares	Company	$(000)	%
180,000	Peoples Energy Corporation (NYSE—PGL)	4,635	4.98
90,000	Syntex Corporation (NYSE—SYN)	4,534	4.87
40,000	Walt Disney Company (NYSE—DIS)	4,480	4.82
120,000	TECO Energy, Inc. (NYSE—TE)	3,540	3.81
100,000	Baxter International Inc. (NYSE—BAX)	2,500	2.69
40,000	Campbell Soup Company (NYSE—CPB)	2,335	2.51

WORKING ASSETS MONEY FUND

230 California Street
San Francisco, CA 94111
Telephones: (800) 533-3863 or
   (415) 989-3200

The nation's largest money market fund, **Working Assets Money Fund** was organized on November 24, 1982. As of April 27, 1990, its assets exceeded $208 million. **Working Assets Limited Partnership** is both adviser to the fund and distributor of its shares.

Working Assets seeks to generate as high a level of current income as possible, while maintaining liquidity and safety of capital. In order to accomplish that, it limits its investments (with minor exceptions) to short-term securities issued or guaranteed by agencies or instrumentalities of the U.S. Government; commercial paper issued by corporations rated A-1 by Standard & Poor's Corporation or P-1 by Moody's Investors Services; and certificates of deposit of commercial banks, thrift institutions and credit unions that are rated A-1 by Standard & Poor's or P-1 by Moody's or which, in the judgment of the fund's adviser, are of comparable quality and present minimal credit risks.

What distinguishes **Working Assets Money Fund** from most other money market funds, however, is not its high financial standards for investments; many other money market funds set equally high standards. Rather, it is the social criteria which it also applies to all of its investments. Indeed, in that sense, it almost stands alone as it appears to cover virtually all the bases of concern to socially responsible investors.

1. *Employment.* The fund attempts to purchase issues that may create jobs and develop the U.S. economy rather than those which just have the effect of rearranging assets through mergers and acquisitions. It also seeks the instruments of financial institutions that reinvest deposits in their local communities.

2. *Housing.* The fund purchases the securities of the **Federal Home Mortgage Association** and the **Federal Home Loan Bank** as well as certificates of deposit in savings and loan institutions that finance moderate-income housing.

3. *Education.* The fund invests in the securities of the **Student Loan Marketing Association** as a means to promote higher education.

4. *Family Farming.* The fund buys securities of the **Federal Farm Credit System** which finances U.S. agriculture and loans guaranteed by the **Farmers Home Administration**.

5. *Equal Employment Opportunity.* The fund does not knowingly invest in companies that discriminate on the basis of race, religion, age, disability, or sexual orientation or which consistently violate regulations of the *Equal Employment Opportunity Commission.* Conversely, it seeks to invest in the securities of firms that promote the economic advancement of women and minorities.

6. *Labor.* The fund seeks to invest in companies that bargain fairly with their employees and have policies that promote their welfare. It does not knowingly invest in companies that consistently violate regulations of the *National Labor Relations Board*, which appear on the national AFL-CIO "Do Not Patronize" list or which have a record, according to the AFL-CIO, of hiring *union-busting* consultants. It also avoids multinational companies with fewer than half their employees in the United

States, unless a majority of their eligible U.S. employees are represented by organized labor.

7. *Nuclear energy.* The fund does not invest in companies that generate nuclear power or manufacture nuclear equipment or materials.

8. *Weapons and defense.* The fund does not invest in companies whose principal business is the manufacture or distribution of weapons. Nor does it invest in U.S. Treasury securities since it believes that those securities are mainly used to finance federal budget deficits caused in part by wasteful defense spending.

9. *Repressive regimes.* The fund does not invest in companies that have a substantial presence in South Africa or other foreign nations controlled by repressive regimes, nor in companies that are part of strategic industries in such countries or assist in financing those regimes.

10. *Environmental Degradation.* The fund does not invest in companies that consistently violate regulations of the *EPA* or *OSIIA*.

11. *Small business.* The fund does seek investments such as *Small Business Administration (SBA)* guaranteed loans which finance the small business sector of the economy.

12. *Charitable contributions.* The fund seeks investments in companies that contribute generously to charities, particularly in their own communities.

13. *Capital flight.* Finally, the fund does not purchase Euro-dollar instruments because it believes these drain capital from productive use in the United States.

A LOOK AT SPECIALIZED FUNDS

One of the advantages of investing in one or another of the socially responsible mutual funds that we have commented on is that they are all *diversified* funds. To be sure, because of their social constraints, they are often forced to exclude companies in certain entire sectors of the economy (such as petroleum or defense). **New Alternatives Fund** does concentrate on stocks in the solar and alternative energy industries and **Calvert-Ariel Growth Fund** does emphasize smaller, less known companies in its portfolio. Despite all that, these funds still manage to diversify sufficiently to merit the description *diversified* and to provide investors with the risk-avoidance benefits of their diversification policies.

There are, however, two sides to this coin. It is possible that you are *not* interested in diversification (despite the value of a diversified portfolio from the strictly financial standpoint of risk-containment), but that you would prefer consciously to *concentrate* your assets in just one or two areas. You might want to do that because you are willing to incur the incremental risk of concentrating, rather than diversifying, your holdings in order to seek higher potential returns than you might reasonably expect from a truly diversified portfolio.

Or you might want to do that because your social concerns are limited to just one or two areas rather than the whole menu of social issues that some others choose to address. If that is the case, you might want to concentrate your investments in just those one or two areas for ethical, if not financial, reasons. If that is how you feel, you might want to consider investing in one of the more specialized funds that are not necessarily regarded as "socially responsible" *per se*, but which still might satisfy your needs even better than the more commonly known and more broadly diversified *ethical* funds.

In particular, you will find that there are many opportunities for you to do this in the environmental area, where a whole host of new mutual funds were launched in 1989 and 1990. In some cases, the motivation underlying their introduction may have been a cynical one: so much publicity was accorded the environmental movement that those funds were readily marketable. In other cases, it may have reflected a strictly rational economic judgment that companies in the environmental area were likely to generate above average investment returns. And in still others, it may have been due to a truly ethical concern that environmental degradation might be the most serious threat confronting not only investors but all of humanity.

Whatever the reason, however, there are now many environmental funds in which you might want to consider investing. One example would be **Freedom Environmental Fund** which completed its initial public offering in October 1989 and was valued at more than $48 million by January 31, 1990. As of that date, the fund's assets were concentrated only in the following environmentally related areas:

Environmental equipment and instruments	17.6%
Water treatment companies	16.3%
Solid waste management	15.9%
Natural gas companies	14.6%
Hazardous waste management	5.0%
Recycling companies	4.6%
Water utilities	3.8%
Waste to energy companies	2.9%
Other environmental companies	10.5%
Net cash equivalents	8.8%

WHY INVEST THROUGH INVESTMENT ADVISERS?

Certainly, there are real advantages to investing in socially responsible funds as we discussed at the beginning of this chapter, including the benefits of diversification, professional management, liquidity, and economies of scale. But there are disadvantages too and mutual funds are not for everyone. Indeed, there are those who, while aware of the benefits that mutual funds provide, still prefer to maintain their own individual accounts with independent investment advisers. Why is that?

Probably the main reason for using an independent adviser rather than a fund is for the individualization or personalization that such an approach may provide. By working directly with an adviser, you can specify exactly what your goals are and how you would like to see them implemented and you need not be bound by the lowest common denominator of all other investors in a pooled fund.

If you don't want to invest in tobacco stocks, for instance, but have no compunctions about buying distilling stocks, that's just fine. Simply instruct your adviser to that effect. Or suppose you are opposed to apartheid but want your opposition to be reflected through carefully thought-out responses to different situations rather than through knee-jerk decisions to divest or to invest in any companies that are signatories to the *Sullivan Principles*. In that case, you might ask your adviser to make situational, rather than blanket decisions based on his analysis of how individual companies actually do function in that country. As a consequence, you might invest in **Johnson & Johnson** (NYSE—JNJ) even though it has not withdrawn from South Africa because of the overall nature of its behavior there, but you might also choose not to invest in **Texaco, Inc.** (NYSE—TX) because of the manner in which it handles its interest in **Caltex** in the same country. In other words, using an investment adviser rather than a mutual fund might enable you to take a rifle shot, rather than shotgun, approach to social problems as you see them.

Since this is the biggest advantage of investing through an individual adviser, rather than through a pooled fund, however, you should make sure that you really will get this advantage. It probably wouldn't make much sense for you to use an individual adviser otherwise—if, for instance, he just pooled your assets with those of his other customers and bought the same securities for all of you anyway. If you're going to pay for individualized treatment, be sure you get what you pay for.

Another reason you might choose to use an individual adviser rather than a mutual fund is because individual advisers can often more easily buy the shares of smaller capitalization companies for their clients than could a larger fund. The biggest funds are often locked in to purchasing only big capitalization companies because of potential liquidity constraints, but that might not be a problem if your individual account were managed independently of the others under your manager's purview.

Of course, you might simply be of the opinion that the skills of the individual money manager you selected were superior to those of the fund managers available to you. And you might be willing to pay up for that.

Finally, you just might want to involve yourself in the investment process, working with your adviser, which really would not be possible for you if you invested through a fund. If such a shared responsibility is what you're looking for, an individual adviser might be right for you.

Bear in mind, however, that you generally do pay a premium for this more individualized service, in the form of higher management fees, larger minimum capital investment requirements, possibly higher commissions, and, depending on the size of your account, possibly less diversification. So be sure that this is really what you want before you opt for it.

In short, if you're just looking for a catch-all approach to socially responsible investing that covers most of the bases, such as that advocated by **Parnassus Fund** or **Working Assets Money Fund**, the individual manager approach probably isn't for you. But if you really want to concentrate in just one area or if you have some unique interests or requirements, then you should certainly consider this as an alternative investment approach.

Evaluating the relative merits of individual investment account managers is more difficult than evaluating mutual funds because, by their very nature, individual investment account managers are engaged in managing both apples and oranges— and pears and peaches and grapes as well. Indeed, they manage all different kinds of accounts which is why you are interested in them in the first place and, as a result, it's extremely difficult to compare their relative performances. But sometimes individual account managers manage pooled funds as well as individual accounts and, when they do, the performance of those pooled funds can provide you with an indication of their relative skill.

More likely though, you'll just have to make more qualitative, rather than quantitative judgments based on such considerations as: How long has the adviser been in business? What is the amount of assets under his management? Has the total amount been growing or shrinking? How large is his professional staff? How long have the specific individuals who will be managing your account been in the business? What is the manager's investment style? Is he a fundamentalist or a technician?

The Social Investment Forum publishes an excellent *Guide to*

Social Investment Services which includes a long list of socially responsible advisers and investment funds. It is available from them at a nominal price.[6]

Four money managers who handle individual accounts in a socially responsible manner are:

The Clean Yield Group
224 State Street
Portsmouth, NH 03801

Franklin Research &
  Development Corporation
711 Atlantic Avenue
Boston, MA 02111

Social Responsibility
  Investment Group, Inc.
The Candler Building,
  Suite 622
127 Peachtree Street, N.E.
Atlanta, GA 30303

United States Trust Company
  of Boston
Asset Management Division—
  Trust Department
40 Court Street, 10th Floor
Boston, MA 02108

But even using an investment adviser isn't the right course for some. There are those who just want to do the whole investment job themselves (perhaps with some help from a concerned and experienced broker), either because of the personal satisfaction that it will give or because they think they could do a better job than either an adviser or a fund manager would do in their behalf. If you feel that way, read on. In the next and final chapter we'll discuss how you might best go about doing just that.

14

How to Manage Your Own Socially Responsible Portfolio

MOTHER, PLEASE, I'D RATHER DO IT MYSELF!

Not everyone wants to invest in mutual funds. Not everyone wants to delegate the responsibility for his investments to an investment adviser either. For a variety of reasons, many people prefer to invest on their own. And you might be one of them.

Perhaps you have such definite ideas regarding the investment process that you hesitate to trust your assets to anyone else. Maybe you think that your own knowledge, intelligence, experience, or attitude qualifies you to do a better job of managing your investments than would a fund manager or investment adviser acting on your behalf. And you might well be right.

Or you might just enjoy the process. Investing as an avocation might be fun for you so that, just as you would not want to pay someone else to play your tennis or golf game, you might not want to pay someone else to manage your investments either.

Or your social values and concerns might be so unique that no mutual fund could really address them adequately and no investment adviser could afford to do the highly individualized job you require economically. If, for instance, South African apartheid and the state of the environment were your major social concerns, you probably wouldn't have much difficulty finding someone to whom you could delegate the job of managing your investments. But if your chief concerns were AIDS research, the importation of coffee from El Salvador, and the marketing of infant formula, finding a good professional to do the job for you might not be nearly as easy.

For whatever reason, however, let's assume that you decided to manage your own investments in a socially responsible manner. How should you actually go about it?

First, you should answer the basic question we raised at the beginning of this book: Do you see yourself as an *avoidance* investor, an *alternative* investor, or an *activist* investor? Let's revisit each of these approaches in turn and see how you actually would use them in managing your own portfolio.

AVOIDANCE INVESTOR

Avoidance investing is the most common sort of socially responsible investing. It simply involves excluding companies with socially undesirable characteristics from investors' portfolios. But, as a practical matter, how might you go about this?

For starters, you might get a long list of potential investments and just eliminate the ones that don't measure up to your standards. It's a bit like the old saw that the way to sculpt an elephant is to obtain a very large block of marble and then just chip away everything that isn't an elephant.

In other words, start with a list of 500, 1,000, or 2,000 companies (such as the *Standard & Poor's 500 Index* or all the stocks followed by the *Value Line Investment Survey*). Then, depending on which social values are important to you, eliminate all those companies which are doing business in South Africa or which don't subscribe to the *Sullivan Principles* (see Chapter 10). Or exclude the 100 largest defense contractors (see Chapter 12). Or screen out all the tobacco companies or manufacturers of alcoholic beverages (see Chapter 6). Or get rid of those companies which perform experiments on animals (see Chapter 11). Or even eliminate all those companies incorporated in Pennsylvania which didn't voluntarily opt out of that state's anti-takeover law (see Chapter 4).

To be sure, every time you applied another screen, your list would get shorter—but that is just what you'd be trying to accomplish. Eventually you'd be down to a manageable number of companies to look at, all of which meet your minimum social criteria. That would complete the first stage of your investment process: screening for socially responsible characteristics.

Then, and only then, it would be time for you to embark on stage two: the evaluation of those companies on the basis of their financial characteristics.

If you were thinking of structuring a balanced portfolio including common stocks, fixed-income securities, and cash equivalents, you'd have to analyze both your potential bond investments and your potential equity commitments. On the fixed-income side, you might begin by ascertaining how the bonds under consideration were rated by Moody's or Standard & Poor's. What are the bonds' coupons and maturity dates? How well covered are fixed charges? Are there sinking fund requirements? Are the bonds callable? Are they convertible?

On the equity side, you'd have to determine whether the stocks you're considering purchasing are selling at low or high price-earnings ratios. Are they paying dividends and, if they are, what are their dividend yields? What are their discounts from (or premiums over) book values? What are the issuing companies' growth rates and their returns on revenues, equity, and capital? Are they gaining or losing market share? What do the professional analysts have to say about them? (Here you might check the investment advisory services and the financial publications, such as *Barron's* or *Forbes*. Or you might ask your broker for the latest opinions of the analysts in his firm's research department.)

Once you've come up with a list of companies in which you *might* want to invest, because they meet both your social and financial requirements, your job would still not be over—not by a long shot. Now you'd come to step three: determining whether these specific stocks and bonds suit your personal needs from a financial standpoint.

For example, if your primary requirement were high current income, you might not want to invest in a non-dividend paying stock even if you believed it to be deeply undervalued and considered the underlying company to be very socially responsible. (However, you *might* be willing to make such an investment if it were undertaken in conjunction with another investment in a high yielding bond, so that the overall yield of the two securities in combination met your objectives, even though the one stock looked at on its own did not; that would be up to you.) Or, if you were willing to incur the risk of investing in the growth stocks of small, emerging companies with relatively illiquid capitalizations, you might not want to invest in a big capitalization, slow-growth, income-producing corporation no matter what its social policies and no matter how statistically undervalued it might be.

Finally, you'd reach stage four: putting it all together. Remember, you want to create a diversified portfolio for yourself, so you probably won't want to own all grocery store companies or pollution control stocks or solar energy issues—no matter how promising their prospects, how statistically undervalued they might be or how particularly suitable they might appear to be for your particular needs. It would still be necessary that they complement one another.

Thus, your goal will be to own some securities in different sectors of the economy (e.g., some consumer stocks or bonds, some financial issues, some basic industrial goods companies, some utilities). Remember, you would be trying to build a diversified portfolio, not just accumulating a list of stocks and bonds. In a sense, what you would want to do is replicate a diversified mutual fund for yourself—only better.

If you decide to limit your investments to common stocks (which is what many socially responsible *avoidance* investors really have in mind since it is as stockholders, or owners, rather than bondholders, or creditors, where they are really in the best position to influence the course of their company's actions), then your job will be somewhat easier. For starters, you wouldn't be building a balanced portfolio but rather an *all-equity* one. So you wouldn't have to do any fixed-income analysis. However, you will still have to do the kind of equity analysis we suggested regarding the selection of stocks, whether for an *all-equity* or a *balanced* portfolio. And your need to diversify would be at least as important.

But let's see how you, as an *avoidance* investor might actually go about structuring a socially responsible investment portfolio on your own. To make the exercise relatively easy to follow, let's assume for now that you're just looking to structure an *all-equity*, rather than a *balanced*, portfolio.

Stage 1: Screening for Social Characteristics

First, you'll have to select some universe of companies that you'll apply your social screens to in order to determine the stocks to avoid. This might be, for instance, the *Fortune 500* list of the largest companies in America, or the companies in the *Standard & Poor's 500 Index* or, if you wanted to be sure to include smaller growth companies as well, those companies traded not only on the New York and American stock exchanges, but also on NASDAQ.

You'll want your initial universe to be sufficiently large so that the application of reasonable screens won't automatically eliminate all of the companies on it. But unless you want to computerize the process, it shouldn't be so large as to be unwieldy.

An initial list of only 30 companies, such as the *Dow Jones Industrial Average*, would not be the best universe for you to use as a starting point since it includes only large, well-established, big capitalization companies listed on the New York Stock Exchange and is skewed, by definition, toward industrial America, with little exposure to transportation companies, financial companies (**American Express** is an exception), or public utilities (here the one exception is **American Telephone and Telegraph**). Thus, if you were to choose, say, the Dow Jones Industrial Average as your starting point, you would really have loaded your sample at the outset not only against smaller, emerging growth companies but also against non-industrial corporations.

For those reasons, a better starting point might be something like the *Value Line Investment Survey's* universe of thousands of companies, large and small, in all sectors of the economy, which would provide you with the potential for far greater diversification.

For the purposes of this exercise, we're going to use the 50 largest companies in terms of market capitalization, as published by *Forbes* in its April 30, 1990 Annual Directory Issue. In that issue, *Forbes* listed the 500 largest U.S. companies in four categories—assets, sales, profits, and market value—and we might well have chosen to use any one of those lists or a part of any one or a combination of any two or more. But the list we've actually selected, the top 10% of "The Forbes Market Value 500" is broad enough to provide us with sufficient raw material from which to structure a diversified portfolio and yet is small enough to be manageable.

(Admittedly, even this list has its shortcomings and we recognize that in using it we are automatically excluding smaller, emerging growth companies from consideration. But that is the price we are willing to pay for the purposes of simplifying this hypothetical exercise.)

The 50 companies are:

Abbott Laboratories (NYSE—ABT)
American Express Company (NYSE—AXP)
American Home Products Corp. (NYSE—AHP)
American Information Technologies Corp. (NYSE—AIT)
American International Group Inc. (NYSE—AIG)
American Telephone and Telegraph Company (NYSE—T)
Amoco Corporation (NYSE—AN)
Anheuser-Busch Companies, Inc. (NYSE—BUD)
Atlantic Richfield Company (NYSE—ARC)
Bell Atlantic Corporation (NYSE—BEL)
BellSouth Corporation (NYSE—BLS)
Boeing Company (NYSE—BA)
Bristol-Myers Squibb (NYSE—BMY)
Chevron Corporation (NYSE—CHV)

Coca Cola Company (NYSE—KO)
Digital Equipment Corporation (NYSE—DEC)
Walt Disney Company (NYSE—DIS)
Dow Chemical Company (NYSE—DOW)
E.I. duPont de Nemours & Co. (NYSE—DD)
Eastman Kodak Company (NYSE—EK)
Exxon Corporation (NYSE—XON)
Ford Motor Company (NYSE—F)
General Electric Company (NYSE—GE)
General Motors Corporation (NYSE—GM)
GTE Corporation (NYSE—GTE)
Hewlett-Packard Company Inc. (NYSE—HWP)
International Business Machines Corporation (NYSE—IBM)
Johnson & Johnson Company (NYSE—JNJ)
Eli Lilly and Company (NYSE—LLY)
McDonald's Corporation (NYSE—MCD)
MCI Communications Corporation (OTC-MCIC)
Merck & Company, Inc. (NYSE—MRK)
Minnesota Mining and Manufacturing Company (NYSE—
    MMM)
Mobil Corporation (NYSE—MOB)
NYNEX Corporation (NYSE—NYN)
Pacific Gas & Electric Company (NYSE—PCG)
Pacific Telesis Group (NYSE—PAC)
PepsiCo, Inc. (NYSE—PEP)
Pfizer, Inc. (NYSE—PFE)
Philip Morris Companies, Inc. (NYSE—MO)
Proctor & Gamble Company (NYSE—PG)
Schering-Plough Corporation (NYSE—SGP)
Sears Roebuck & Company (NYSE—S)
Southwestern Bell Corporation (NYSE—SBC)
Texaco, Inc. (NYSE—TX)
US West, Inc. (NYSE—USW)
USX Corporation (NYSE—X)
Wal-Mart Stores, Inc. (NYSE—WMT)
Waste Management, Inc. (NYSE—WMX)
Westinghouse Electric Corporation (NYSE—WX)

Now, before you can go any further, you'll have to determine what your personal social concerns are. They might include the environment, equal employment opportunities for women, alcohol, animal rights, or any of the other issues that we have discussed in this book (or, indeed, any others of your own choosing). For the sake of this exercise, though, let's assume that your principal social concerns are your opposition to South African apartheid, tobacco, alcoholic beverages, and armaments. Then you might want to establish the following socially responsible guidelines for yourself:

A.   *Exclude companies doing business in South Africa.* But what exactly does this mean? Do you just want to exclude companies with ownership interests in South Africa? Or do you want to exclude even those which only have licensing, distribution, sales or marketing arrangements there?

If you would be satisfied with the first and milder standard, only excluding companies with direct ownership interests in South Africa and accommodating those with licensing or distribution agreements if they have no outright ownership interests, you would still have to exclude the following 10 companies from your portfolio:

> **Abbott Laboratories**, which employs nearly 150 people through a subsidiary in South Africa distributing pharmaceuticals, hospital products, and infant food.
>
> **Bristol-Myers Squibb**, which employs more than 500 people in South African subsidiaries that manufacture and market pharmaceuticals and toiletries.
>
> **Chevron Corporation**, which owns 50% of **Caltex Petroleum**, the largest remaining American-owned oil company doing business in South Africa.
>
> **E.I. duPont de Nemours**, which, through a subsidiary, maintains a South African branch office with 32 employees.
>
> **Johnson & Johnson**, which produces and markets pharmaceuticals and consumer products through four subsidiaries or affiliates in South Africa, employing more than 1,400 people in the process.

Eli Lilly, which employs approximately 170 people in a South African subsidiary which markets pharmaceuticals and agricultural equipment.

Minnesota Mining & Manufacturing, which has several subsidiaries and affiliates in South Africa, marketing adhesives, abrasives, pharmaceuticals, and *Scotch* brand products and operates retail photography stores, employing over 800 people.

Pfizer, which employs nearly 200 people in South Africa in the marketing of pharmaceuticals and animal health products.

Schering-Plough, which employs more than 160 people in a South African affiliate marketing pharmaceuticals.

Texaco, Inc. which owns the other half of **Caltex Petroleum Corp.**

If, however, you feel even more strongly on this issue and also want to exclude companies with any sort of marketing, direct or indirect sales, technical support, licensing, underwriting, or distribution agreements in South Africa, whether or not they have any ownership interests there, you'd also have to exclude the following 21 companies: **American Express, American Home Products, Boeing, Coca Cola, Digital Equipment, Dow Chemical, Exxon, Ford, General Electric, General Motors, GTE Corporation, Hewlett-Packard, International Business Machines, MCI Communications, Merck, PepsiCo, Philip Morris, Procter & Gamble, Sears Roebuck, USX,** and **Westinghouse Electric**.

For the sake of this exercise, let's assume that you're satisfied with the milder ownership standard. On that basis, you'll just exclude **Abbott Laboratories, Bristol-Myers Squibb, Chevron, DuPont, Johnson & Johnson, Eli Lilly, Minnesota Mining & Manufacturing, Pfizer, Schering-Plough**, and **Texaco** from your potential portfolio. That will still leave you with 40 other stocks to choose from. Now you're ready to apply your second screen.

B. *Exclude tobacco and alcohol companies.* This is an easy one. Just look at the lists of companies in the tobacco and alcohol industries that were provided in Chapter 6. You'll find that of the

50 largest companies in terms of market capitalization on the *Forbes* list, the only tobacco or alcohol companies are **Anheuser-Busch** (which manufactures beer) and **Philip Morris** (which manufactures cigarettes and beer). So exclude them. That will still leave you with 38 stocks to choose from and will bring you to your third and last social screen.

C.   *Exclude major defense contractors.* The first thing you'll have to decide here is what you mean by *defense contractors* and then what you mean by *major*. If a company sells millions of dollars worth of food, tobacco, or clothing to the military, is that the kind of contractor you want to exclude from your portfolio or do you just intend to exclude the manufacturers of guns, tanks, planes, and other armaments?

And what do you mean by *major*: $10 million in annual revenues or $100 million? Or should the determinant be the percentage of a company's total business accounted for by sales to the military, rather than the total dollar amount?

Again, for the sake of simplicity, let's assume that you have defined major defense contractors as the 100 companies which did the largest dollar volume of business, of whatever sort, with the Department of Defense in 1989. By that standard, the following 17 companies from among the 50 largest in terms of market capitalization would have to be excluded from your portfolio: **American Telephone and Telegraph, Amoco, Atlantic Richfield, Boeing, Chevron, Digital Equipment, Eastman Kodak, Exxon, Ford, General Electric, General Motors, GTE, Hewlett-Packard, International Business Machines, Mobil, Philip Morris**, and **Westinghouse Electric**.

(Two of these companies, **Chevron** and **Philip Morris**, were already excluded based on the apartheid or tobacco screens; this would be just one additional reason for avoiding them.)

Thus, after screening for these three social criteria, you would be left with the following 23 companies (out of the original 50 in the *Forbes* list of the largest capitalization companies) which have *no* ownership interests in South Africa, do *not* manufacture tobacco or alcohol products, and are *not* among the nation's 100 leading defense contractors in 1989: **American Express, American Home Products, American Information Technologies,**

American International Group, Bell Atlantic, BellSouth, Coca Cola Company, Walt Disney, Dow Chemical, McDonald's, MCI Communications, Merck, NYNEX, Pacific Gas & Electric, Pacific Telesis, PepsiCo, Proctor & Gamble, Sears Roebuck, Southwestern Bell, US West, USX, Wal-Mart Stores, and **Waste Management**.

Stage 2: Screening for Investment Value

At this point, it would be necessary for you to determine which, if any, of these companies also represented good values from a financial, not social, standpoint. The answer to that would vary with time. A stock might represent an excellent value when it is selling, say, at $30 per share and yet be terribly unattractive at $60. So we cannot give you any absolute answers on this one since we can't know where any of these stocks will actually be selling at the time you're reading this book.

Between mid-October 1989 and mid-October 1990, for instance, the Dow Jones Industrial Average declined a little less than 7%. But during that period, **Proctor & Gamble** appreciated more than 24% and **Coca Cola** climbed more than 28% while **American Express** declined more than 44%. So, all other things being equal, it might be reasonable to assume that **Proctor & Gamble** and **Coca Cola** had become *less* statistically attractive while **American Express** had become *more* reasonably priced over that time.

But, of course, all other things never are equal. Companies' prospects change. They introduce new products. They are confronted by new competition. Their earnings improve or deteriorate. Managements change. Technological breakthroughs and demographic changes enhance their prospects and cost structures—or make their product lines less competitive or even obsolete. None of this can be predicted with certainty.

So this is the point at which you must do a lot of homework. Read the financial press and company news releases. Talk to brokers and request research reports from them on these companies. Calculate price-earnings ratios, discounts from book values, earnings growth rates, cash flows, and so on based on the latest information available to you. Then decide which, if any, of these stocks are attractively priced at the time you're thinking of making your investment.

But let's assume for now, just to keep things moving along, that you've done all that and, remarkable as it may seem, all 23 of these companies show up as reasonably valued potential investments. Does that now mean you should invest in all of them? Not necessarily. You still don't know if they're the right stocks for *you*, based on your *own* personal investment goals and constraints.

Stage 3: Screening for Personal Goals

So now you have to look at your own financial goals. That might include long-term growth of capital with limited risk through investments in well-established companies. Or you might be willing to assume somewhat greater risk in shooting for higher returns by investing in emerging growth stocks. Or you might be interested in short-term trading profits through speculative buying and selling techniques.

For the purposes of this example, let's assume that you are relatively conservative and that your main goal is a relatively high level of current dividend income which is likely to increase over time as a hedge against inflation. In that event, you might decide only to invest in companies with current yields of at least 4%, records of having paid dividends for at least five years without an omission or cut, and some evidence that those companies' dividends have been increased over time.

From any one of a number of standard investment manuals, such as Moody's, Standard & Poor's, or the *Value Line Investment Survey*, and from the latest newspapers, you could now extract the following information:

Which, if any, of these companies, pay dividends?

How long have these dividends been paid?

Which have increased their dividend rates over time?

Which have reduced or omitted them?

What are their current yields?

This is what you'll discover: Neither **MCI Communications** nor **USX** would suit your needs, **MCI** because it only paid its first dividend in 1990 and **USX** because its dividend record has been spotty. (**USX** has paid dividends annually since 1940 but the dividend frequently has been cut; indeed, it paid less in 1990 than it did in the late 1970s.)

Proctor & Gamble and **Coca Cola** wouldn't meet your standards either, even though they have both paid dividends since the 1890s. That's because current yields in both cases (as of September 30, 1990) were less than 3.0%. Similarly, neither **McDonald's** nor **American International Group** would meet your needs: although **McDonald's** has paid and increased its dividends annually since 1976, its yield as of September 30, 1990 was only 1.3%; and, although **American International Group** has paid dividends since 1969 and has increased them annually since 1986, its yield as of the same date was only 0.7%.

Several other companies, including **Merck, PepsiCo, Walt Disney, Wal-Mart Stores**, and **Waste Management** also wouldn't quite make the grade for the same reasons. To be sure, all of them boast long records of dividend payments and increases. But in all those cases too, current yields, as of the end of September 1990, were less than 3%.

However, the seven regional telephone companies formed when the **American Telephone & Telegraph Company** was broken up in 1984—**American Information Technologies (Ameritech), Bell Atlantic, BellSouth, NYNEX, Pacific Telesis, Southwestern Bell**, and **US West**—all have paid dividends annually since then. And yields on those seven stocks (as of September 30, 1990) ranged from 4.6% to 6.5%. Any of those might meet your criteria.

The remaining five companies on our original list of 50 also might suit your needs:

American Express has paid dividends annually since 1870, has increased its rate annually since at least 1974, and yielded 4.4% as of September 30, 1990.

American Home Products has paid dividends annually since 1919, has increased its rate annually since at least 1974, and yielded 4.6% as of September 30, 1990.

Dow Chemical has paid dividends annually since 1911, has increased its rate annually since 1986, and yielded 6.7% as of September 30, 1990.

Pacific Gas & Electric has paid dividends since 1919. It yielded 7.2% as of September 30, 1990.

Sears Roebuck has paid dividends annually since 1935, has raised or sustained the dividend annually since 1977, and yielded 7.9% as of September 30, 1990.

So let's sum up where this leaves us: A total of 12 companies including **American Information Technologies (Ameritech), Bell Atlantic, BellSouth, NYNEX, Pacific Telesis, Southwestern Bell, US West, American Express, American Home Products, Dow Chemical, Pacific Gas & Electric**, and **Sears Roebuck** have all paid dividends annually at least since 1986 (and, in some cases, back to the last century), all have enviable records of having raised dividends over time, and all yielded over 4% as of September 30, 1990.

Stage 4: Putting It All Together

But your job is not quite over yet. Sure, you could just buy equal amounts of those 12 companies and call it quits. If you did, you would own a number of stocks that met the specific social and investment criteria you'd established. None of the 12 have ownership interests in South Africa. None manufacture tobacco products or alcoholic beverages. None are major armaments manufacturers. All have outstanding records of dividend rate increases. Each yields more than 4%. But notwithstanding all that, you'd still have created a pretty undiversified and, therefore, less than totally desirable portfolio.

The fact remains that more than half of the companies you would have bought would be regional telephone companies, one would be an electric utility, one would be a major financial company, and only three (**American Home Products, Dow Chemical**, and **Sears Roebuck**) would be industrials. What might make sense, therefore, would be for you to buy only one or two of the regional telephone company stocks, instead of all seven, in order to avoid excessive overweighting in any one sector. If you did that, just purchasing **NYNEX**, for example, your final portfolio would look like this:

Stock	Industry	Yield
American Express	Financial services	4.4%
American Home Products	Drugs	4.6%
Dow Chemical	Chemicals	6.7%
NYNEX	Telephone	6.5%
Pacific Gas & Electric	Electric utility	7.2%
Sears, Roebuck	Retail trade	7.9%

Certainly, we do not mean to suggest that this would constitute the perfect portfolio for every socially responsible investor. On the contrary: If your concerns were the environment, equal employment opportunity, or animal rights, rather than apartheid, tobacco, alcohol, and armaments, entirely different stocks might be much more suitable for you. Moreover, even if your primary social concerns are apartheid, alcohol, tobacco, and armaments, this portfolio might not work for you if you are more interested in capital appreciation potential than in dividend income. Finally, even if these are your social concerns and if dividend income is your primary investment goal, it is still true that this is not a perfectly well-diversified portfolio: it holds no energy stocks, transportation issues, technology companies, or natural resources stocks.

Still, it isn't just a hodge-podge of issues either. It was structured to meet the specific social and investment requirements of a particular hypothetical investor and, given the artificial constraint of the original 50-stock universe with which we began, it appears to have done that quite well. Certainly it is as diversified as one might reasonably expect of just a six-stock portfolio including one consumer cyclical (**Sears, Roebuck**) one consumer staple (**American Home Products**) one basic industrial (**Dow Chemical**) one electric utility, one telephone utility, and one financial services company.

Of course, if this level of diversification was not sufficient for you, you could always go back to square one and expand your original universe to include, say, the 100 largest capitalization companies, rather than just the top 50. Or you could relax your social standards, accepting, say, companies manufacturing alcoholic beverages, so long as they don't deal with South Africa and aren't major defense contractors. You could relax your financial requirements, accepting stocks yielding less than 3%.

To summarize, in structuring your own socially responsible all-equity *avoidance* portfolio, these are the rules you might follow:

1.   Choose a reasonably large universe of at least 50 companies with which to begin. Recognize that the universe you choose will predetermine some of the characteristics of your ultimate portfolio. If, for instance, you wanted to end up with some smaller growth companies in your portfolio, you shouldn't start out with a universe of big capitalization companies, or even companies ranked by sales volume or assets.

2.   Decide what your own socially responsible priorities are—and be precise. It isn't enough simply to decide that you are opposed to apartheid with no further elaboration. As we've seen, you must decide whether that means that you'd only be willing to invest in companies that subscribe to the *Sullivan Principles* or that you'd only be willing to invest in companies that have no ownership interests in South Africa or that you'd only invest in those which have absolutely nothing to do with South Africa. Each of these policies may be described correctly as *anti-apartheid*, but the fact remains that the consequences of their implementation differ markedly from one another.

The same kind of considerations would enter into virtually any social issue: If equal employment opportunity is of major importance to you, does that mean you favor or oppose affirmative action or comparable worth programs? Arguments may be made on both sides of the question and it is for you to decide.

3.   Screen your list, eliminating those companies which fail to meet the social critera you have established.

4.   Screen the remaining stocks on your list for value. Use all

the resources and statistical help you can get: brokerage house research reports, company reports, the financial press, and so on.

5.   Decide what your personal financial goals and constraints are: preservation of capital, current income, long-term capital appreciation, trading profits. Decide how much risk you're willing to assume.

6.   Screen out those companies that don't meet your personal objectives.

7.   Put it all together with reasonable diversification, seeking representation in a variety of economic sectors and industries. If you wish, you could weight each economic sector respresented in your portfolio equally (e.g., consumer staples, energy, technology, financial, consumer cyclicals, basic industry, capital goods). Or you might want to weight the holdings of your portfolio in line with the weightings of the *Standard & Poor's 500 Stock Index*.

ALTERNATIVE INVESTOR

The *alternative* approach to socially responsible investing is really the flip side of *avoidance* investing: it entails seeking out companies that are doing positive good, rather than simply avoiding those which might do harm.

Investors interested in this approach fall into two categories:

1. Investors who seek to invest in specific community-targeted programs, often church sponsored, which are designed to encourage or support low-income housing and minority businesses through the provision of low interest rate loans. Investors in this category might begin by referring to The Social Investment Forum's *Social Investment Services Guide to Forum Members* which includes a listing of more than 30 organizations involved in the financing of socially responsible community programs.[1]

2. Investors who are interested in investing in the same *kinds* of marketable securities (stocks and bonds) that

appeal to *avoidance* investors but who wish to be pro-active in seeking out companies that do good, rather than re-active in merely avoiding companies that do harm.

Investors in the second category have a more difficult task, or at least a less structured task, ahead of them. For them, the best starting point might be to subscribe to one or more of the invest-ment advisory services that focus on the investment merits of socially responsible companies, such as *The Clean Yield* or *Frank-lin's insight: The Advisory Letter for Concerned Investors*.

In addition, *alternative* investors might be well-advised to subscribe to other information services (e.g., those provided by the Council on Economic Priorities or the Interfaith Center on Corporate Responsibility) that call attention not only to the harm done by some companies but also to the good done by others. (Their addresses may be found in Bibliography and Information Sources in this book.)

Finally, *alternative* investors ought avail themselves of the information to be found in the press. This would not only include standard sources such as *Barrons, Forbes*, or *Fortune*, but also speciality or niche publications directed primarily at women or minorities, such as *Black Enterprise*.

Of course, if you're an *alternative* investor seeking investment ideas among publicly owned companies, you might also want to make note of some of the companies that were singled out for especially favorable mention in this book in one regard or anoth-er. To refresh your memory, the following are but 10 of them.

American Telephone & Telegraph Company (NYSE—T). In 1989, **American Telephone** was nominated by the environmen-tally progressive Council on Economic Priorities for a *Corporate Conscience Award in Environmental Stewardship* for its paper recycling program. In 1990, it was nominated again for its pro-gram to end all use of ozone-depleting chlorofluorocarbons by 1994. However, in early 1990, the company also announced that it no longer would make annual $50,000 contributions to the Planned Parenthood Federation of America because of that or-ganization's advocacy of abortion rights. Depending on your own pro-life or pro-choice attitude, that represented either the height of corporate responsibility or an act of moral cowardice.

Ben & Jerry's Homemade, Inc. (OTC-BJICA). A manufacturer and marketer of super-premium ice cream, **Ben & Jerry's** may be the most visible example of the extremes to which corporate social concerns can go. *Franklin's insight*, published by **Franklin Research and Development Corporation** has given **Ben & Jerry's** its very highest Social Assessment Rating on all counts: South Africa, employee relations, environment, citizenship, energy, product, and weapons.

The company contributes 7.5% of pre-tax profits to charity (compared to a corporate average of 1%). It pays no employee more than five times what it pays its lowest paid worker. It has introduced rain forest crunch ice cream which utilizes items from the tropical rain forest to call attention to that issue. It opposes the use of growth hormones that increase milk production in cows. And it is an active recycler, printing its own annual report on recycled paper.

E. I. duPont de Nemours & Company (NYSE—DD). The largest chemicals company in the United States, **DuPont** has carved out a major niche for itself in recent years in several areas of environmental concern. It has spent $1 billion on pollution control equipment, $800 million annually to operate it, and $500 million to clean up its own old environmental problems.

It has developed a line of herbicides which break down quickly, posing less of a threat to the groundwater. It is recycling a billion pounds of its own polymers in waste reduction programs. It has entered into a joint venture with **Waste Management Inc.** to recycle plastic bottles into **DuPont** products. It runs the largest waste water treatment operation in the country. Through its **Conoco** subsidiary, it was the first company to announce that it would build all its future oil tankers with double hulls in order to reduce the risks of oil spills.

In 1988, it announced that it would *totally* end production of chlorofluorocarbons by the year 2000—or even earlier, if possible (that was years earlier than required by law and meant that

Socially Responsible Investing

DuPont was walking away from a $750 million a year business in which it dominated the industry). By 1990, **DuPont** had already spent $170 million in the development of products to replace chlorofluorocarbons in cleaning, refrigeration, and other uses and had committed to invest up to $1 billion in that effort. In terms of lost work days due to accidents or work-related illnesses, **DuPont** has the best record of any major corporation in the country.

On the negative side, the company was the largest emitter of toxic wastes in the nation in 1988. But it has committed itself to reducing that by 60% by 1993.

H.J. Heinz Company (NYSE—HNZ). A major food processor with one of the most extraordinary records of consistent earnings growth in corporate America and an evident concern for social issues, **Heinz** was the first major corporation to announce that it would not buy tuna caught in nets that also trap and kill dolphins. In 1990, it also voluntarily opted out of Pennsylvania's anti-takeover law, announcing that "The anti-takeover provisions of the law weren't . . . helpful with respect to our long-term objective of enhancing shareholder value."[2] And in April 1990, **Heinz** said that it would introduce a new "recyclable" ketchup bottle in 1991.

Johnson & Johnson (NYSE—JNJ). Another exceptional company in terms of on-the-job safety, with a record of lost work days that is well below its industry's average, **Johnson & Johnson** is equally concerned about its workers' overall wellness: its ambitious *Live for Life* program is designed to encourage employees to stop smoking, improve their eating habits, get exercise, and generally improve their health. The company provides free use of a gymnasium wherein its average headquarters' employee works out twice a week. It provides a selection of *healthy heart* foods in the employees' cafeteria. Its child-care centers for its workers' children are among the best in corporate America. The company's outstanding and well-earned reputation for the quality of its products and its paramount concern for its customers was exemplified in 1982 by its immediate and voluntary recall of its *Extra-Strength Tylenol* capsules at a cost to the company in excess of $100 million in the face of a cyanide scare.

However, **Johnson & Johnson's** most controversial social activities involve its refusal to withdraw from South Africa, despite considerable pressure on it to do so, preferring instead to subscribe to the *Sullivan Principles*, to finance housing for many of its mostly black 1,400 employees there, and to help build schools and hospitals in South African townships. Whether or not you agree with **Johnson & Johnson** on this issue, there is little doubt that the company has been motivated by principle, rather than potential profits, in adopting this policy.

Lands' End, Inc. (NYSE—LE). **Lands' End**, a mail order catalog vendor of classic-styled clothing, has always given high priority to its customers' interests and delivered more than might be expected of it. Company volunteers, including the company's founder and its chief executive officer, personally respond to the approximately 50,000 letters which they receive annually from customers. Telephone orders are answered within three rings. Shipments go out the very next day after orders are received. And the company guarantees its products unequivocally, accepting returns for any reason.

McDonald's Corporation (NYSE—MCD). Operating a chain of over 11,000 fast-food restaurants throughout the world, **McDonald's** social record is as impressive as its financial one: It has played important roles in providing youths with entry level jobs, in combatting racism in the workplace, and in breaking new ground environmentally.

Black Enterprise magazine has cited **McDonald's** as one of the 50 best corporations for blacks to work for in America. The company provides one out of every 15 Americans with their first jobs. Half of its store managers started with the company as low-paid hamburger flippers; 40% of its board of directors worked for the company at one time for hourly wages; and 17% of its managers are black. Relative to other franchisers, **McDonald's** also ranks first by a large margin in the number of its units owned by blacks: out of a total of 4,900 franchised units, 418, or more than 8.5%, were owned by blacks in 1990.

In April 1990, **McDonald's** announced a program called *McRecycle USA* to create a $100 million a year market for recycled materials for its restaurants, over and above the millions of dollars it had been spending annually for recycled paper products. In August 1990, it entered into a joint venture with the Environmental Defense Fund to study its solid wastes program and, three months later, it announced that it would abandon its use of polystyrene packaging.

McDonald's has also taken some clearly socially responsible actions in the nutritional area: it has agreed to fry its potatoes in vegetable oil rather than animal fats, it has voluntarily posted nutritional information in its restaurants, and it has developed a number of nutrition education programs for elementary school children.

Merck & Co., Inc. (NYSE—MRK). One of the nation's leading pharmaceutical companies with annual revenues approximating $7 billion, **Merck & Co.** is justifiably one of the most admired corporations in the country. In 1990, it ranked Number 1 (out of 305 companies in *Fortune's* annual survey) for the fifth consecutive year, placing first in four out of eight categories (ability to attract, develop, and keep talented people; innovativeness; financial soundness; and quality of products or services), second in three (community and environmental responsibility; use of corporate assets; and value as a long-term investment), and third in the eighth (quality of management). In April 1990, the company announced that it would reduce the prices of its prescription drugs to Medicaid patients, making them available to them at the lowest prices it charges its volume purchasers.

Minnesota Mining and Manufacturing Co. (NYSE—MMM). Commended by *Black Engineer* magazine for having one of the best minority recruitment programs in the United States, **Minnesota Mining and Manufacturing** recruits from 75 colleges and universities and makes a special point of encouraging minority participation in the sciences. Similarly, it sends many of its women scientists and technicians to schools to encourage girls to consider embarking on scientific careers.

Polaroid Corporation (NYSE—PRD). A leading manufacturer of instant photographic cameras, films, and other optical, chemical, and electronic products, **Polaroid** was the first U.S. corporation to refuse to sell its products in South Africa.

Of course, the fundamental difference between the investment approaches adopted by *avoidance* and *alternative* investors relates only to their initial selection processes on social grounds. Where the one begins by excluding what he *doesn't* want, the other starts out by looking for what he *does* want. But once that has been done, both must still make the same kinds of decisions regarding their evaluations of the relative attractiveness of the securities they are considering investing in, the suitability of those issues for their own particular needs, and the manner in which they ought to be combined to provide appropriate diversification.

At this point, therefore, the *alternative* investor ought simply to behave much as we recommended that the *avoidance* investor should. Having developed a preliminary list of stocks in which he might want to invest, he should now consider the various financial factors that we alluded to earlier (i.e., price-earnings multiples, dividend yields, research recommendations, returns on capital, sector diversification, etc.).

ACTIVIST INVESTOR

In theory, the socially responsible *activist* investor might actually seek out socially *irresponsible* companies in which to invest, so that he might bring maximum pressure to bear on the companies doing the most harm (by his lights) to encourage them to change their ways. Or he might ignore corporations' social characteristics at the outset, only concerning himself with their financial attributes, with the intention of postponing any social concerns he might have until after he had invested and could take action as an investor, not a potential investor.

In fact, however, most *activist* investors understandably really start out as *avoidance* or *alternative* investors in their own right and only overlay their activism on top of that. So, even if you see yourself as an *activist*, in structuring your initial portfolio, you probably should simply follow one of the first two approaches already discussed in this chapter and elsewhere.

Once you've done that, however, the time for your potential activism will have arrived. From time to time, some or all of the companies in your portfolio will act in a manner that you disapprove of in at least some area and, when that occurs, it will be time for you to let your feelings be known. As a stockholder, you have the right—indeed, some would even claim that you have the responsibility—to communicate with management regarding those issues which concern you.

Certainly you should write or call. And you should make a special point of being aware of any issues to be voted on at the annual meetings of those companies in which you have invested, especially those issues which may have been introduced by other interested stockholders such as yourself.

One group of which you, as an *activist* investor, should be aware, is the Interfaith Center on Corporate Responsibility in New York. The Interfaith Center is a leader in the coordination of shareholder proxy resolutions on a variety of socially responsible subjects. As a lone investor, any actions you might take might not be nearly as effective as those taken in concert with other like-minded individuals and the Interfaith Center, as a clearing house on a variety of issues, might prove invaluable to you in that respect.

Bibliography
and Information Sources

The following newspapers, magazines, and newsletters were of particular value in researching this book: *Adweek's Marketing Week; The Amicus Journal* (published by the Natural Resources Defense Council); *Barron's; Black Enterprise; Business and Society Review; Business Week; The Corporate Examiner* (published by the Interfaith Center on Corporate Responsibility); *Council on Economics Priorities Newsletter; The Economist; Financial Services Week; Forbes; Fortune; The Forum* (published by The Social Investment Forum); *Franklin's insight: Investing for a Better World* (published by Franklin Research & Development); *Garbage; inside PR; Money; Natural History* (published by American Museum of Natural History); *New York Magazine; The New York Times; Pensions & Investments; Policy Review, Prudential-Bache Securities Strategy Weekly; reason; Shearson Lehman Hutton research; Smithsonian; Time*; and *The Wall Street Journal*.

In addition, the following books provided important background and reference material from a variety of perspectives for many of the ideas discussed herein:

Allaby, Michael, *A Guide to Gaia* (New York: E.P. Dutton, 1990).

The Animal Rights Handbook (Los Angeles: Living Planet Press, 1990).

Baldwin, Stuart A.; Tower, Jay W.; Litvak, Lawrence; and Karpen, James F., *Pension Funds & Ethical Investment*, Council on Economic Priorities (New York: St. Martin's Press, 1986).

Bluestone, Barry, *The Social Responsibility of Business: Market, Goods, Human Rights and Social Externalities.*

Bradshaw, Thornton and Vogel, David, *Corporations and Their Critics* (New York: McGraw-Hill, 1981).

Commoner, Barry, *Making Peace with the Planet* (New York: Pantheon Books, 1990).

Corson, Ben; Marlin, Alice Tepper; Schorsch, Jonathan; Swaminathan, Anitra; and Will, Rosyln, *Shopping for a Better World* (New York: Council on Economic Priorities, 1989).

Dickinson, Lynda, *Victims of Vanity* (Toronto, Ontario, Canada: Summerhill Press, 1989).

Domini, Amy L. and Kinder, Peter D., *Ethical Investing* (Reading, MA: Addison-Wesley, 1989).

Edgar, Robert E., *Sanctioning Apartheid* (New Jersey, Africa World Press, 1990).

French, Peter A., *Collective and Corporate Responsibility* (New York: Columbia University Press, 1984).

Friedman, Milton, *Capitalism and Freedom* (Chicago and London: University of Chicago Press, 1962).

Hollender, Jeffrey, *How to Make the World a Better Place*, (New York: William Morrow, 1990).

Johnson, M. Bruce, *The Attack on Corporate America*, Law and Economics Center, University of Miami School of Law (New York: McGraw-Hill, 1978).

Knight, Richard, *Unified List of United States Companies Doing Business in South Africa* (New York: The Africa Fund, 1990).

Leach, Graham, *South Africa* (London: Methuen London, 1987).

Linowes, David F. *The Corporate Conscience* (New York: Hawthorn Books, 1974).

Lydenberg, Steven D.; Marlin, Alice Tepper; Strub, Sean O'Brien; and the Council on Economic Priorities, *Rating America's Corporate Conscience* (Reading, MA: Addison-Wesley, 1986).

Millstein, Ira M. and Katsh, Salem M., *The Limits of Corporate Power* (New York: Macmillan, 1981).

Null, Gary, *Clearer, Cleaner, Safer, Greener* (New York: Omni Publications International, Villard Books, 1990).

Ontiveros, Suzanne Robitaille, *Corporate Social Responsibility* (Santa Barbara, CA and Oxford, England: ABC-Clio, 1986).

Schonberger, Richard J., *Building a Chain of Customers* (New York: The Free Press, 1990).

Silk, Leonard and Vogel, David, *Ethics and Profits* (New York: Simon & Schuster, 1976).

Simon, John G.; Powers, Charles W.; and Gunnemann, Jon P., *The Ethical Investor* (New Haven and London: Yale University Press, 1972).

Singer, Peter, *Animal Liberation* (New York: Avon Books, 1975).

Smith, Adam, *The Wealth of Nations* (1776), Canaan ed. (London, 1930).

Social Investment Services: A Guide to Forum Members, May 1, 1990 Edition (The Social Investment Forum).

Sombke, Laurence, *The Solution to Pollution* (New York: MasterMedia Limited, 1990).

Perhaps of greatest value, however, were the various background publications and general news and informational releases available from the following profit-making and non-profit organizations:

The Africa Fund
198 Broadway
New York, NY 10038

Animal Rights Front (ARF)
P.O. Box 3307
Yale Station
New Haven, CT 06520
(203) 776-1928

Animal Rights Mobilization (ARM!)
P.O. Box 1553
Williamsport, PA 17703
(717) 322-3252

The Clean Yield Group
Box 1880
Greensboro Bend, VT 05842
(802) 533-7178

Council on Economic Priorities
30 Irving Place
New York, NY 10003
(212) 420-1133

Co-op America
2100 M Street, N.W.
Suite 310
Washington, DC 20063
(800) 424-COOP or (202) 872-5307

First Affirmative Financial Network
370 East 76 Street, Suite A-704
New York, NY 10021
(212) 628-1108

Franklin Research & Development Corporation
711 Atlantic Avenue, 5th Floor
Boston, MA 02111
(617) 423-6655

INFORM, Inc.
381 Park Avenue South
New York, NY 10016
(212) 689-4040

Interfaith Center on Corporate Responsibility
475 Riverside Drive, Room 566
New York, NY 10115
(212) 870-2295

Investor Responsibility Research Center
P.O. Box 50
Plainfield, NH 03781
(603) 675-9274
or
1755 Massachusetts Avenue, NW
Washington, DC 20036
(202) 939-6500

Kinder, Lydenberg, Domini & Co., Inc.
7 Dana Street
Cambridge, MA 02138
(617) 547-7479

National Wildlife Federation
1400 Sixteenth Street, N.W.
Washington, DC 20036-2266

Natural Resources Defense Council
40 West 20 Street
New York, NY 10011
(212) 727-2700

People for the Ethical Treatment of Animals (PETA)
P.O. Box 42516
Washington, DC 20015
(301) 770-7444

The Social Investment Forum
430 First Avenue North #204
Minneapolis, MN 55401
(612) 333-8338

Notes

Preface

1. "Protecting the Dolphins," *The Wall Street Journal*, April 17, 1990, p. A22, and "Double Whammy," *The Wall Street Journal*, May 7, 1990, p. A14.

Chapter 1

1. *Social Investment Services: A Guide to Forum Members, May 1, 1990 Edition* (The Social Investment Forum), p. 1.
2. Richard Knight, "Sanctions, Disinvestment, and U.S. Corporations in South Africa," *Sanctioning Apartheid*, Robert E. Edgar, ed. (Africa World Press, New Jersey, 1990), p. 69.
3. Milton Friedman, *Capitalism and Freedom* (Chicago and London: University of Chicago Press, 1962), p. 133.
4. *Ibid.*, p. 133.
5. Harold M. Williams, "Corporate Accountability." Address before the Securities Regulation Institute, San Diego, California, January 18, 1978. Quoted in *Pension Funds & Ethical Investment*, Stuart A. Baldwin; Tower, Jay W.; Litvak, Lawrence; Karpen, James F. (New York: St. Martin's Press, 1986), p. 4.

335

6. Steven D. Lydenberg, Alice Tepper Marlin, Sean O'Brien Strub, and the Council on Economic Priorities, *Rating America's Corporate Conscience* (Reading, Massachusetts: Addison-Wesley, 1986), p. 11.

7. "Ben & Jerry's," *Franklin's insight: Equity Brief*, January 1990, p. 1.

8. Barry Bluestone, *The Social Responsibility of Business: Market, Goods, Human Rights and Social Externalities*, p. 128.

9. John Holusha, "Talking Business with Cook of Atlantic Richfield," *The New York Times*, 3 April 1990, p. D2.

10. *Passive* investors invest in broadly diversified indexed portfolios structured so that their performance results should replicate those of some popular market average, such as the Standard & Poor's 500 Stock Index. Their goal is to do as well as, but not necessarily better than, the market, while incurring no greater risk than that inherent in the overall market itself.

11. *Active* investors seek out individual investment opportunities that they believe will provide them with superior returns. Their goal is to do better than the market and they are prepared to accept the incremental risk involved.

12. Paul M. Barrett, "Doing Good and Doing All Right: Investors Applying Ethical Values," *The Wall Street Journal*, 5 August 1986.

13. *Socially Responsible Investing: We Believe You Don't Have to Sacrifice Profits for Principles*, Shearson Lehman Hutton, New York, 7 March 1990, p. 4.

14. *Ibid.*, p. 4.

15. Steven Lydenberg and Rosalyn Will, "Funds Thrive as Awareness Gains," *Council on Economic Priorities Newsletter*, June 1986, p. 6.

16. *Ibid.*, p. 6.

17. Paul M. Barrett, *op. cit.*

18. Margaret Price, "Performance clouds issue of divestment," *Pensions & Investments*, 29 October 1990, p. 22.

19. "The SRI Alternative," *Financial Services Week*, 24 April 1989, p. 21.

20. Carole Gould, "Mutual Funds: Betting on the 'Green' Group," *The New York Times*, 1 April 1990, p. 16.

21. Penelope Wang, "Mutual Funds: What's Hot," *Money*, March 1990, p. 113.

22. Earl C. Gottschalk, Jr., "Pure Plays: Investments Promoted as Ecologically Clean Pop Up Like Weeds," *The Wall Street Journal*, 10 April 1990, p. A1.

23. Stuart A. Baldwin, Jay W. Tower, Lawrence Litvak, and James F. Karpen, *Pension Funds & Ethical Investment*, Council on Economic Priorities, New York, 1986, p. 80.

24. *Ibid.*, p. 82.

25. *Ibid.*, pp. 77–78.

26. Adam Smith, *The Wealth of Nations* (1776), Cannan, ed. (London, 1930), p. 421.

27. Michael Novak, "The Ecumanicacs," *Forbes*, 17 September 1990, p. 100.

28. Mark Melcher, "Social Investing: The Changing Face of the Investing Community," *Prudential-Bache Securities Strategy Weekly*, New York, 28 February 1990, p. 28.

Chapter 2

1. *Golden parachutes* are lucrative contracts granted to corporate executives providing them with added benefits in the event their companies are taken over by other corporations resulting in their loss of employment. Golden parachutes might include severance pay, bonuses, or stock options.

   Poison pills are corporate strategies by takeover target companies designed to make their stocks less attractive to potential acquirers by providing, for instance, that in the event of a takeover, target company shareholders could redeem preferred stock at a premium price or purchase additional shares of their own company or the acquirer company at bargain prices.

Greenmail is the payment by a takeover target company to a potential acquirer to repurchase shares in the target company owned by the potential acquirer at a premium price, in exchange for a commitment by the potential acquirer to terminate its takeover attempt.

2. Gelvin Stevenson, "The Complete Return on Investment," *The New York Times*, 25 March 1990.

3. *Ibid.*

4. Anthony Ramirez, "From Coffee to Tobacco, Boycotts Are a Growth Industry," *The New York Times*, 3 June 1990, section 4, p. 2.

5. August Felando, "Dolphin-Safe Tuna: No Real Net Gain," *The Wall Street Journal*, 12 June 1990, p. A21.

6. Rick Wartzman and Karen Blumenthal, "Lockheed Wins Proxy Battle with Simmons," *The Wall Street Journal*, 11 April 1990, p. A3.

Chapter 4

1. Milton Friedman, *Capitalism and Freedom* (Chicago and London: University of Chicago Press, 1962), p. 133.

2. Jason Zweig, "Socialism, Pennsylvania Style," *Forbes*, 14 May 1990, p. 42

3. "Contempt for Shareholders," *The Economist*, 28 April 1990, p. 16.

4. Diana B. Henriques, "Wall Street: A Paradoxical Anti-Takeover Bill," *The New York Times*, 8 April 1990, p. 15.

5. *Ibid.*

6. *Ibid.*

7. Leslie Wayne, "Pennsylvania Lends Force to Anti-Takeover Trend," *The New York Times*, 19 April 1990, p. D7.

8. *Ibid.*

9. Leslie Wayne, "Anti-Takeover Proposal Gains in Pennsylvania," *The New York Times*, 4 April 1990.

10. Vindu P Goel, "Many Pennsylvania Firms, Labor Groups Oppose Adoption of Anti-Takeover Bill," *The Wall Street Journal*," 16 April 1990, p. A14.

11. Leslie Wayne, "Many Companies in Pennsylvania Reject State's Takeover Protection," *The New York Times*, 20 July 1990, p. D4.

12. *Ibid*, p. D4.

13. Judith H. Dobrzynski and Eric Schine, "Commentary: Lockheed's Lesson: It's Open Season on Yes-Man Boards," *Business Week*, 16 April 1990, p. 25.

14. Leslie Wayne, "As Proxy Use Widens, New Rules Are Urged," *The New York Times*, 15 June 1990, p. D1.

Chapter 5

1. Susan Caminitri, "Romance: Lands' End Courts Unseen Customers," *Fortune*, 13 March 1989, p. 45.

2. Milton Friedman, *Capitalism and Freedom* (Chicago and London: University of Chicago Press, 1962), p. 133.

3. Susan Caminitri, *op. cit.*

4. Patricia Sellers, "Getting Customers to Love You," *Fortune*, 13 March 1989, p. 48.

5. "Managing: Put Quality First," *Fortune*, 9 April 1990.

6. Sarah Smith, "America's Most Admired Corporations" and "Leaders of the Most Admired," *Fortune*, 29 January 1990, pp. 40–88.

7. Ron Winslow, "Merck Plans Medicaid Price Cut," *The Wall Street Journal*, 23 April 1990, p. B1.

8. Stephen Philips, Amy Dunkin, James B. Treece, and Keith H. Hammonds, "King Customer," *Business Week*, 12 March 1990, p. 88.

9. "Where's the BEEF?," *inside PR*, July 1990, p. 16

10. *Ibid*.

11. *Ibid*. p. 17.

Chapter 6

1. "SEC Rules Companies Must Include Anti-Tobacco Resolutions in 1990 Proxy Statements to Shareholders," *News from the Interfaith Center on Corporate Responsibility*, 22 February 1990.

2. "Passive Smoke Harms Heart," *The New York Times*, 21 May 1990, p. A19.

3. Sonia L. Nazario, "California Ads Attack Cigarettes," *The Wall Street Journal*, 11 April 1990, p. B1.

4. Tamar Lewin, "Harvard and CUNY Shedding Stocks in Tobacco," *The New York Times*, 24 May 1990, p. A1.

5. Kevin Sack, "Cuomo Weighs Move to Drop Tobacco Stocks," *The New York Times*, 9 June 1990, p. 25.

6. *Ibid.*, p. 28.

7. "SEC Rules Companies Must Include Anti-Tobacco Resolutions in 1990 Proxy Statements to Shareholders," *op. cit.*

8. "Prohibition Blues," *inside PR*, July 1990, pp. 9–11.

Chapter 7

1. Bil Gilbert, "Earth Day plus 20, and counting," *Smithsonian*, April 1990, p. 47.

2. Michael Parfit, "Earth First!ers wield a mean monkey wrench," *Smithsonian*, April 1990, p. 198.

3. *Ibid.*, p.198.

4. *Ibid.*, p.192.

5. Ari L. Goldman, "Focus on Humans, Cardinal Cautions," *The New York Times*, 23 April 1990, p. B12.

6. "Darman on the Environment," *The New York Times*, 2 May 1990, p. A22.

7. Andrew Rosenthal, "Bush, on West Coast, Skirts Two Conservation Issues," *The New York Times*, 22 May 1990, p. A20.

8. Richard L. Berke, "Oratory of Environmentalism Becomes the Sound of Politics," *The New York Times*, 17 April 1990, p. A1.

9. *Ibid.*

10. Barbara Rosewicz, "Friends of the Earth: Americans Are Willing to Sacrifice to Reduce Pollution, They Say," *The Wall Street Journal*, 20 April 1990, p. A1.

11. Matthew L. Wald, "Guarding Environment: A World of Challenges," *The New York Times*, 22 April 1990, p. 24.

12. John Holusha, "Market Place: Rulings May Aid Waste Companies," *The New York Times*, 12 April 1990, p. D8.

13. *Ibid.*

14. *Ibid.*

15. Earl C. Gottschalk, Jr., "Pure Plays: Investments Promoted As Ecologically Clean Pop Up Like Weeds," *The Wall Street Journal*, 10 April 1990, p. A1.

16. Barnaby J. Feder, "Market Place: Browning-Ferris's Strategic Retreat," *The New York Times*, 9 April 1990, p. D6.

17. *Ibid.*

18. Michael J. McCarthy, "Recycled Plastic Wins Converts: Coke and Pepsi," *The Wall Street Journal*, 5 December 1990, p. B1.

19. Bill Paul, "Recycling Waste Is Gaining Popularity Among Americans, Group's Poll Shows," *The Wall Street Journal*, 4 May 1990, p. B3B.

20. Dena Kleiman, "How Do You Fix a Broken Planet," *The New York Times*, 25 April 1990, p. C1.

21. John Holusha, "Some Smog in Pledges to Help Environment," *The New York Times*, 19 April 1990, p. D1.

22. John Holusha, "Packaging and Public Image: McDonald's Fills a Big Order," *The New York Times*, 2 November 1990, p. A1.

23. Peter Nulty, "Recycling Becomes a Big Business," *Fortune*, 13 August 1990, p. 84.

24. Barry Meier, "Is Degradability a Throwaway Claim?," *The New York Times*, 17 February 1990.

25. *Ibid.*

26. John Holusha, "Diaper Debate: Cloth or Disposable?," *The New York Times*, 14 July 1990, p. 46.

27. "Day-Care Centers Stick with Disposables," *The Wall Street Journal*, 17 May 1990, p. B1.

28. John Holusha, "Ed Woolard Walks DuPont's Tight-rope," *The New York Times*, 14 October 1990, Section 3, p. 6.

29. *Ibid.*, Section 3, p.1.

30. Julian Simon, "Earth Day Isn't Getting Any Easier," *The New York Times*, 22 April 1990, p. D13.

31. Barnaby J. Feder, *op cit.*

32. Gail E. Schares, "Berzelius: They Cart Waste Away, Treat It—And Then Sell It," *Business Week*, 21 May 1990, p. 132.

33. "AIG Issues Forum: Why It's Important to Put Cleanup First and Establish a National Environmental Trust Fund." Advertisement in *The Wall Street Journal*, 16 May 1990, p. A13.

34. *Ibid.*

35. Marian Burros, "New Urgency Fuels Effort to Improve Safety of Food," *The New York Times*, p. D11.

36. Joan O'C. Hamilton and Vicky Cahan, "A Tempest in a Cottonfield," *Business Week*, 9 April 1990, p. 46.

37. William K. Stevens, "Worst Fears on Acid Rain Unrealized," *The New York Times*, 20 February 1990.

38. "Geraghty & Miller," *Fortune*, 9 April 1990.

39. Alan R. Gold, "After Years of Becoming Cleaner, New York City Air Grows Dirtier," *The New York Times*, 18 April 1990, p. A1.

40. "Ozone." Leaflet, New York State Department of Environmental Conservation.

41. Gary Null, *Clearer, Cleaner, Safer, Greener*, (New York: Omni Publications International, Villard Books, 1990), p. 22.

42. Peter Passell, "Economic Scene: Penny-Wise on Ozone?," *The New York Times*, 16 May 1990, p. D2.

43. Michael Allaby, *A Guide to Gaia* (New York: E.P. Dutton, 1990), pp. 168–170.

44. Daniel Berg, "Letter to the Editor," *The New York Times*, 16 May 1990, p. A26.

45. *Ibid.*

46. Robert Buderi, "Gasoline vs. Electric: The Trade-Offs Are Tricky," *Business Week*, 14 May 1990, p. 61.

47. *Ibid.*

48. David Woodruff, with John Rossant and Karen Lowry Miller, "GM Drives the Electric Car Closer to Reality," *Business Week*, 14 May 1990, p. 60.

49. David J. Jefferson, "California Adopts Strictest Smog Laws in the Nation to Reduce Auto Pollution," *The Wall Street Journal*, 1 October 1990, p. A3.

50. *Ibid.*

51. Matthew L. Wald, "A Bid for Scrap, to Cut Pollution," *The New York Times*, 27 April 1990, p. A16.

52. Matthew L. Wald, " 'Gasohol' May Cut Monoxide but Raise Smog, Study Asserts," *The New York Times*, 9 May 1990, p. D2.

53. John E. Yang, "Legislation Would Assist Corn Farms, Ethanol Firm," *The Wall Street Journal*, 4 April 1990.

54. *Ibid.*

55. Thomas C. Hayes, "Shortage of Additive Limits Clean Gasoline," *The New York Times*, 18 April 1990, p. D1.

56. Peter Nulty, "Global Warming: What We Know," *Fortune*, 9 April 1990, p. 104.

57. William K. Stevens, "Clouds Are Yielding Clues to Changes in Climate," *The New York Times*, 24 April 1990, p. C1.

58. Philip Shabecoff, "European Officials Dispute Bush Over Global Warming," *The New York Times*, 18 April 1990, p. B4.

59. Bob Davis, "Bid to Slow Global Warming Could Cost U.S. $200 Billion a Year, Bush Aide Says," *The Wall Street Journal*, 16 April 1990, p. B4.

60. Philip Shabecoff, "Bush Denies Putting Off Action on Averting Global Climate Shift," *The New York Times*, 19 April 1990, p. B4.

61. Rose Gutfeld and Barbara Rosewicz, "Clean-Air Accord Is Reached in Congress That May Cost Industry $25 Billion a Year," *The Wall Street Journal*, 23 October 1990, p. A2.

62. *Ibid.*

63. Rose Gutfeld, "Pure Plays: For Each Dollar Spent on Clean Air Someone Stands to Make a Buck," *The Wall Street Journal*, 29 October 1990, p. A1.

64. Gordon Davidson, "SIF Announces Valdez Principles with $150B Worth of Backers, Wide Press Coverage," *The Forum*, Winter 1989, p. 4.

65. "The Valdez Principles," *Franklin's insight*, 15 April 1990, p. 2.

66. Press release of The Social Investment Forum (711 Atlantic Avenue, Boston, MA 02111), September 17, 1989.

Chapter 8

1. Donald M. Atwater, John Cogan, and Allen Hyman, "Should EEOC-mandated Affirmative Action Programs Be Expanded for Corporations?" in *The Attack on Corporate America*, M. Bruce Johnson, Ed., Law and Economics Center, University of Miami School of Law (New York: McGraw-Hill, 1978), p. 57.

2. *Ibid.*, p. 58.

3. John H. Bunzel, "Inequitable Equality on Campus," *The Wall Street Journal*, 25 July 1990, p. A12.

4. Peter T. Kilborn, "Wage Gap Between Sexes Is Cut in Test, but at a Price," *The New York Times*, 31 May 1990, p. A1.

5. Lynne Kilpatrick, "In Ontario, 'Equal Pay for Equal Work' Becomes a Reality, but Not Very Easily," *The Wall Street Journal*, 3 March 1990, p. B1.

6. "Women Get Access to Jobs with Risk," *The New York Times*, 19 May 1990, p. 9.

7. Peter T. Kilborn, "Who Decides Who Works at Jobs Imperiling Fetuses?," *The New York Times*, 2 September 1990, p. 28.

8. Mark Landler and Walecia Konrad, "Consumers Are Getting Mad, Mad, Mad, Mad at Mad Ave," *Business Week*, 30 April 1990, p. 70.

9. Isabel Wilkerson, "Challenging Nike, Rights Group Takes a Risky Stand," *The New York Times*, 25 August 1990, p. 10.

10. *Ibid*.

11. Chip Johnson, "Rights Group to Kick Harder at Sneaker Firm's Policies," *The Wall Street Journal*, 17 August 1990, p. B1.

12. Wilkerson, op. cit.

13. Ben Wildavsky, "McJobs," *Policy Review*, Summer 1989, quoted by Martin Morse Wooster in "Grab a Bucket and Mop," *reason*, March 1990, p. 39.

14. Walecia Konrad, "Welcome to the Woman-Friendly Company," *Business Week*, 6 August 1990, pp. 48–55.

15. Janice Castro, "Get Set: Here They Come!," *Time*, Vol. 136, No. 19, Special Issue: Women: The Road Ahead, Fall 1990, p. 51.

16. Claudia H. Deutsch, "Putting Women on the Fast Track," *The New York Times*, 16 December 1990, Section 3, p. 25.

17. Claudia H. Deutsch, "Using Money to Change Executive Behavior," *The New York Times*, 20 May 1990, Section 3, p. 29.

18. Wiley Woodward, "Exploring New Frontiers: Franchise Overview—Black Enterprise Franchise 50," *Black Enterprise*, September 1989.

19. Lockheed Corp. Advertisement in *Black Enterprise*, August 1990, p. 129.

20. Brent Bowers, "Black Owners Fight Obstacles to Get Orders," *The Wall Street Journal*, 16 November 1990, p. B1.

21. "Blacks, Whites and Greens," *Time*, 6 August 1990, p. 29.

22. Jaime Diaz, "Augusta and Baltusrol May Admit First Black Members," *The New York Times*, 2 August 1990, p. B7.

23. Rinker Buck, "Wielding New Power, Marketers Drive Golf Beyond the Color Barrier," *Adweek's Marketing Week*, 6 August 1990, p. 5.

Chapter 9

1. Harold M. Williams, "Corporate Accountability." Address before the Securities Regulation Institute, San Diego, California, January 18, 1978. Quoted in *Pension Funds & Ethical Investment*, Stuart A. Baldwin, Jay W. Tower, Lawrence Litvak, and James F. Karpen (New York: St. Martin's Press, 1986), p. 4.

2. *Church Proxy Resolution*, January 1990, Interfaith Center on Corporate Responsibility, New York, p. 21.

3. Thomas N. Cochran, "Happy Workers," *Barron's*, 26 February 1990.

4. Corey Rosen, "Do ESOP's Improve Corporate and Stock Performance?" and "You Want To Be A What? Persuading Your Company to Say Yes to Employee Ownership," *Franklin's insight*, 15 July 1990.

5. Ron Winslow, "Safety Group Cites Fatalities Linked to Work," *The Wall Street Journal*, 31 August 1990, p. B8.

6. Albert R. Karr, "This Corporate Race Belongs to the Safest," *The Wall Street Journal*, 15 July 1990, p. B1.

7. Shawn G. Kennedy, "Drawing Developers into Day Care," *The New York Times*, 26 August 1990, Section 10, p. 1

8. Gregory A. Patterson and Joseph B. White, "UAW Is Expected to Make Job Security Top Demand in Big Three Contract Talks," *The Wall Street Journal*, 22 May 1990, p. A3.

9. Gregory A. Patterson, "GM Wins Arbitration in UAW Dispute Over Firm's Closing of Michigan Plant," *The Wall Street Journal*, 30 March 1990.

10. Gregory A. Patterson, "GM Agrees to Postpone Plant Closing for Five Years in Settlement of Walkout," *The Wall Street Journal*, 15 August 1990, p. A4.

11. Peter T. Kilborn, "When Plant Shuts Down, Retraining Laid-Off Workers Is Toughest Job Yet," *The New York Times*, 23 April 1990, p. A14.

Chapter 10

1. Sarah Smith, "America's Most Admired Corporations," *Fortune*, 29 January 1990, p. 54.

2. Graham Leach, *South Africa* (London: Methuen London, 1987), p. 271.

3. Frederick H. Katayama, "Did Mobil Help or Hurt Apartheid," *Fortune*, 5 June 1989, p. 17.

4. Steven D. Lydenberg, Alice Tepper Marlin, Sean O'Brien Strub, and the Council on Economic Priorities, *Rating America's Corporate Conscience* (Reading, Massachusetts: Addison-Wesley, 1987), p. 32.

5. Frederick H. Katayama, *op. cit.*

6. Richard Knight, "Sanctions, Disinvestment, and US Corporations in South Africa," *Sanctioning Apartheid*, Robert E. Edgar, Ed. (Trenton, New Jersey: Africa World Press, 1990) p. 70.

7. *News from the Interfaith Center on Corporate Responsibility*, New York, 21 March 1990, p. 2.

8. Christopher S. Wren, "Praising de Klerk, Bush Offers Help on Sanctions," *The New York Times*, 25 September 1990, p. A7.

9. James S. Henry, "Even if Sanctions Are Lifted, Few Will Rush to South Africa," *The New York Times*, 28 October 1990, Section 3, p. 5.

Chapter 11

1. Peter Singer, *Animal Liberation* (New York: Avon Books, 1975), p. ix.

2. *WHAT IS ARF?* Pamphlet distributed by Animal Rights Front, New Haven, Connecticut, 1990.

3. Warren E. Leary, "Interior Secretary Questions Law on Endangered Species," *The New York Times*, 12 May 1990, p. 8.

4. Teri Agins, "Fur Retailers Post Flat Winter Sales, Begin Using New Marketing Strategies," *The Wall Street Journal*, 30 March 1990.

5. Lynda Dickinson, *Victims of Vanity* (Toronto, Ontario, Canada: Summerhill Press, 1989), p. 19.

6. "Animals' Advocates Seen as 'Terrorists' by Health Secretary," *The New York Times*, 8 June 1990, p. A10.

7. "A.M.A. Assails Tactics of Animals' Advocates," *The New York Times*, 5 October 1990, p. A22.

8. *Ibid*.

Chapter 12

1. Deborah L. Jacobs, "Corporate Donations Under Attack," *The New York Times*, 30 September 1990, Section 3, p. 23.

2. Kevin Kelly, "Dayton Hudson Finds There's No Graceful Way to Flip-Flop," *Business Week*, 24 September 1990, p. 50.

3. Leonard Buder, "Large Pension Fund Criticizes A.T.&T. Over Family Agency," *The New York Times*, 18 April 1990, p. B3.

4. Michael Lev, "A.T.&T. Chief Defends Decision on Abortion," *The New York Times*, 19 April 1990, p. A14.

5. "Church Investors Challenge Weapons Producers," News from the Interfaith Center on Corporate Responsibility, New York, 28 March 1990, p. 1.

6. Murray Weidenbaum, "Defense 'Conversion'—An Empty Promise," *The New York Times*, 20 August 1990, p. A15.

7. Janice Castro, "Biting the Bullets," *Time*, 30 April 1990, p. 70.

8. Nancy J. Perry, "The Arms Makers' Next Battle," *Fortune*, 27 August 1990, p. 88.

9. Janice Castro, *op cit.*

10. ICCR Brief, Vol. 15, No. 3, 1986, *The Corporate Examiner*, Interfaith Center on Corporate Responsibility, p. 30.

Chapter 13

1. Calvert-Ariel Growth Fund prospectus.

2. New Alternatives Fund prospectus.

3. Parnassus Fund prospectus.

4. Penelope Wang, "Money Pro: A True Believer who Does Well By Seeking to Do Good," *Money*, May 1990, p. 177.

5. *Ibid.*

6. The Social Investment Forum is located at 430 First Avenue North, #204, Minneapolis, MN 55401.

Chapter 14

1. The Social Investment Forum is located at 430 First Avenue North, #204, Minneapolis, MN 55401. Telephone:

(612) 333-8338. The *Social Investment Services Guide to Forum Members* may be purchased directly or as part of a membership package.

2. Diana B. Henriques, "Wall Street: A Paradoxical Anti-Takeover Bill," *The New York Times*, 8 April 1990, p. 15.

Index

Time Warner, Inc., 67–68
TIPS, 110
Tobacco, 26–27, 95–105
Tobacco Divestment Project,
99–100, 280
Topfer, Klaus, 166
Toronto Sun Publishing, 184
*Toxic 500: The 500 Largest
Releases of Toxic Chemicals in the
U.S. 1987*, 30
Toxic wastes, 30
Toyota Motor Corp., 91, 194, 209
Traditional investing, 47–49
Training for Intervention
Procedure by Servers of Alcohol,
110
TransAmerica Corporation, 75
Travelers Corporation, 100
Tropicana, 109
TRW Incorporated, 91–92
Tucker, Anthony Inc., 126
Tuna companies, 35
Tutu, Archbishop, 221
Tyson, Luther E., 295

U

U.S. Surgical, 247
U.S. Trust Company of Boston,
16, 33, 170, 276, 304
U.S. West Inc., 191
Unilever, 133
Union Carbide Corporation, 171
Union Pacific, 171
United Auto Workers Union, 209,
210
United States Trust Company of
Boston, 16, 33, 170, 276, 304
United Technologies Corporation,
261
United Telecommunications, 193

Universal Corp., 103
Universities, and South African
investments, 220
Unocal Corporation, 161, 169
Upjohn, 245
USAir Group Inc., 75
UST Inc., 103, 109
USX Corporation, 75, 163

V

Valdez Principles, 169–73
Valkyrie Three, 108
Van Kamp Seafood Company, 36
Vegetarians, and animal rights,
240–41
VF Corporation, 71, 72
Viney, Robert, 133

W

W.R. Grace & Co., 161
Waste Management, Inc., 124,
125, 130, 141, 171, 324
Waste-to-energy facilities, 128–29
Water pollution, 146–51
Weidenbaum, Murray, 262
Wellness programs, 206–7
Wendy's International, Inc., 88–89
  recycling efforts, 138
Westcott, Bruce, 16
Westinghouse Electric Corporation,
71, 72, 129, 253
Westmoreland Coal Company, 169
Wheelabrator Technologies Inc.,
129
White, Bob, 220
Wieles, Dr. Torsten, 246
Wildavsky, Ben, 190